T0260252

Digital Analytics for Marketing

This second edition of *Digital Analytics for Marketing* provides students with a comprehensive overview of the tools needed to measure digital activity and implement best practices when using data to inform marketing strategy. It is the first text of its kind to introduce students to analytics platforms from a practical marketing perspective.

Demonstrating how to integrate large amounts of data from web, digital, social, and search platforms, this helpful guide offers actionable insights into data analysis, explaining how to "connect the dots" and "humanize" information to make effective marketing decisions. The authors cover timely topics, such as social media, web analytics, marketing analytics challenges, and dashboards, helping students to make sense of business measurement challenges, extract insights, and take effective actions. The book's experiential approach, combined with chapter objectives, summaries, and review questions, will engage readers, deepening their learning by helping them to think outside the box.

Filled with engaging, interactive exercises and interesting insights from industry experts, this book will appeal to undergraduate and postgraduate students of digital marketing, online marketing, and analytics.

Online support materials for this book include an instructor's manual, test bank, and PowerPoint slides.

Dr. A. Karim Feroz is a research scientist with expertise in digital transformation, digital business strategy, and Industry 4.0. He has an MBA (strategic management focus) and a PhD in the field of ICT (information and telecommunication technology) management from South Korea's number one ranked elite research university, KAIST (Korea Advanced Institute of Science and Technology). He has more than five years of research experience in academic, policy, business, and strategic management settings. He has experience in the government and private sectors as well as in NGOs in Afghanistan and South Korea.

Dr. Gohar F. Khan is a computational social scientist with expertise in digital business, data analytics, and network science. He specializes in both quantitative and qualitative research methods. His work has been published in several refereed journals, conference proceedings, and books.

Marshall Sponder holds a dual appointment as a faculty lecturer at Zicklin School of Business, Baruch College, USA, where he teaches digital analytics, text analytics, and Internet marketing to graduate and undergraduate students and an associate professor of professional practice at Rutgers Business School, USA.

Business Analytics

Marketing Analytics
Statistical Tools for Marketing and Consumer Behaviour
using SPSS
José Marcos Carvalho de Mesquita and Erik Kostelijk

Digital Analytics for Marketing, 2e
A. Karim Feroz, Gohar F. Khan, Marshall Sponder

Digital Analytics for Marketing

Second Edition

A. Karim Feroz, Gohar F. Khan, and Marshall Sponder

NEW YORK AND LONDON

Designed cover image: © NicoElNino

Second edition published 2024
by Routledge
605 Third Avenue, New York, NY 10158

and by Routledge
4 Park Square, Milton Park, Abingdon, Oxon, OX14 4RN

Routledge is an imprint of the Taylor & Francis Group, an informa business

© 2024 Marshall Sponder, Gohar F. Khan, and A. Karim Feroz

The right of Marshall Sponder, Gohar F. Khan, and A. Karim Feroz to be identified as authors of this work has been asserted in accordance with sections 77 and 78 of the Copyright, Designs and Patents Act 1988.

All rights reserved. No part of this book may be reprinted or reproduced or utilised in any form or by any electronic, mechanical, or other means, now known or hereafter invented, including photocopying and recording, or in any information storage or retrieval system, without permission in writing from the publishers.

Trademark notice: Product or corporate names may be trademarks or registered trademarks, and are used only for identification and explanation without intent to infringe.

First edition published by Routledge 2017

British Library Cataloguing-in-Publication Data
A catalogue record for this book is available from the British Library

Library of Congress Cataloging-in-Publication Data
Names: Sponder, Marshall, author. | Khan, Gohar F., author. | Feroz, A. Karim, author.
Title: Digital analytics for marketing / Marshall Sponder, Gohar F. Khan and A. Karim Feroz.
Description: Second Edition. | New York, NY : Routledge, 2024. | Series: Mastering business analytics | Revised edition of Digital analytics for marketing, 2017. | Includes bibliographical references and index.
Identifiers: LCCN 2023034387 (print) | LCCN 2023034388 (ebook) | ISBN 9780367457921 (hardback) | ISBN 9780367456412 (paperback) | ISBN 9781003025351 (ebook)
Subjects: LCSH: Internet marketing. | Social media.
Classification: LCC HF5415.1265 S658 2024 (print) | LCC HF5415.1265 (ebook) | DDC 658.8/340285—dc23/eng/20230721
LC record available at https://lccn.loc.gov/2023034387
LC ebook record available at https://lccn.loc.gov/2023034388

ISBN: 978-0-367-45792-1 (hbk)
ISBN: 978-0-367-45641-2 (pbk)
ISBN: 978-1-003-02535-1 (ebk)

DOI: 10.4324/9781003025351

Typeset in Helvetica Neue
by Apex CoVantage, LLC

Access the Support Materials: www.routledge.com/9780367456412

Contents

Figures

Tables

Preface

We present this updated and expanded version of the previous book, *Digital Analytics for Marketing*. I am thankful to Marshall Sponder and Gohar F. Khan, the original authors of the first edition, for providing me this great opportunity to work with them on this book. I am privileged and honored to have them as my co-authors. Their work on the first edition laid the foundation for this book. In this second edition of the book, we build upon the previous work and new research to provide updates on digital marketing analytics.

As we know, digital technologies have penetrated every aspect of our lives in this rapidly evolving digital age. The emergence of new digital technologies such as artificial intelligence, big data analytics, blockchain, IoT, cloud and mobile, and social media analytics plays a fundamental role in enabling organizations to bring changes to their business models and core operations in radical ways or to create entire new business models and new ways for operations. This process is called digital transformation, which is challenging the traditional business models, and organizations have no choice but to go digital. This coupled with the fact that consumers these days are more informed creates additional challenges for organizations to understand their needs and rethink their value creation strategies.

Like any other sector, the world of marketing has undergone a remarkable transformation due to the influence of these technologies. The fast-changing environment enabled by digital technologies warrants transforming value creating processes and business models to meet evolving customer needs. Relying on traditional marketing methodologies to reach and engage customers is not an option in the modern digital age. Organizations understand that data-driven strategic insights hold the key to unlocking unparalleled opportunities for growth and success in the digital marketing arena. Since the release of the first edition, the landscape of digital marketing has evolved at an unprecedented pace, driven by technological advancements, changing consumer behaviors, and emerging trends. In this new edition, we aim to equip readers with the latest insights, strategies, and tools to navigate this ever-evolving digital ecosystem.

In this book, our goal is to understand the dynamics of digital marketing analytics and equip marketers, students and any other readers with practical and theoretical knowledge and skills necessary for succeeding with digital marketing in today's complex digital environment. Hence, we have created Digital RAA (Readiness, Analytics, Action) framework, that provides guidelines to organizations to utilize novel digital technologies for digitalizing marketing and creating value with it. This book is categorized into three main parts with chapters for each of the components of Digital RAA Framework. We take an integrated approach to studying the entire digital marketing analytics process. The book starts off with an introduction, talks about the objectives and selecting metrics for data collection, analysis, and visualization, digital marketing analytics tools, digital ecosystems, and creating digital value from digital analytics for marketing. With a strong emphasis on real-world examples and case studies, we illustrate how digital marketing analytics can be applied across various industries and marketing channels.

This book introduces new chapters that delve into cutting-edge topics and emerging trends. Specifically, Chapter 1 provides an overview of digital marketing analytics and introduces Digital RAA framework that binds all the remaining chapters. We have removed some chapters from the previous book as they were no longer relevant in today's digital marketing environment. We have introduced new topics that are closely related to the industrial trends these days and are considered hot topics such as generative AI and Google analytics 4, etc. We explore the impact of artificial intelligence and machine learning on digital marketing analytics, discussing how these technologies can enhance personalization, automation, and predictive modeling. Furthermore, we delve into the realm of social media analytics, which is both science and art. For the science part, we discuss skilled data analysts, sophisticated tools and technologies; and data and for the art part of it, we discuss the important of interpreting and aligning analytics with business objectives and goals.

We extend our sincere gratitude to our readers, whose support and feedback have been invaluable in shaping this second edition. We have taken your suggestions to heart and strived to provide an even more comprehensive and insightful exploration of digital marketing analytics. We hope this book serves as a valuable tool on your journey to master the art and science of digital marketing analytics.

A. Karim Feroz
Gohar F. Khan
Marshall Sponder
June, 2023

Introduction to Digital Marketing and Analytics

CHAPTER OBJECTIVES

After reading this chapter, readers should understand the following:

- What is Marketing?
- Marketing Mix and Other Marketing Frameworks
- What is Digital Marketing?
- Digital Marketing Channels
- Digital Marketing Analytics and Digital RAA Framework

Marketing

Marketing is the process of identifying, anticipating, and satisfying customer needs and wants through the creation, promotion, and distribution of products and services. With the enormous growth of the Internet and digital technologies, marketing-related activities have skyrocketed. Consumers are exposed to an unprecedented number of advertisements on a daily basis through social media, TVs, emails, and online streaming, etc. Despite the takeover of digital media, traditional media such as newspapers, magazines, and other print publications still carry advertisements. The rise of digital media has rendered these kinds of marketing activities ineffective in terms of reaching a broader audience with lower costs. Marketing teams use various strategies, techniques, and online and offline communication channels to reach a target audience and persuade them to purchase products and/or services offered by business organizations.[1-3]

Generally speaking, marketing covers a wide range of activities within an organization, such as market research, product development, branding, advertising, and sales. The ultimate goals of marketing are to drive sales, increase revenue, and expand market share for a business. Marketing is conducted in many ways. For example, doing consumer and market research to better understand the target audience and their needs and wants is a form of marketing. Similarly, developing a new product or service that addresses a specific customer need, carrying out campaigns for a strong brand image, or developing strategies to

DOI: 10.4324/9781003025351-1

differentiate brands from competitors are examples of marketing. Other marketing examples include

- Organizing and running advertising campaigns through social media or offline events to increase brand awareness
- Utilizing public relations and mass media to manage and improve reputation and brand image
- Using digital marketing techniques such as analytics, content marketing, search engine optimization (SEO), or email marketing to reach customers worldwide online
- Using promotions, public relations, influencer events, and other tactics for increasing brand awareness and attracting new audience

The operations of business organizations and enterprises can be divided into two main pillars, namely core functions and support functions. Core business functions are a set of internal and external activities of an organization that are collectively utilized for the production of final goods and/or services. Companies usually categorize their core business functions into four departments: inbound and outbound operations, marketing and sales, human resources, and finance. This may differ across different companies depending on their business models, operations, and corporate strategy. Marketing is one of the most important core business functions of an organization in terms of efficient resource allocation to advertisement campaigns and prioritizing promotions related decision-making.[4, 5] Successful marketing activities have multiple advantages for organizations for gaining visibility, improving brand image, and expanding market share. Support business functions, on the other hand, are set of activities aimed at backing the core functions. Customer service, R&D, communications, PR, IT, and quality management are some of the examples of support functions. The two pillars come together in a perfect union to create and deliver value for customers by meeting their needs and wants.

Marketing is all about putting the right products and/or services at the right place in the right time at the right price! Companies undertake marketing activities to expand the reach of their final goods and services to the end users. Marketing activities mainly include selling, promotions, advertising, and mass media campaigns, etc. However, marketing activities can come in other different forms and shapes. For instance, warranty and return policy, packaging, attending trade shows and events, customer relations, discounts, and brand building, etc.

Figure 1.1 outlines all the general functions of marketing. All of them constitute the traditional marketing mix or 4Ps of marketing, which refers to four broad levels of marketing decision, that is, product, price, promotion, and place (4Ps framework), which has gone through substantial modifications through years of scholarly work in the field. In summary, marketing is a multifaceted activity which involves many departments in an organization where various different techniques and channels are used to promote and sell products and services to the target audience. We define and explain various marketing concepts in this chapter (see Table 1.3).

Marketing Frameworks

Marketing mix or 4Ps of marketing is a widely accepted traditional conceptual framework for marketing. It was as originally proposed by Jerome McCarthy in

Market Information and Research	• Gathering and analyzing information about the demands, needs and wants of consumers • Analyzing competition, decision-making for successful marketing of products and service
Product Design, Development, and Management	• Developing and improving a product or a product to create and capture consumer value • Product life cycle management
Markering Information Management	• Gathering, storing and analyzing all the information involving the consumers, the product, the competitors, and the market iteself • Helps with making sound buisness decisions across an organization
Costing and Financing	• Involves decisions of charging consumers for products and services and allocating budgets for marketing campaigns • Generally involves multiple departments in an organization
Customer Support and Services	• Includes sales and after-sales services • Highly focused on building long-term relationships with the consumers

Figure 1.1 General Functions of Marketing
Source: A. Karim Feroz

the 1960s. Marketing mix can be seen as a way of translating marketing *planning* into *practice*. Over the years, marketing mix has transitioned from 4Ps through modifications into 7Ps (three additions: people, process, physical evidence), and 4Cs, etc. In Table 1.1, we provided definitions and explanations of each of 4Ps and 4Cs with key relevant activities.

Digital Marketing

Information and communication technologies (ICT) offer new ways of connecting with consumers and carrying out business activities. Digital technologies have fundamentally altered the way marketing activities are carried out and value is created for customers. With the emergence of digital technologies, organizations have transformed the way they connect with their customers and promote their products and services. For example, companies are now able to connect with customers from across the globe in real time, which wouldn't have been possible without the growth and penetration of Internet and ICTs in business. There is no to physically visit a store to purchase something. It can be entirely done online. From purchase to delivery and post-purchase decisions, everything has done online. Everything is literally just a few clicks or touches (in case of smart phones, tablets) away! This use of digital communication channels and other technologies such as digital analytics, social media and analytics, email, and websites for marketing goods and services is called digital marketing.[6, 7]

Here are some examples of digital marketing.

• **Social media marketing:** Social media platforms are powerful online tools for the promotion of products and services. Organizations can reach a diverse audience through these channels. Examples of social media marketing includes

Table 1.1 Marketing Mix Framework

4Ps/4Cs	Definitions/ Explanations	Key Activities	Sources
Product/ Customer	Customers are the end users of products and services. Companies should make wise investment decisions regarding product attributes and their quality that the customers will be willing to pay for. If customers don't see the value in the final goods or services, they will not be willing to pay for them.	– Product development – Product design – Branding – Packaging – Services	8, 9
Price/ Cost	This marketing mix refers to the price structure and level. Price constitutes the total cost of delivering final products and services.	– Pricing strategies – Costs and breaking even – Employing various pricing tactics – Discounts, etc.	10, 11
Place/ Convenience	This includes all the distribution efforts aimed at ensuring a smooth delivery of products to the consumers. Digital technologies (e.g., the Internet) have greatly impacted this mix in terms of shortening the distance between the final goods and consumers.	– Channel identifications – Location assessments – Market coverage – Opening franchises – Delivery and distribution strategies – Warehousing	12, 13
Promotion/ Communication	This mix deals with investment in making the product visible to the consumers. Companies invest money in advertising, publicity, communications to expand their reach through various promotional mix strategies.	– Public relations – Advertising – Communication strategies – Identifying communication channels – Direct marketing	14, 15

creating a Facebook ad campaign to promote a new product launch, making and uploading products or services-related videos to YouTube, and running a Twitter page, etc.

- **Search engine optimization (SEO):** Search engines are important digital channels that can help expand an organization's reach. Almost everyone relies on Google to help them find something they need. This provides a great opportunity for customers to find you. But you have to ensure that you are easy to find. Organizations can optimize their websites for specific keywords that can result in ranking them higher in search engine results pages. This enhances the ability of organizations to reach broader audience.
- **Email marketing:** Email is one of fastest way to reach customers! Emails serve as the direct link between you and your potential customers. Sending promotional emails to a list of subscribers to promote a product or service can result in gaining visibility.
- **Content marketing:** Content marketing has gained popularity with the growth of social media and the Internet. One way to connect with the customers is creating and distributing valuable, relevant, and consistent content. This can help in attracting and engaging an audience, with the goal of driving profitable customer action.
- **Influencer marketing:** Partnership with individuals who have a large following on social media platforms for promotions and brand awareness can be expensive financially but can definitely pay off in expanding audience base.
- **Affiliate marketing:** Affiliation and partnering has become easier with digital marketing. It is a mutually beneficial relationship that businesses can capitalize on to promote their companies.
- **PPC (pay per click) marketing:** In this type of digital marketing, companies can pay to have a website's link appear at the top of search engine results pages or on other websites through programmatic advertising.

Lasted Digital Technologies

Digital marketing heavily relies on digital technologies and digital communication channels for the promotion of goods and services. In fact, digital marketing is all about the effective use of digital channels to promote a product or service.[16, 17] It allows for targeted and measurable campaigns, with the ability to track the success of various strategies in real time. Research has shown that digital marketing can be highly effective in reaching and engaging with consumers and can lead to increase in sales for businesses and that it is more effective than traditional marketing methods in terms of cost and ROI.[18, 19] However, there are also challenges to digital marketing, such as the need for constantly evolving strategies to stay ahead of the competition and the potential for oversaturation in certain online channels. Businesses must stay up-to-date on the latest digital marketing trends and technologies to remain competitive. Overall, digital marketing has become an essential tool for businesses looking to reach and engage with their target audience, but it's important to stay up-to-date on the latest trends and technologies to be effective.[20, 21]

The digitalization of organizational practices and operations and the proliferation of digital technologies in industries and markets have created a number of previously unavailable ways to conduct marketing activities. With the help of digital technologies such as social media, mobile devices and applications, the Internet and other search engines, email, desktop computers and tablets, companies are now able to reach large swaths of the population.[6, 17] Today's consumers are more knowledgeable than ever and have easy access to information to make informed purchase and post-purchase decisions. Digital marketing considers the data-driven nature of consumers and takes personalized approaches to individual marketing. Recent developments in artificial intelligence and machine learning have further narrowed down the scope of personalized digital and, as a result, organizations greatly benefit from targeted individual marketing campaigns. For example, if you search for a particular product or services on Google, then you will likely get ads on similar products on your Facebook or YouTube account.

"I was recently looking to buy a car here in the United States. I followed some car dealership pages and looked at the Facebook pages of local used cars shops in my area. And guess what? Now, I keep getting these 'recommended' car sale posts on my feed. The AI knows that I am looking for a vehicle" (Personal example from A. Karim Feroz).

Digital Marketing Frameworks

There are several frameworks available for digital marketing analytics that can help businesses track and measure the effectiveness of their digital marketing efforts. Below we discuss a few examples of the frameworks available for digital marketing analytics. Each framework has its own unique focus and can be used in different ways to help businesses track and measure the effectiveness of their digital marketing efforts.

1. Digital RAA Framework

In this book, we introduce digital RAA (stands for digital readiness, digital analytics, and digital action) framework that provides guidelines to organizations to utilize novel digital technologies for digitalizing marketing and creating value with it.

2. The AIDA Framework

AIDA stands for attention, interest, desire, and action. This framework helps businesses to understand how to create effective marketing campaigns that capture attention, generate interest, create desire, and drive action.[22, 23]

3. The SMART Framework

SMART stands for specific, measurable, achievable, relevant, and time-bound. This framework can help businesses to set clear and measurable goals for their marketing campaigns.[24, 25]

4. The PESTLE Framework

PESTLE stands for political, economic, social, technological, legal, and environmental. This framework helps businesses to understand the external factors that can impact their marketing efforts.

5. The RACE Framework

RACE stands for reach, act, convert, and engage. It's a digital marketing framework that helps businesses to plan, manage, and optimize their online activities to reach their target audience, act on their insights, convert visitors into customers, and engage with their customers to drive repeat business.

6. The Funnel Framework

This framework provides a visual representation of how customers move through different stages of the sales process, from awareness to purchase. This framework helps businesses understand how to optimize different stages of the funnel to improve conversion rates.

Digital Marketing Communication Channels

Digital marketing is possible because of the invention of digital communication channels. With the advent of social media and web-based technologies, marketing communication has become easier, less expensive (as compared to print media), and efficient. Digital marketers receive valuable insights from these channels because of the time that modern consumer spent and the data they share on social media and other online platforms. The followings are some of the digital communication channels.

1. Social Media Communication Channels

Social media has become a very popular communication channel for companies to stay connected with their clients. Particularly, over the past decade, the emergence of various kinds of social media platforms like Facebook, Twitter, Instagram, and YouTube has provided unprecedented opportunities for organizations to open new digital communication channels and engage in marketing. Using modern social media platforms for digital marketing has many benefits. Most modern social media platforms have built-in engagement and analytics metrics for analyzing data, which is very useful and valuable in terms of understanding the customers. There are many paid ads such as google ads and Facebook ads that provided targeted and personalized marketing services on social media to promote the business. Staying connected with social media is not only a great way to build and improve relationships with customers but also to attract new clients and enhance brand image. Nonetheless, organizations should have specific communication and content development strategies in order to successfully engage with their perspective clients. Such strategies should cover the scope, scale, and frequency of the materials uploaded to the social media platforms.

2. Website Communication Channels

A website is very powerful communication channel as it is usually the primary source online that represents the brand of an organization. Promotion of this channel is imperative to get more traffic on the website, which can lead to the retention of existing customers and the attraction new ones. Companies should have sound web development strategies in place in order to attract and retain customers. The strategies should have specific plans to ensure that website channels are user-friendly, fast, accurate, mobile friendly, easy to navigate and have simple hierarchal structures. Utilizing more than one channels simultaneously can help companies more audience and attract more customers. For instance, business social media can be used to promote website channels and vice versa by linking one to another.

3. Mobile Communication Channels

Mobile technologies have come a long way since their inception. Smartphones and tablets provide an easy access to information online and enable quick communication among various parties. Companies rely on mobile communication channels to carry out digital marketing to reach specific audience through SMS, MMS, social media, mobile applications, and more. Digital marketing through mobile technologies offers marketers direct access to their perspective clients. Through personalized content and location-based marketing techniques organizations have the opportunity to create highly individualized ads on mobile devices to promote products and services. For instance, many companies rely on location-based marketing techniques to target potential customers who are within a few miles/ close proximity of their business.[26] A unique advantage of mobile channels is that audiences can be reached anytime, anywhere across the globe. Furthermore, mobile communication channel paves way for organizations to utilize other communication channels through it, for example, social media, apps push notifications, and text messaging, etc.

4. Email Communication Channels

Email has revolutionized personalized digital marketing. This channel comes at a very low cost for companies and can provide them with instant access to their clients. Email communications enable organizations to not only engage in digital marketing and advertising but can also be used as a platform to connect with clients for support and after-sales services. This channel effectively serves as a bridge and directly brings companies and customers closer. We have all experienced using this channel to communicate with organizations. It enables a two-way communication and each party can greatly benefit from highly personal interactions. With the amount of information out there and a deluge of emails being sent out by online marketers, potential consumers may be overloaded and never get a chance to open marketed emails. Therefore, it is imperative that companies develop a sound and effective email communication strategy that addresses how to avoid being spammed by potential customers.

5. Instant Messaging and Live Chat Communication Channels

Developments in information and communication technologies have created more innovative ways to engage in marketing campaigns. Instant messaging is a fast way to communicate. Many organizations nowadays employ chatbots and other live chat application to shorten the distance with their customers and provide faster and more efficient services and support. Customers often want fast access to services and technical support. In this regard, these communication channels can become essential tools and elevate the quality of customer experiences.

6. AI-based "Human-Like" Marketing

We have all head of the generative AI-based ChatGPT and other human-like chats and instant messaging apps. Given the rise of these applications, there are enormous implications for industries, businesses, societies, and governments around the globe, which will accelerate as time marches on. Like every other discipline and field, marketing is also going to be deeply impacted by AI.[27, 28] AI-based marketing practices offer exciting opportunities for businesses to explore new arenas but also carry risk at the same time. AI tools for marketing rely on machine learning algorithms to assist marketers in various aspects of their work, such as personalized recommendations, content generation, and automation of routine activities, etc.

Digital Marketing Advantages

Unlike the traditional marketing, digital marketing is more efficient in terms of engaging, communicating, and interacting with customers. Digital marketing communication channels offer faster and cheaper ways of connecting with customers regardless of geographic distance and different time zones. Digital marketing can bring many benefits for organizations and can be leveraged to achieve business objectives. Table 1.2 outlines the advantages and objectives of digital marketing.

Marketing Analytics

Marketing analytics is a subdomain of business analytics that deals with extraction, collection, management, and analysis of huge of data to support insightful marketing-related decision.[29] The building block of marketing analytics is data, which is used to evaluate the effectiveness and success of marketing activities. Marketing analytics take organizations further into consumers' minds and helps them gain valuable insights from data to make more effective marketing strategies. Studies have shown that marketing analytics have a positive impact on marketing decision-making and product development management, which in turn impact the long-term competitive advantage, among other things (ibid). Tools and technologies are available in market, which help businesses access a wide array of marketing data to measure varies marketing activities. Amazon Web Services (AWS), for example, allows businesses to acquire millions of usage behavior data points, identify latent demand through pattern spotting, and match real-time demands effectively. To design and assess various marketing initiatives and aid marketing decisions, marketing analytics mostly employ structure data, such as customer demographics data, transaction data, and sales data.

Table 1.2 Objectives and Advantages of Digital Marketing

Objective and Advantages	Examples/Explanations
Expanding market share	Digital marketing can help companies expand their market share by attracting more customers through online promotion campaigns. In today's highly connected world, consumers have access to unlimited amount of information. Consumers spend a lot of time online, which makes them available to be targeted through online marketing. Companies can always develop individual strategies to improve customers' online journeys and make them more memorable and gain their loyalty. Many digital tools can be employed to know who the customers are automate and track digital marketing activities.
Brand building and awareness	Brand awareness is very important for firm's any growth as it represents a business's prowess to stand out in the crowd. Digital marketing is a great way for organizations to increase brand awareness. The availability of a diverse audience online provides excellent opportunities for companies to portray themselves uniquely, develop different tones across different channels, and follow a strategy of consistent branding.
Improving communication	The competitiveness of markets and technologically advanced businesses warrant that the flow of communication in any direction is seamless. Improved communication is key to retaining customers, delivering the best services, building relationships with various stakeholder and engaging in other corporate activities. Digital marketing tools, if utilized effectively, can make communication across all channels.
Streamlining customer experiences	Digital marketing can increase the quality of customers' online experiences by reducing the wait times of service delivery by providing all the essential information about products and services to aid in buying decision and by offering flexible channel options.
Lowering costs	The utilization of multiple digital marketing channels makes communication more effective and the delivery of services more efficient, which can help organizations to lower costs. In addition to that, companies can benefit from automated online chatbots to replace expensive human operators. The key to success is to balance convenience with lower costs.
Enhancing global and local reach	Many big and small corporations these days operate beyond their local boundaries. Digital marketing has made the beyond reach customers reachable by enabling real-time communication across online channels. Companies can now easily promote their goods and services and target potential customers whenever and wherever.

Source: Authors

Digital Marketing Analytics (DMA)

Digital marketing analytics is a subdomain within marketing analytics, and it is defined as the science and art of extracting, management, and analyzing of vast amount of semi-structural and unstructured digital data (such as text, images, and network data) to enable informed digital marketing decision. DMA is mostly focused on extracting, management, and analyzing of digital data the comes from social media platforms such as Facebook, Twitter, and search engines. The goal is to translate all the consumer behavior data into actionable business insights on which organization will capitalize to create and capture value.

Table 1.3 A Summary of Definitions of Various Marketing-Related Terms Discussed in This Chapter

Concept	Definition	Source
Marketing	Putting the right products and services in the right place in the right time at the right price.	11, 14
Digital marketing	Digital marketing is the application of digital media, data, and technology to achieve marketing objectives.	29
	Digital marketing is a set of integrated techniques, technologies, and information that enables marketing to create new products and services; enter new markets; improve the processes needed to engage in a dynamic conversation with people who are influencers and buyers; and ultimately target, acquire, and retain customers.	30
	An adaptive, technology-enabled process by which firms collaborate with customers and partners to jointly create, communicate, deliver, and sustain value for all stakeholders.	31
Marketing analytics	Marketing analytics, a subdomain of business analytics, refers to the collection, management, and analysis of data to extract useful insights to support marketing decision-making.	32
Digital marketing analytics	The science and art of extracting, management, and analyzing of vast amount of structural, semi-structural, and unstructured digital data (such as text, images, and network data) to enable informed digital marketing decision.	This book

Source: Authors

Digital Marketing Analytics Capabilities

DMA capabilities are necessary for organizations to successfully translate raw data into useful insights for value chain processes. In a study, Shahriar Akter et al. (2022) identified marketing analytics capabilities of cloud sharing platforms.[33] DMA capabilities can enable organizations to engage in better and more focused digital marketing by driving thought leadership and generating leads for potential market expansion.

Digital RAA Framework

The explosive growth of modern digital technologies has enabled average consumers to become smarter, more informative, and choosier when it comes to buying decisions. These days, a typical customer goes through several loops, steps, information, and channels (both online and offline) before making the actual purchase.[34, 35] Making a purchase is the first stage of entire consumer journey that includes post-purchase cognitive and emotional feelings experienced by the customers. These feelings and activities spearhead consumers' decisions to evaluate, buy, enjoy, advocate, and bond with the products and services. Digital technologies have impacted the activities and organizational processes associated with buying decisions and consumer experiences.

Figure 1.2 This Book's Structure in Relation to Digital RAA Framework
Source: Authors

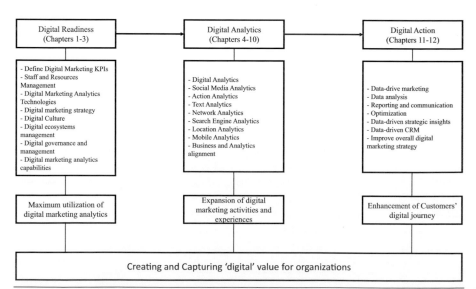

Figure 1.3 Digital RAA Framework for Digital Marketing Analytics
Source: Authors

Hence, organizations must employ digital marketing in every stage of the consumers' journey to create and capture value. Taking the importance of digital technologies, we have created, Digital RAA (readiness, analytics, action) framework that provides guidelines to organizations to utilize novel digital technologies for digitalizing marketing and creating value with it. This book can be divided into three main parts as shown in Figure 1.2 with chapters for each of the component of Digital RAA Framework as shown next:

Digital RAA framework, shown in Figure 1.3, has been developed based on theories and concepts of marketing and digital analytics to help manage and improve results from digital marketing. The framework allows researchers and marketers to adopt a customer-centric perspective and map the multiple ways in which digital marketing affects consumers and provides a strong and diverse conceptual framework for understanding digital marketing analytics. The discussions in this book are centered around this framework, and each chapter will cover various analytics tools and strategies to conceptualize the different types of digital data generated that can potentially be used to make informed marketing decision. The framework conceptualizes digital marketing as a four staged process, where each stage consists of several activities that leads to an outcome culminating in the final outcome for organizations.

Stages of Digital RAA Framework

1. Digital Readiness

Outcome: *Maximize the utilization of digital marketing analytics*

Digital readiness consists of all the digital activities involved in preparing organizations to embark on digitalizing marketing practices. Digital readiness equips organizations with capabilities and skills necessary for measuring and expanding the audience volume by utilizing multiple digital channels. The key concepts regarding this stage covered in this book are as follows:

- Define digital marketing KPIs
- Staff and resources management
- Digital marketing analytics technologies
- Digital marketing strategy
- Digital culture
- Digital ecosystems management
- Digital governance and management
- Digital marketing analytics capabilities

2. Digital Analytics

Outcome: *Expansion of digital marketing activities and experiences*

This stage involves collecting, storing, analyzing, and managing data from all digital marketing channels, such as social media, email, and website analytics. This data should include metrics, such as website traffic, engagement, conversion rates, and customer demographics. In this book, we explore digital analytics for marketing in great detail. Key topics in this stage that will be covered in this book are as follows:

- Digital analytics
- Social media analytics

- Action analytics
- Text analytics
- Network analytics
- Search engine analytics
- Location analytics
- Mobile analytics
- Business and analytics alignment

Digital Action

Outcome: *Enhancing of consumers' digital journey*

In the final step, organizations should to act on the insights gained from the data analysis. This includes creating and implementing a plan to optimize and improve marketing efforts. The action plan should include specific, measurable goals and objectives, and should be regularly monitored and evaluated. The ultimate goal of organizations should be to digitalize every aspect of marketing in order to create and capture digital value. Emerging digital technologies such as artificial intelligence, big data and analytics, blockchain, Internet of Things (IoT), cloud, mobile and social media technologies are changing the fundamental structures of the supply chain, business models, and value creation processes. These technologies enable digital transformation and their influence and reach are expanding exponentially. Organizations should utilize them in digital marketing practices and take advantage of the exciting new ways of creating value for customers. Digital action requires the following activities:

- Data-driven marketing
- Data analysis
- Reporting and communication
- Optimization
- Data-driven strategic insights
- Data-driven CRM
- Improve overall digital marketing strategy

Review Questions

1. What is marketing and digital marketing?
2. What are digital marketing channels?
3. What is digital marketing analytics?
4. What is RAA Framework?

Chapter 1 Citations

1. A. Krizanova, G. Lazaroiu, L. Gajanova, J. Kliestikova, M. Nadanyiova, and D. Moravcikova, "The effectiveness of marketing communication and importance of its evaluation in an online environment," *Sustain.*, vol. 11, no. 24, pp. 1–19, 2019, doi: 10.3390/su11247016.

2. S. S. Chun, H. Kim, J. R. Kim, S. Oh, and S. Sull, "Fast text caption localization on video using visual rhythm," *Lect. Notes Comput. Sci. (including Subser. Lect. Notes Artif. Intell. Lect. Notes Bioinformatics)*, vol. 2314, pp. 259–268, 2002, doi: 10.1007/3-540-45925-1_24.

3. N. H. Tien, "The role of international marketing in international business strategy," *Int. J. Res. Mark. Manag. Sale*, vol. 1, no. 2, pp. 134–138, 2020.

4. K. R. Kumar and G. C. Hadjinicola, "Resource allocation to defensive marketing and manufacturing strategies," *Eur. J. Oper. Res.*, vol. 94, no. 3, pp. 453–466, 1996, doi: 10.1016/0377-2217(95)00101-8.

5. K. Raman, M. K. Mantrala, S. Sridhar, and Y. E. Tang, "Optimal resource allocation with time-varying marketing effectiveness, margins and costs," *J. Interact. Mark.*, vol. 26, no. 1, pp. 43–52, 2012, doi: 10.1016/j.intmar.2011.05.001.

6. K. de Ruyter, D. Isobel Keeling, and L. V. Ngo, "When nothing is what it seems: A digital marketing research agenda," *Australas. Mark. J.*, vol. 26, no. 3, pp. 199–202, 2018, doi: 10.1016/j.ausmj.2018.07.003.

7. N. Morris, "Understanding digital marketing: Marketing strategies for engaging the digital generation," *J. Direct, Data Digit. Mark. Pract.*, vol. 10, no. 4, pp. 384–387, 2009, doi: 10.1057/dddmp.2009.7.

8. L. G. Pinto, L. Cavique, and J. M. A. Santos, "Marketing mix and new product diffusion models," *Procedia Comput. Sci.*, vol. 204, pp. 885–890, 2022, doi: 10.1016/j.procs.2022.08.107.

9. B. R. Londhe, "Marketing mix for next generation marketing," *Procedia Econ. Financ.*, vol. 11, no. 1964, pp. 335–340, 2014, doi: 10.1016/s2212-5671(14)00201-9.

10. R. Helm and S. Gritsch, "Examining the influence of uncertainty on marketing mix strategy elements in emerging business to business export-markets," *Int. Bus. Rev.*, vol. 23, no. 2, pp. 418–428, 2014, doi: 10.1016/j.ibusrev.2013.06.007.

11. S. Purohit, J. Paul, and R. Mishra, "Rethinking the bottom of the pyramid: Towards a new marketing mix," *J. Retail. Consum. Serv.*, vol. 58, no. August 2020, p. 102275, 2021, doi: 10.1016/j.jretconser.2020.102275.

12. J. R. K. Wichmann, A. Uppal, A. Sharma, and M. G. Dekimpe, "A global perspective on the marketing mix across time and space," *Int. J. Res. Mark.*, vol. 39, no. 2, pp. 502–521, 2022, doi: 10.1016/j.ijresmar.2021.09.001.

13. T. H. Thabit and M. B. Raewf, "The evaluation of marketing mix elements: A case study," *Int. J. Soc. Sci. Educ. Stud.*, vol. 4, no. 4, 2018, doi: 10.23918/ijsses.v4i4p100.

14. M. Boisen, K. Terlouw, P. Groote, and O. Couwenberg, "Reframing place promotion, place marketing, and place branding – moving beyond conceptual confusion," *Cities*, vol. 80, no. August 2017, pp. 4–11, 2018, doi: 10.1016/j.cities.2017.08.021.

15. O. Mintz, T. J. Gilbride, P. Lenk, and I. S. Currim, "The right metrics for marketing-mix decisions," *Int. J. Res. Mark.*, vol. 38, no. 1, pp. 32–49, 2021, doi: 10.1016/j.ijresmar.2020.08.003.

16. P. De Pelsmacker, S. van Tilburg, and C. Holthof, "Digital marketing strategies, online reviews and hotel performance," *Int. J. Hosp. Manag.*, vol. 72, no. February, pp. 47–55, 2018, doi: 10.1016/j.ijhm.2018.01.003.

17. G. Kaur, "The importance of digital marketing in the tourism industry," *Int. J. Res. – GRANTHAALAYAH*, vol. 5, no. 6, pp. 72–77, 2017, doi: 10.29121/granthaalayah.v5.i6.2017.1998.

18. D. C. Edelman, "Four ways to get more value from digital marketing," *McKinsey Q.*, no. March, pp. 1–8, 2010.

19. A. Djakasaputra, O. Y. A. Wijaya, A. S. Utama, C. Yohana, B. Romadhoni, and M. Fahlevi, "Empirical study of indonesian SMEs sales performance in digital era: The role of quality service and digital marketing," *Int. J. Data Netw. Sci.*, vol. 5, no. 3, pp. 303–310, 2021, doi: 10.5267/j.ijdns.2021.6.003.

20. D. Jayaram, A. K. Manrai, and L. A. Manrai, "Effective use of marketing technology in Eastern Europe: Web analytics, social media, customer analytics, digital campaigns and mobile applications," *J. Econ. Financ. Adm. Sci.*, vol. 20, no. 39, pp. 118–132, 2015, doi: 10.1016/j.jefas.2015.07.001.

21. R. Ioannis, N. Angelos, and T. Nikolaos, "Digital marketing: The case of digital marketing strategies on luxurious hotels," *Procedia Comput. Sci.*, vol. 219, no. 2022, pp. 688–696, 2023, doi: 10.1016/j.procs.2023.01.340.

22. S. Hassan, S. Z. A. Nadzim, and N. Shiratuddin, "Strategic use of social media for small business based on the AIDA model," *Procedia – Soc. Behav. Sci.*, vol. 172, pp. 262–269, 2015, doi: 10.1016/j.sbspro.2015.01.363.

23. F. U. Rehman, T. Nawaz, M. Ilyas, and S. Hyder, "A comparative analysis of mobile and email marketing using AIDA model," *J. Basic Appl. Sci. Res.*, vol. 4, no. 6, pp. 38–49, 2014.

24. D. Chaffey and D. Bosomworth, "Digital marketing strategy planning template," *Smart Insights*, no. January, pp. 1–14, 2013, [Online]. Available: http://www.enterprisebucks.co.uk/wp-content/uploads/2014/09/digital-marketing-plan-template-smart-insights1.pdf.

25. A. Dwivedi and N. Pawsey, "Examining the drivers of marketing innovation in SMEs," *J. Bus. Res.*, vol. 155, no. PB, p. 113409, 2023, doi: 10.1016/j.jbusres.2022.113409.

26. S. Banerjee, S. Xu, and S. D. Johnson, "How does location based marketing affect mobile retail revenues? The complex interplay of delivery tactic, interface mobility and user privacy," *J. Bus. Res.*, vol. 130, no. November 2018, pp. 398–404, 2021, doi: 10.1016/j.jbusres.2020.02.042.

27. Y. A. Jeon, "Let me transfer you to our AI-based manager: Impact of manager-level job titles assigned to AI-based agents on marketing outcomes," *J. Bus. Res.*, vol. 145, no. March, pp. 892–904, 2022, doi: 10.1016/j.jbusres.2022.03.028.

28. A. Haleem, M. Javaid, M. Asim, R. Pratap, and R. Suman, "International Journal of Intelligent Networks Artificial intelligence (AI) applications for marketing: A literature-based study," *Int. J. Intell. Networks*, vol. 3, no. July, pp. 119–132, 2022, [Online]. Available: https://doi.org/10.1016/j.ijin.2022.08.005.

29. D. Shah and B. P. S. Murthi, "Marketing in a data-driven digital world: Implications for the role and scope of marketing," *J. Bus. Res.*, vol. 125, no. June 2020, pp. 772–779, 2021, doi: 10.1016/j.jbusres.2020.06.062.

30. Gartner, "Digital marketing," *2021*. https://www.gartner.com/.

31. M. Wedel and P. K. Kannan, "Marketing analytics for data-rich environments," *J. Mark.*, 2016, doi: 10.1509/jm.15.0413.

32. H. Li, Y. Wu, D. Cao, and Y. Wang, "Organizational mindfulness towards digital transformation as a prerequisite of information processing capability to achieve

market agility," *J. Bus. Res.*, no. October, pp. 1–13, 2019, doi: 10.1016/j. jbusres.2019.10.036.

33. S. Akter, U. Hani, Y. K. Dwivedi, and A. Sharma, "The future of marketing analytics in the sharing economy," *Ind. Mark. Manag.*, vol. 104, no. September 2021, pp. 85–100, 2022, doi: 10.1016/j.indmarman.2022.04.008.

34. C. Del Bucchia, C. Lancelot Miltgen, C. A. Russell, and C. Burlat, "Empowerment as latent vulnerability in techno-mediated consumption journeys," *J. Bus. Res.*, vol. 124, no. February 2019, pp. 629–651, 2021, doi: 10.1016/j. jbusres.2020.03.014.

35. L. Lundin and D. Kindström, "Digitalizing customer journeys in B2B markets," *J. Bus. Res.*, vol. 157, no. January, 2023, doi: 10.1016/j.jbusres.2022.113639.

2

Digital Marketing KPIs, Strategy, Ecosystems, Governance, and More

---

CHAPTER OBJECTIVES

After reading this chapter, readers should understand the following:

- KPIs for digital marketing
- Digital marketing analytics tools
- Digital culture and digital resource management
- Digital governance and ecosystems management
- Digital marketing analytics capabilities

Digital Marketing KPIs

Key performance indicators or KPIs are a set of quantifiable measurements that organizations can use to quantify the business's overall long-term performance.[1] KPIs are important parameters that can enable organizations to keep track of their progress towards marketing.[2, 3] Setting up clear and concise digital marketing KPIs will assist you to determine your company's overall digital marketing objectives. Before starting any digital marketing campaigns, it is essential to define clear business objectives and KPIs that will be used to measure the success of the digital advertisement and other marketing campaigns. This will help to align the analytics efforts with the overall business goals of the organization. By defining measurable goals and objectives, KPIs provide a clear direction and focus for digital marketing efforts. They enable organizations to track and evaluate their performance, identify areas of improvement, and make data-driven decisions. In Chapter 12, we explain how KPIs can help in adjustments and repositioning of digital marketing initiatives.

One of the steps that analysts and business consultants are often called into organizations to do is to help them identify what their business goals are and how they map to digital marketing. As many studying the digital marketing are aspiring or actually the people responsible for implementing digital strategies and analytics/insights, it is important to collect all the needed information at the beginning of any project or implementation plan that will be used for setting up digital marketing and analytics,

DOI: 10.4324/9781003025351-2

along with the advertising part. The first step after collecting relevant information would be to start setting up KPIs. Some examples of digital marketing KPIs may include

- Which marketing channels are driving the most traffic and conversions these days?
- Which digital communication channels are more effective?
- What are the key drivers of social media customer engagement?
- Which digital advertisement campaigns are most effective in reaching target audiences?
- How satisfied are our customers, and what steps can we take to improve their satisfaction levels?
- How engaged is our audience on social media, and what strategies can we implement to boost engagement metrics such as likes, shares, and comments? (This specific KPI is related to actions analytics covered in Chapter 7.)

Organizations should customize digital marketing KPIs for their needs, which can vary depending on the business and value creation mechanism. When setting up KPIs for digital marketing, it is important to keep in mind that they should be measurable, achievable, and credible.[4] There are various KPIs that can be used for digital marketing. For example, website traffic, which measures the number of visitors coming to an organization's website. The number of visitors indicate the level of interest, and it can help to evaluate the effectiveness of digital marketing campaigns and digital content. Newer web analytics platforms such as Google Analytics 4 have built-in engagement metrics that measure the engagement of a user or a session. There are various tools available to track website traffic through tools, such as Google Analytics 4 and Adobe Analytics. Google Analytics 4 enables you to track and analyze a wide range of data about an organization's website visitors, including how many people are visiting the site, where they are coming from, what pages they are viewing, and how long they are staying on the site, etc. In the following Table 2.1, we provide a list of some of the KPIs for digital marketing along with the measurement tools.

Other examples of web analytics tools that help in KPI measurements include Clicky (https://clicky.com/), which is a real-time website traffic monitoring tool that provides real-time data on visitor behavior, heatmaps, and conversion tracking. Piwik is a free,

Table 2.1 KPIs for Digital Marketing and Measurement Tools

No.	KPIs	Explanations	Tools
1.	Online traffic monitoring	It refers to the total number of visits to the website of an organization over a specific period of time.	Tools that can be used to measure this KPI include Google Analytics, Adobe Analytics, and Matomo, etc.
2.	Social media engagement	This KPI can be measured in terms of number of likes, comments, shares, retweets, and followers on different social media platforms such as Facebook and Twitter.	Social media analytics tools such as Sprout Social and Hootsuite can be used for measuring this KPI.

No.	KPIs	Explanations	Tools
3.	Conversion rate measurement	Refers to the percentage of website visitors into potential buyers. Either through purchase or filling out of a form.	Tools for measurement include Google Analytics, Adobe Analytics, and Kissmetrics.
4.	Click-through rate (CTR)	It measures the percentage of users who click on an ad or link compared to the number of impressions.	Examples include Google Ads and Facebook Ads
5.	CPC (cost per click)	It measures the average cost incurred for each click on an ad that marketers have put on websites or social media, based on the number of clicks the ad receives.	Some examples of the tools include LinkedIn Ads, Google Ads, and Facebook Ads, etc.

open source website analytics tool that provides insights into website traffic, visitor behavior, and conversion tracking. Similarly, other KPIs like conversion rate measures the percentage of website visitors who take the desired action on the website, such as making a purchase, filling out a form, or subscribing to the newsletter.

Staff and Resource Management

After the KPIs are identified, organizations should plan for staffing and resources management because it is an integral part of running any successful digital marketing campaigns. The effective management and use of staff and resources will speed up the process to achieve marketing goals. Investment in building a team with the right skill set to handle digital marketing analytics is very important. The team will require a variety of staff and resources to support its operations and growth. Some key roles and resources that may be needed include the following:

Technical Leadership

The commitment of leadership to employ technical capabilities for extracting insights from big data for organizations is essential to the expansion of digital reach. Leadership capabilities and technical skills are equally important to stay ahead of the competition given the rapid market changes and emergence of new digital technologies. Technical leadership should be able to make timely and concise decisions, share their knowledge, mentor individuals, and use their abilities to equip their teams with skills and resources to leverage technology for digital marketing.

Data Analysts and Scientists

Analyzing huge amounts of data and making sense of it is at the core of marketing analytics. Key staff working on data should include analysts and scientist who will be responsible for collecting, cleaning, and analyzing data to inform marketing decisions. This team usually performs descriptive analytics applies statistical techniques and data mining methods to identify patterns and trends. They will also be responsible for creating and maintaining data pipelines and data models. They will have to work with other departments and teams such as the business team to understand the requirements of the organization and provide data-driven recommendations.

Digital Marketing Analysts and Specialists

Alongside the data analysts and data scientist, organizations will need digital marketing analysts, and specialists who will be responsible for analyzing and interpreting the data collected by the data analysts and scientists. They will work closely with the data analysts and marketing analysts to ensure that campaigns are targeting the right audiences and that they are delivering the desired results. They will also be responsible for creating dashboards and reports that can be used by the marketing team to make decisions. Other functions will include, setting up, configuring, and maintaining the tools used for marketing automation, such as email marketing platforms, etc.

Other Technical Staff

These individuals will be responsible for maintaining and managing the organization's technology systems and infrastructure, including hardware, software, and networks. This may include roles such as system administrators, network administrators, and software developers, IT staff, security staff, and legal teams. The IT staff usually oversee the security and maintenance of the organization's data and systems. They will also be responsible for providing technical support and troubleshooting. IT security staff work towards protecting the organization's digital assets and data from cyber threats. Roles may include cybersecurity analysts, penetration testers, and incident responders. The legal and compliance staff are there to ensure that the organization is following relevant laws and regulations and for protecting the organization's intellectual property. Roles may include legal counsel and compliance officers.

Digital Marketing Analytics Technologies

In addition to staff, a digital marketing analytics team will require various resources such as marketing analytics and automation tools, data storage and management systems, and office space. The team will also need to have access to large amounts of data, such as web analytics, social media data, and customer data, to be able to perform their analysis. Overall, the tools described later will help you to understand how your target audience interacts with your website and campaigns, and how to optimize them to achieve better results. We have categorized the tools into different groups as shown in Figure 2.1.

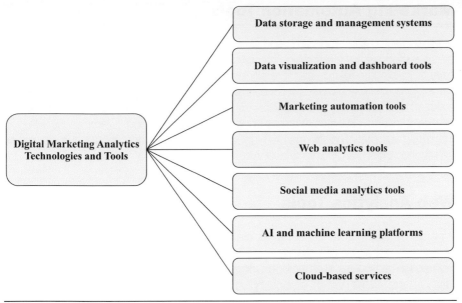

Figure 2.1 Digital Marketing Analytics Tools
Source: Authors

Data Storage and Management Systems

Digital marketing analytics deal with very large amounts of unstructured data. These systems are used to store and manage the large amounts of data that are collected for analysis. The size and scale of these systems will depend on the overall data infrastructure of the organization. This can include data warehousing and business intelligence systems, as well as cloud-based storage solutions. Traditional databases are not suitable for unstructured data. Non-relational databases such as NoSQL can offer much more flexibility in handling unstructured and semi-structured data. In addition, organizations can also employ data lakes that can store vast amounts of structured, semi-structured, and unstructured data in its raw form.

Data Visualization and Dashboard Tools

Data visualization is a great way for analyzing marketing trends. It makes analysis easier for analysts by enabling graphical representation of data through the use of various visual elements, such as charts, graphs, maps, and other formats. It is also a great way to simplify complex data findings. It makes reporting and communicating of the results to the stakeholders very easy and enables non-expert users to quickly grasp the meaning. It also makes it a lot easier for the executive and leaders (upper management) to make business decisions. Thanks to the advances in digital technologies, a plethora of tools are available to create interactive dashboards and reports that can be used by the marketing team to make decisions. Examples include Tableau, Power BI, and Looker Studio (formally Google Data Studio).

Marketing Automation Tools

Marketing automation tools are used to automate repetitive tasks and to segment and target audiences. By streamlining marketing tasks, these tools can help marketers to save time, allocate resources more efficiently, and enhance personalized marketing campaigns. There are various tools available for the automation of digital marketing tasks. The employability of these tools will depend on the organization's specific marketing needs, analytics strategy, budget, scale, and scope. Examples include marketing automation platforms like HubSpot, Marketo, Pardot, and Eloqua, as well as A/B testing tools like Optimizely and VWO.

Web Analytics Tools

Website marketing is very effective for creating a customer base. In this regard, web analytics tools can be used to track and analyze website traffic, user behavior, and conversion rates. Examples include Google Analytics, Adobe Analytics, and Piwik, etc. Website visibility which is about how discoverable your website is, can be very helpful in attracting potential customers and achieving online success. Search engine optimization (SEO) tools track and measure website visibility and performance in search engine results. Examples include Ahrefs, SEMrush, and Moz. To enhance website visibility, the marketing team should consider various things, such as site speed, quality of the content, and user experience. For example, with the emergence of mobile devices, it is very crucial to having a mobile-friendly website. They should ensure that the organization's main website is responsive and provides optimal user experience on various screen sizes and devices. Many people use their mobile devices when searching for products or services. Hence, they would naturally give preference to mobile-friendly websites in search results.

Social Media Analytics Tools

Social media analytics play an important role in digital marketing. Thanks to the advances in digital technologies, many tools are now available for marketers to analyze huge chucks of social media data and gain valuable insights into the performance and effectiveness of social media campaigns. These tools are used to track and analyze social media metrics, such as likes, shares, and engagement. Examples include Hootsuite Insights, Brand24, and Sprout Social. By successfully utilizing these tools marketers can bring many advantages for businesses, such as performance tracking, content optimization, competitor analysis, customer sentiment analysis, and ROI measurement, etc.

AI and Machine Learning Platforms

As we discussed in Chapter 1, AI and machine learning are enabling fundamental changes in digital marketing practices. Because of the new processes and tools enabled by these platforms, organizations are able to analyze large, complex data sets, identify patterns and insights, and make market predictions. Examples include TensorFlow, PyTorch, and R-Studio. AI tools are incredibly helpful in terms of analyzing consumer behavior and buying habits. Organizations can personalize marketing campaigns by employing AI-driven and track progress in real time.

Cloud-Based Services

Modern digital marketing practices rely on collaboration across a network of digital platforms and between departments within an organization. Hence, there is a need for cloud-based services. These services provide marketing teams with the flexibility, scalability, and cost-effectiveness they need to store valuable data and collaborate with other departments and platforms. For example, cloud-based collaboration tools like Google Drive, Microsoft Office 365, and Asana facilitate team collaboration within an organization, speed up the process of content creation, and enhance project management. There are also cloud-based advertising platforms like Google Ads, Facebook Ads Manager, and LinkedIn Ads which are good tools for creating and managing digital advertising campaigns. In short, by using cloud-based applications and services marketers can collaborate on documents, share files, and track progress in real time, which can lead to the improvement of overall productivity and organizational coordination.

Digital Marketing Strategy

Digital marketing strategy should identify digital communication channels for expanding the reach of organizations. Digital technologies have enabled the creation of previously unavailable digital communication channels that make it possible to go beyond borders and reach the untapped diverse global audience. Digital presence on these channels significantly contributes to brand awareness, widens the horizons, and enables organizations to reach a vast diversity of clients. In this regard, social media is a highly important digital channel that can expand the reach of organizations and attract new customers. Organizations should develop a sound and comprehensive social media strategy that can enable digital marketers to reach local and global audience. The strategy should lay out clear plans and mechanisms that consider long-term brand and is focused on digital contents. It's all about numbers. Increase the numbers of followers! Social media presence is pivotal to not only retain the existing customers but also to attract new ones and convert non-customers into customers. Social media is very effective to capitalize customer loyalty and maintain long-term relationships with them at comparatively lower costs to the organization. To maintain social media, organizations should develop a good ***digital content strategy.*** The creation and maintenance of good content is fundamental to communicating the values of organizations and boosting engagement with clients.

Digital Culture

It is imperative for organizations to encourage digital culture, which refers to the values, norms, and behaviors that shape how employees interact with and use technology in their workplace. It encompasses the way in which employees use digital tools and systems to complete their work, as well as the ways in which technology shapes communication and collaboration within the organization. A positive digital culture in an organization can lead to increased productivity and innovation, as employees are empowered to use technology to their fullest potential. Some elements that can foster a positive digital culture in an organization include

- **Change management:** Digital technologies bring changes in every aspect of organization. The top management should adapt to these changes and encourage the employees to be open to new technologies and ways of working. Organizations should ensure the readiness for changes due to digital transformation of value generating processes.
- **Organization-wide collaboration:** Collaboration and working together facilitates the achievement of organizational goals. In this regard, utilized digital technologies can contribute to smoothening collaboration and communication across teams and departments inside the organization.
- **Employee empowerment and development:** Empowerment of employees to key to the successful implementation of digital transformation-driven changes in an organization. The top management should ensure that employees have timely access to the tools, training, and autonomy they need to be successful in their roles.
- **Innovation and creativity:** Leadership should create a conducive environment for creativity and working with new tools and methods. They should encourage employees to suggest new ideas and ways of using technology to improve the organization.
- **Digital security and safety:** With the increasing cyber threats, it has never been more important to focus on the digital security of organizations. Hence, implementing robust security measures to protect the organization's digital assets and data is key to creating a safe environment for using new technologies for organizational affairs.
- **Feedback and improvements:** Feedback is important for bringing positive changes into the digital culture of an organization. The leadership should regularly review and update the organization's digital culture and technology to ensure it remains aligned with the organization's goals and objectives. For instance, with the rise of remote works, they should encourage and enable employees to work remotely with digital tools. They should also let the data enlighten the way and use data and analytics to make informed decisions and improve performance.

Digital Ecosystems Management

The recent development in digital technologies, such as AI, bigdata, analytics, and mobile technologies are changing the global digital ecosystem very fast. Information and communication technologies (ICT) offer tremendous opportunities for growth and success. Organizations capitalize on ICT-enabled mechanisms to expand their reach and benefits from the new industry dynamics and market trends. Organizations must develop strategies and mechanisms in order to successfully manage all the digital ecosystems players, such as suppliers, customers, trading partners, applications, third-party data service providers and all respective technologies. In this regard, investments in information technology initiatives are paramount to the success of digital ecosystems management as they can help feed the rest of digital activities. Organizations should consider acquiring new talents, technology equipment, and utility software, etc., to maximize the impact of ICT on their overall marketing strategy. In this regard, artificial intelligence is a great avenue for investments. AI-based marketing analytics can enable organizations to acquire excellent precision in terms of targeting certain segments of the market and thus, bring more efficiency in digital marketing.

Data Governance and Management

Data governance and management refers to the overall management and control of an organization's digital assets and infrastructure. It involves the establishment of policies, processes, and standards to ensure the quality, integrity, security, and usability of the organization's data. Data governance and management is crucial for ensuring that data is accurate, reliable, and secure. This includes creating guidelines and protocols for data collection, storage, and sharing, and designating roles and responsibilities for data management within the organization. It's important to note that this is a dynamic process and should be iterative, regularly monitoring and collecting data, analyzing it, and taking appropriate actions. This will enable marketers to continuously improve their digital marketing strategy and tactics. In this regard, organizations should develop digital governance framework which is a set of policies, procedures, and guidelines that organizations use to manage and govern their digital assets and technology systems. Data governance framework can vary across different organizations. However, it should include elements such as the structure, data management, risk management, compliance, change management, collaboration, and incident management, etc.

Digital Marketing Analytics Capabilities

Digital technologies are disrupting societies, industries, and value chain processes.[5, 6] Digital transformation allows organizations to digitally alter their revenue-generating mechanisms, digitalize operations, and foster efficiency. Digital transformation of organizational processes that accommodate digital marketing practices can enhance the ability of organizations to encourage going digital and maximize the positive impacts of digitalization. These days consumers are more intelligent, informative, and sophisticated because of the availability of information, thanks to the advancement in digital technologies. Their needs have evolved and they have become pickier because of plethora of choices and almost no switching costs to them. Hence, organizations should develop big data and marketing analytics capabilities to better understand consumers' behaviors and take charge. Organizational dynamic capabilities are particularly important when it comes to adapting new digital technologies for value creating processes.[7] Digital marketing analytics capabilities are necessary to extract, manage, and analyze vast amount of structural, semi-structural, and unstructured digital data (such as text, images, and network data) to enable informed digital marketing decision.

Review Questions

1. What are some examples of KPIs for digital marketing?
2. What resources are needed for digital marketing analytics?
3. Explain digital ecosystems for digital marketing
4. What is digital culture?
5. Why are digital marketing analytics capabilities important?

Chapter 2 Citations

1. J. Singh, G. S. Kushwaha, and M. Kumari, "The role of KPIs and metrics in digital marketing," *Res. Rev. Int. J. Multidiscip.*, vol. 4, no. 1, pp. 1053–1058, 2019, [Online]. Available: https://www.researchgate.net/publication/337111093_The_Role_of_KPIs_and_Metrics_in_Digital_Marketing.

2. K. Raman, M. K. Mantrala, S. Sridhar, and Y. E. Tang, "Optimal resource allocation with time-varying marketing effectiveness, margins and costs," *J. Interact. Mark.*, vol. 26, no. 1, pp. 43–52, 2012, doi: 10.1016/j.intmar.2011.05.001.

3. D. Velimirovi, M. Velimirovi, and R. Stankovi, "Role and importance of key performance indicators measurement," *Serb. J. Manag.*, vol. 6, no. 1, pp. 63–72, 2011.

4. J. R. Saura, P. Palos-Sánchez, and L. M. C. Suárez, "Understanding the digital marketing environment with kpis and web analytics," *Futur. Internet*, vol. 9, no. 4, pp. 1–13, 2017, doi: 10.3390/FI9040076.

5. A. K. Feroz, H. Zo, and A. Chiravuri, "Digital transformation and environmental sustainability: A review and research agenda," *Sustainability*, vol. 13, no. 3, p. 1530, February 2021, doi: 10.3390/su13031530.

6. P. C. Verhoef *et al.*, "Digital transformation: A multidisciplinary reflection and research agenda," *J. Bus. Res.*, no. September, 2019, doi: 10.1016/j.jbusres.2019.09.022.

7. A. K. Feroz, H. Zo, J. Eom, and A. Chiravuri, "Identifying organizations' dynamic capabilities for sustainable digital transformation: A mixed methods study," *Technol. Soc.*, vol. 73, no. April, 2023, doi: 10.1016/j.techsoc.2023.102257.

The Evolution of Digital Analytics and the Internet

CHAPTER OBJECTIVES

After reading this chapter, readers should understand the following:

- Structured and unstructured data
- Introduction to the Internet and the World Wide Web
- Evolution of the Web

How Digital Analytics Began

Digital analytics is the study of various forms of business data to improve the online experience of a business and its customers. In other words, digital analytics involve the collection, measurement, analysis, and interpretation of large chucks of data from various online resources to optimize digital marketing activities. Access to data is important for analytics. Other than the internal organizational data that is easily accessible for analysts working for the organization, various, there are many sources from which external data can be collected, such as websites, mobile applications, social media, and other digital platforms. The data collected from these channels can be used to understand user behavior, optimize user experience, and make data-driven decisions. The insights obtained from data analytics can help businesses to improve performance by understanding consumer behavior, identifying trends and opportunities, measuring the effectiveness of certain program like marketing campaigns, and optimizing online presence.

The evolution of digital analytics took place simultaneously with the development of digital marketing. For our purposes, once Internet technology was developed, it was made to be accessible and extensible to the public. The Internet allowed search engines and social media to emerge as specific online marketing disciplines that students and practitioners could study and master. Also, the development of the Google search engine and its associated web services supplemented this change and revolutionized the manner and ease with which we access and use data.

DOI: 10.4324/9781003025351-3

Structured Versus Unstructured Data

More than 50 years ago, the data we had collected was mostly structured. Structured data is data with a high level of organization, such as balance sheets (cash, accounts payable), medical devices (heart rate, blood pressure), or census records (birth, employment). The structure is provided in the collection of the data through certain objectives so that once the data is captured, it occupies a specified field. Nowadays, we capture a great deal of unstructured or semi-structured data. The emergence of social media platforms such Facebook, TikTok, and Twitter, etc., has resulted in an unprecedented amount of content generation by users. In other words, tons of unstructured data is created on a daily basis. Other than the social data, unstructured data can come in various forms, including text documents, emails, social media posts, audio and video files, images, and sensor data, etc. Structured data can be processed easily in a relational database or spreadsheet. Unstructured data is information that does not exist in a row and column database. To be able to capture unstructured data, we must modify and create special tools that manipulate the data into intelligible results. Otherwise, when left unmanaged, data can become overwhelming, making it difficult to organize and work with. Hence, in terms of analysis and insights extraction, three types of data exit.

The first one (structured) makes is very easy for data scientists and perhaps business analysts to organize and extract meaning from it. The second (unstructured) does contain valuable information, but it is extremely challenging to analyze it using traditional data processing techniques (See Figure 3.1). Special analytics techniques are required to analyze and interpret that data. There is an additional state of data that is termed "semi-structured". It consists of information that is nearly prepared and ready to be organized, but it lacks the cleaning and organization necessary for it to be processed; for example, resolving misspellings and spacing errors in a column of data. Businesses are interested in mining unstructured data because of the possible benefits of the data-driven insights, such as reducing operation costs, responding more quickly to changing market conditions, and innovative market research. Once the unstructured and semi-structured data is organized for analysts to use, the applications created with the newly structured data can be organized and shared across the various business, non-profit, and educational enterprises.

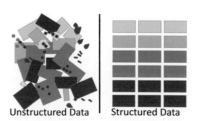

Unstructured Data | Structured Data

Figure 3.1 Structured vs. Unstructured Data
Source: Authors

The Evolution of the Internet

The Internet, formerly called Arpanet by the Department of Defense (DOD), is a global network of interconnected networks that was created in 1983 as a way for researchers to quickly and freely communicate. In 1990, the now famous computer scientist Tim Berners-Lee created the World Wide Web, which opened the network for everyone, nationally and internationally.

Tim Berners-Lee and the World Wide Web

Tim Berners-Lee is most famous for his creation of the World Wide Web. When Berners-Lee worked at CERN (the European Organization for Nuclear Research, founded in 1954, which operates the largest particle physics laboratory in the world), he encountered a problem: physicists from all over the world came to CERN, worked for a period, and then left. To fix the disorganization between the multitude of platforms and protocols, Berners-Lee created the World Wide Web, a universal medium to link information (and people) together. In November 1989, he created the three protocols – HTTP, URL, and HTML – that we now know as the "Web", which brought him global fame. With the rise of mobile devices, the World Wide Web continues to maintain its level of significance in the modern world, much as it did in the early 1990s. Berners-Lee recently[1] commented on the growing trend of Internet users to favor native applications (that are experienced by users individually) instead of Web apps that can sustain a wider conversation and community. Berners-Lee would like to see companies and developers focusing on building Web apps using HTML5, so content and experiences are more shareable than dedicated Web apps designed to run exclusively on mobile devices. HTML5 pages render faster and identically across all Web browsers (mobile and desktop), while requiring less coding.

Network Types

Web networks are logical constructs or ways of representing and simplifying complexity that help both humans and computers understand how data spreads across several interconnected devices. The data is moved over phone lines, cables, and satellites and sent to the intended devices via intelligent network devices, such as switches, hubs, and routers. For the most part, the communications infrastructure remains invisible to the average user, unless it breaks. Once that happens, interruptions and error messages become more noticeable and cryptic, uncovering a vast group of protocols and interconnections that are often difficult to troubleshoot. Today, there are at least five methods to connect to the Internet and the World Wide Web, including

- Public Internet
- Intranet: network that runs internally in an organization

- Extranet: two or more joined networks that share information
- Mobile: the mobile Internet used by our handheld devices connecting through Internet providers
- Internet of Things: devices talking to devices – creates intelligent Web

Internet Timeline

- 1950s: After WWII, the Cold War spawns the need for new ways to communicate more quickly, hence Arpanet originated for military uses.
- 1960s: Arpanet became available to researchers around the world.
- 1970s: Apple and IBM developed personal computers in the late 1970s, which appeal to a new audience who can run simple word processing and spreadsheet applications on them.
- 1980s: Transmission Control Protocol/Internet Protocol (TCP/IP) created as a basic communication language for the Internet. The National Science Foundation operated the backbone and banned commercial traffic.
- 1980s: Web 1.0 or the first stage in the World Wide Web developed, which was entirely made up of static, non-interactive Web pages connected by hyperlinks.
- 1990s: Venture capital funding poured into untried and uniquely individual business models.
- 1991: Gopher developed as: a TCP/IP for searching and distributing documents over the Internet. Hyper Text Mark-up Language (HTML) developed for creating Web pages and Web applications.
- 1993: Mosaic was the first freely available browser, which soon spawned Netscape. Mosaic supported Gopher, file transfer protocol, and network news transfer protocol.
- 1995: Yahoo! Search Engine debuted and initially used Google algorithms up until 2004, where it began investing in its algorithms.
- 1998: Google Search founded on September 4, 1998 by Larry Page and Sergey Brin. Google Search differentiated itself from other search engines by focusing on the relevance of pages based on patterns formed in hyperlinks.
- 2000–2002: Businesses failed during the 2000s, which led to the disappearance of venture capital funding.
- 2004–2009: The popularity of the WWW equated to a rapid growth in users, content, and sales, both B2C and B2B. As a result of the popularity, there is an emergence of new players, such as Facebook, Twitter, Foursquare, YouTube, and LinkedIn – the social networks we are familiar with today.

An Introduction to the World Wide Web and How It Works

The World Wide Web is a set of protocols and services enabling devices to communicate with each other, and it provides the basis for the study of digital analytics, whereas the Internet is the global network of interconnected devices, such as personal computers, smartphones, switches, routers, satellites, and cables. Through the interrelationships, the Internet is composed of several technologies, and one of the underlying software technologies is the WWW, or simply the Web. In its simplest form, the Web is composed of interlinked hypertext documents (e.g., websites) that can be accessed through Web browsers such as Google Chrome, Apple Safari, Firefox, and Microsoft Edge/Internet Explorer. The Internet functions as a large phone book or digital directory that can translate an almost infinite number of names into numbers as well as numbers into names.[2] The numbers point back to logical network addresses. These networks point to nodes on the network using Internet routing, protocols. Computers and software require the logical address of the port numbers that communications are directed to and from. Services communicate with each other, on the same computer and other computers connected to the network. However, the rest of the underlying communication that powers the web is transparent to users.

Note: The World Wide Web represents only 1% of the entire Internet; the Dark Web, Deep Web, and their vast ecosystem make up the rest. The Dark Web is part of the World Wide Web content existing on overlay networks that use the public Internet but require specific software, configurations, or authorization to access.[3] The Deep Web is the part of the World Wide Web whose contents are not indexed by standard search engines for many reasons. The Deep Web is opposite to the World Wide Web.[4]

The Seven-Layer OSI Model

The most common way to visualize communications on the Web is by using the operating systems interconnection (OSI) seven-layer model. Data packet communications are broken down from a physical layer device, such as an Ethernet or wireless port of a network node, which is usually a computer or mobile device. Communications are transformed from the physical level all the way up to the application level, where users interact with the communications and reply. The process of traversing the seven layers of connectivity happens several times each second, and the result is the Web that we interact with.

The Evolution of the Web

The Web has radically evolved since it was first created, the earliest version being referred to as Web 1.0. As Table 3.1 shows, the Web has three distinct phases, and we cover each of them in this chapter.

Web 1.0

Web 1.0, read-only web, is an early version of the Internet and is static in nature. It has a one-to-many fashion of sharing information. In Web 1.0, Web developers and designers create websites and content for users to consume. The design of the site prevents users from contributing to the content or crafting a response. Web 1.0 users are only passive recipients of the information and content, which means

Table 3.1 Web 1.0 to Web 4.0

Web 1.0	Web 2.0	Web 3.0	Web 4.0
Read-Only	Read-Write	Personal, Portable, Extensible	Converged
Company & Business focused	Community, Social focused	Focused on the Individual	Personal Assistants (Siri/ Google Now Cortana)
Home Page	Blogs, logging, Wikis	Streaming media, Live streaming, Data Waves	Bots/Intelligent Agents/Drones
Own Your Content	Share Your Content	Collect & Content	Programmable Content & Content on Demand
Web Forms	Web Applications	Smart/ Autonomous Applications	Artificial Intelligence/ Algorithms
Web Directories and Folders	Content Tagging	User Behavior/ Quantified Self	Private Cloud, Internet of Things
Page Views	Cost Per Click (CPC)	User Engagement via Collected Metrics	Cross Channel Measurement
Banner Ads	Interactive Ads	Behavioral Ads & Targeting	Programmatic Advertising
Britannica Online	Wikipedia	Semantic Web	Transparent Web/ WikiLeaks
HTML and Web Portals	XML/RSS	RDF/RDFS/OWL	Quantum Computing, AI

Source: Authors

they would be considered the readers, not contributors, of the content. Web 1.0 is another channel of narrow information distribution like other conventional one-to-many technologies, such as radio and television. Web 1.0 websites are only used for information presentation purposes and not used for generating information or content.

Web 2.0

Web 2.0 is the version of the World Wide Web that most of us have experience of. It is characterized by the shift from static webpages to user-generated content and the emergence of social media and mobile technologies. Web 2.0 alters the WWW landscape by turning the Web into a collaborative ecosystem where users could create content, share ideas, and offer actual products and services. Web 2.0 allows two-way and many-to-many information flow and user-generated content.[5] The content generated by users over social media platforms is known as user-generated content (UGC). Some tools of this collaborative ecosystem: are podcasts, blogs, tags, social bookmarks, social networks, wikis, etc. One thing to note is that Web 2.0 is not a technical standard or an update to the first standard, Web 1.0. However, it reflects the changes in the way people use the Web and how programmers design websites. Due to changing societal norms, webmasters and programmers develop platforms allowing users to create, monetize, and share their content.

Features of Web 2.0

- **Scalability of software:** This refers to the ability to gather behavioral data via cookies and clickstream analytics. A clickstream is a path or order of pages that visitors choose when navigating through a site. (Note: clickstreams, when applied to the Web, are the categories of websites that users visit on a regular basis – the clickstream is used for retargeting purposes.) Users emerge as co-developers, and software begins harnessing the collective Intelligence of developers and users.
- **Long tail:** This is a term popularized by *Wired Magazine* editor Chris Anderson in 2004. It refers to many products that sell in small quantities and is contrasted with the limited number of best-selling products, new platforms and revenue models are tailored to an individual's needs and desires. For example, Amazon and eBay are powered by organic and paid search engines to serve individuals better. Businesses begin to make a living by serving people. In a micro-audience but at a global level. People could also build their personal brand easier now because artists could find their niches earlier and invest in a small, but a constant number of patrons. As an effect, businesses are currently focused on a long tail keyword strategy and specific keyword phrases to capture and guide interested Web users to their products and services.
- **New business models:** Collaborative economy business models, such as Airbnb and Uber, begin to threaten the survival of older business models, such as hotels and cabs.
- **Device agnostic software development:** Mobile software development toolkits, such as the Android SDK, aid in the development of programs that run on the largest number of devices possible.
- **Web analytics:** Web analytics matures as a platform to measure Web 1.0 and Web 2.0 digital activities.
- **Search engines:** These pick up specific keywords that when used in a search and can narrow down results from the infinite amounts of unstructured data.
- **Semantic web:** This is an extension of the Internet which makes the Web intuitive and intelligent by separating the presentation of content from its meaning. The Semantic Web simplifies the way in which we can customize and personalize communications.
- **Social media:** Social media are websites and applications that focus on communicating and sharing through mobile devices and stimulate social networking.
- **Anywhere Internet:** This speaks to the expansion of the Internet to nearly half of the global population in the 2010s. In turn, there is a rise of automated advertising, also known as programmatic, which would have been impossible without Web 2.0.

- **Geo-location:** Mobile devices broadcast their location to Internet Service Providers via global positioning system (GPS), near field communication (NFC), and geofencing. GPS simplifies navigation by eliminating the need for physical maps, which saves time and energy.

Web 3.0

Web 3.0 is the next iteration of the World Wide Web. Web 3.0 marks the era of a connected Web operating system where most software components (e.g., application programs and operating systems) and data processing reside on the Internet. Web 3.0 is smarter, quicker, and more reliable at connecting data, concepts, applications, and people. A critical dimension of Web 3.0 is the Semantic Web or Linked Data. The Semantic Web is known as the "web of data" (W3 2015) and aims to make huge amounts of data and the relationship among the datasets Web-available in a machine-readable format, such as Resource Description Framework (RDF) format, for applications to query it. RDF is a general-purpose language for representing information on the web (W3 2015).[6] The World Wide Web became more personalized with an on demand approach. Below are examples of the changes the World Wide Web experienced:

- **Democratization:** Everyone can become a content creator and content consumer. Most businesses are transforming to align with the new capabilities developed through Web 1.0 and Web 2.0 with the extensibility and automation of Web 3.0. For example, baggers can create their blog, post public content to their blogs, and collaborate with other content creators to promote virality in their posts.
- **Intelligent Applications:** Intelligent applications customize and personalize the user's web experience with, insights forged by geo-location services, predictive analytics, and big data. Through the invention of intelligent devices and software, the Internet of Things was produced.
- **Collaborative Economy:** Business models that leverage/network and Internet technology to satisfy needs, such as Uber and Airbnb.
- **Smart Fabric:** Smart fabric refers to processed and shared information, and its location, whether it is in cloud computing, Hadoop, iBeacons, mesh networks, intelligent devices, or data lakes.

Recent Examples of Web 3.0-Driven Business Acquisitions

In 2015, IBM purchased the Weather Company to predict consumers' purchase behavior based on weather changes.[7] Because of the acquisition, IBM collects billions of sensors' data from around the world while releasing real-time information and insights to tens of millions of users via Watson Analytics.

Also, in 2015, Verizon acquired AOL. Verizon created a synergy as an ISP and coupled it with the large content publisher, AOL. Verizon's acquisition allowed it to combine viewer's programming preferences collected from set-top boxes and cellular communications of Verizon subscribers. About a year later, Verizon acquired Yahoo! to shape the digital advertising marketplace. With these insights, the programmatic advertising and targeting technologies that AOL developed could be deployed to create competent advertising solutions against Google and Facebook.[8]

Web 4.0

Web 4.0 is relatively new and directed to emerging technologies such as the Internet of Things, quantified self, private clouds, intelligent computing, embedded intelligence, predictive analytics, and artificial intelligence.[9] There are many interesting Web 4.0 developments, and we will cover the subject in the next edition of this textbook.

Common Internet Terms

URL (Uniform Resource Locator)

The basic building block of the World Wide Web is webpages. Webpages are assigned a virtual address defined as an URL. A Uniform Resource Locator (URL), also known as a Uniform Resource Identifier (URI), is a web address specifying its location on a computer network and a mechanism for retrieving it. An URL is the representation of a URI, although many people use the two terms interchangeably (See Figure 3.2). Note that URN refers to the Uniform Resource Name, which is a means to call a network regardless of its numerical address or URI (which often changes on a regular basis).

A typical URL could have the form http://www.example.com/index.html, which indicates a protocol (HTTP), a hostname (www.example.com), and a file name (index. html). URLs occur most commonly to reference web pages (HTTP), for file transfer (FTP), email (email to), database access (JDBC), and many other applications.[10] Tim Berners-Lee defined URLs with Request for Comments (RFC) 1738 in 1994 to the URI working group of the Internet Engineering Task Force (IETF).

Domain Name

Simply, a domain name is a location where a collection of pages lives or can live, and when there is a topology or map of a domain. For example, the domain ESPN. com provides visitors with popular sports scores while nytimes.com provides news reporting and commentary. Domain names are an extension of our concept of location: we live on the Earth, in a country, in a city, and at a physical address. To send and receive mail, we must specify the address we are sending it to, and usually we want to include our address, just in case the mail cannot be delivered. Moreover, we built a system on the Web that operates the same way, except it is for computers, networks, and services. The naming and address resolution system in place is called the Domain Name Services (DNS) and has existed since the Internet, or World Wide Web appeared.

- Root domains are set to apply universally.
- Once a web domain is set up, subdomains are created within their domain.
- Administration of subdomains is set up within an organization's Domain Name Service.

DNS Servers
The Domain Name Service is a distributed global registry that resolves domain names to Internet IP addresses and vice versa. One of the hallmarks of the Domain Name Service is its scalability and extensibility – DNS can resolve every domain

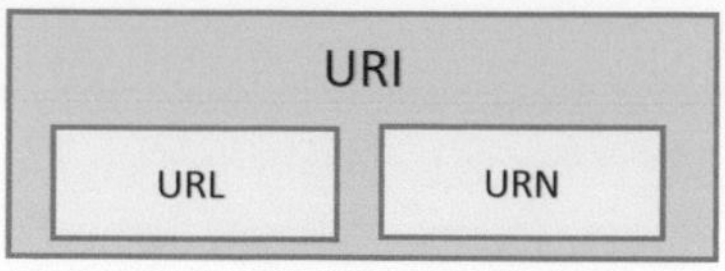

Figure 3.2 URI Structure
Source: Marshall Sponder

and subdomain to the correct IP address on the planet! DNS is extensible because network administrators can control the names and IP addresses of all the devices on their internal networks, also called Intranets, with full confidence that the designations are propagated across the entire global DNS network. DNS servers communicate with each other so the mapping and routing of messages can reach their destinations and vice versa. The network map is both resilient and easy to update. It is also one of the most successful examples of democratized control of resources. Local network administrators can handle the details of addresses in subdomains they oversee.

Servers

Servers are computer programs or machines capable of accepting requests from clients and responding to them. When a server is running on hardware, it can usually be accessed over a network. A server can run unattended without a computer monitor, input device, and USB interfaces. Many systems and user processes are called servers and work with clients that are programs and individual addresses (or identities) that work.

IP Address (Internet Protocol)

The IP address is the key aspect of how Internet traffic goes back and forth from an address to the rest of the Web (which includes Intranets or organization internal domain). Internet Protocol address (IP address) is a numerical label assigned to each device (e.g., computer, printer) participating in a computer network that uses the Internet Protocol for communication. There are two versions in use: IP Version 4 and IP Version 6. Each version defines an IP address differently. IP address typically still refers to the addresses defined by IPv4.

- An IP address is written out in both numeric forms (Version 4 & Version 6) so that we can understand it.
- Hexadecimal addressing is used for computer programming so that the address can be computed and operated on by the various routing mechanisms (e.g., routers, intelligent switches). Routers move information back and forth throughout the Internet or Intranet (Note: The Intranet is a private Internet that allows communication with an organization without going through the Web).

Browser

A Web browser is a software application for retrieving, presenting, and traversing information resources on the World Wide Web. An information resource is identified by a Uniform Resource Identifier (URI/URL); it may be a webpage, image, video, or other content. Modern browsers, however, go beyond surfing the Web through the addition of plug-in applications that extend the capabilities of the browser.

Transport Layer Security (TLS)

Transport Layer Security (TLS) is a protocol that ensures privacy between communicating applications and their users on the Internet. When a server and client communicate, TLS ensures that no third party may eavesdrop or tamper with any message. TLS is the successor to the Secure Sockets Layer (SSL).

Web Hosting

Web hosting is a type of Internet hosting service that allows individuals and organizations to make their website accessible via the World Wide Web. Web hosts are companies that provide space on a server owned or leased for use by clients, as well as providing Internet connectivity, typically in a data center. The location of web hosting services varies widely. The most basic are webpages and small-scale file hosting, where files are uploaded via file transfer protocol (FTP) or a web interface. The files are usually delivered to the web as is or with minimal processing. Many Internet service providers (ISPs) offer this service free to subscribers. Personal website hosting is typically free, advertisement-sponsored, or inexpensive. Business website hosting has a higher expense depending on the size and type of the site.

Cloud Computing

Computing and data storage on public clouds, private clouds, or hybrid clouds has revolutionized data processing and brought the era of big data to fruition. Public and private cloud suppliers, such as Amazon, Apple, Salesforce, and Backspace are used by corporations and government agencies to keep and process data. Cloud computing may have conceptually been possible before its start date in 2008, but it did not take off until programming stacks were created alongside with virtual storage systems and virtual processing to leverage it.[11] Cloud resources are often shared by multiple users and dynamically reallocated according to demand. This reallocation makes sense, as the data is often processed where it is located rather than moved to another data repository first. Clouds allow economies of scale and rapid updates of the data, which is faster than previously thought possible. For the user and application developer, no hardware is needed for cloud computing. The cloud provider handles the hardware, so there are no upfront charges for purchasing and maintaining servers. In turn, organizations only use and pay for the resources they need.

Cloud Computing Uses
- Web-based email
- Mobile apps
- Real-time geo-location systems (Google Waze, Google Maps)
- Store photos or videos online
- Use apps like Google Docs, Google Analytics, Adobe Creative Suite

- Store or backup files online with Dropbox or similar platform
- Customer intelligence (e.g., Salesforce, Oracle, and Adobe Marketing and Sales Clouds)

Cloud Computing Issues

- Certain types of input and output operations are much slower (e.g., copying a file system to Dropbox may take several hours).
- Usage charges can creep up when data processing needs rapidly increase.
- Clouds occasionally crash. Vital services and applications can suddenly stop functioning. Even applications that do not directly pull from the cloud may be vulnerable. It occurs when a component references software or data located in the cloud. Clouds are complex constructs with high fault tolerance, but they are also susceptible to errors that are difficult to troubleshoot.
- Clouds provided by different vendors or platforms are usually not interoperable. Some organizations have high security and continuity of service requirements and want to avoid a single point of failure. Having multiple clouds with different vendors or providers would be desirable to ensure a quality product or service with no failures but could be incredibly costly.
- Information stored in a cloud environment may be insecure, even when it is encrypted.

Introduction to First-Party and Third-Party Data

We are approaching a time when a complete curation of the customer experience is within our sights. Barriers in C2B information sharing are slowly fading as the initial privacy concern shock begins to fade away. Soon, a customer driving past Walmart will be shown an ad in their self-driving vehicle reminding them that the TV they were searching for on Amazon is available for a discount. As they enter to pull up or to park, they could be informed of the benefits of installing the Walmart app. Once they enter the store, the app could then guide them towards the TV, but only after exposing them to curated ads via iBeacon technology from their favorite brands. As they then leave the store, they will be given incentives to review their experience so that this whole process can be optimized. The landscape of marketing has changed quite a bit. There was once not enough information about clients, but now there is too much.

Marketers collect more customer data than they can act on. Conversely from a customer perspective, customers should turn off geo-location notifications broadcast from applications on their mobile devices when they are not needed. First-party data is data collected by the website for use in tools, such as Adobe, Google Analytics, or customer relationship management (CRM). The CRM data can be very useful and tell many things about websites. For example, it can tell how many visited a site, pageviews, time spent on a page, bounce rate, and conversion funnels among many other things. The CRM data can be segmented to show what is valuable to stakeholders. For example, stakeholders may want to segment by demographics (age and gender) and affinities to gain a better understanding of consumers, along with the type of advertising campaign that would be helpful to run.

Consider all the avenues of interaction with a person that can now be quantified and stored, knowingly or not: mobile app, social, on-site, blog, in person, and on the phone. There is much uproar over the sharing of personal data for marketing purposes, based on first-, second-, and third-party data or cookies. These marketing, efforts could be considered by some be an invasion of stranger's personal privacy. Most consumers are unaware their information is being examined at this level and they have not given their permission.

Text Analytics

Text analytics did not formally exist until about 1975. The simplest way to explain text analytics is the method of turning text into numbers, similar in structure to a spreadsheet so that statistics and other types of analysis can be run on the data. In the "What's the Big Data?" infographic,[12] text analytics evolved with other data science disciplines since its inception. The public awareness of text analytics is low, although organizations have been examining text for some time. In fact, the Google search engine – and all search engines – is powered by text analytics. Most people do not realize the rich intelligence that can be extracted from text documents (details on this subject in later chapters).

Digital Analytics History

Digital Analytics is as old as the Internet, see Figure 3.3. Web analytics is a solution for businesses that want to gather behavioral data from their websites. Web data helps businesses gain a better understanding of their customers and thus improve customer experience, which leads to benefits, such as more sales or conversions. The existing platforms were developed for webmasters and IT professionals in the early to mid-1990s to keep track of downloads, file input or output, etc. The first web analytics platforms were developed to analyze Web server logs and provide diagnostic readouts.

With the advent of JavaScript in the late 1990s, newer and more adaptive tracking methods using Web cookies evolved. A web cookie is a small piece of data sent

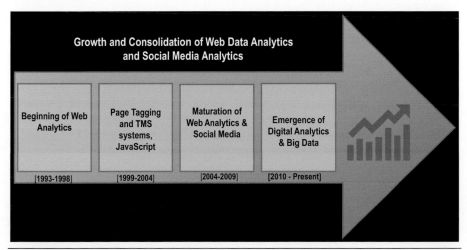

Figure 3.3 Evolution of Digital Analytics
Source: Marshall Sponder

from a website and stored on the user's computer by the user's Web browser, while the user is browsing. Cookies are chosen by the Web server to identify users, prepare customized webpages, or to save site login information about users so they do not need to re-enter the same login information every time they visit a website. Web tracking shifted away from installing software to a third-party hosted solution. Web analytics no longer needed dedicated servers to collect or process the data. It became the basis of a new page-tagging approach using JavaScript beacon scripts.

However, the broad adoption of JavaScript and remotely hosted analytics software turned out to be a mixed bag that came with several positives and negatives. While the JavaScript improved tracking of some web activities, it missed tracking others, such as file downloads. Tracking rich media required more analytics enablement and was often neglected. Thus, JavaScript tracking led to gaps in basic data collection.

The Era of Massive Data Growth – Data Is the New Oil

Every year, the amount of information being generated surpasses almost all the information humanity has created in its entire history, and most of the data being generated is unstructured. Welcome to the world of big data! Structured data is what we have in spreadsheets with rows and columns and the information already organized. Unstructured data is becoming just about everything else. Data is created so massively and quickly that new ways to process and store it have become necessary. Data growth requires individuals who know how to work with the data.

Massive Growth of Unstructured Data

Turning information from its unstructured form and providing it with structure has been compared to alchemy, the ancient science claiming it was possible to turn lead into gold. The term "data is the new oil" reflects the current consensus that the most valuable asset an organization has is its data.

Examples of turning data into dollars:

- Credit card companies detect unusual spending patterns of their customers using sophisticated algorithms that examine massive datasets. Customers are immediately alerted of the suspicious activities by phone or email. This activity saves customers and credit card companies billions of dollars a year.
- Major retailers use unstructured data collected for customer transactions to refine their online search engines and to encourage customers to buy more products.
- Food and beverage suppliers merge customers, logistics, and manufacturing data to improve their plant operations significantly.

As the Internet and its capabilities evolved, it became the driving force behind decisions about what makes sense now, along with the data and analytics to both power and understand these new abilities and their impact and implications.

As popularity is increased with the Internet, online marketing and advertising rose to match with businesses' new strategy of "staying connected" by increasing the resources and capabilities a consumer could perform. In this context, "staying connected" refers to the emphasis we place on being reachable through online communications or various messaging applications at any given time. Spending is expected to increase in developed countries, including the United States, parts of Europe and Asia, and in small pockets of Latin America and the Middle East. Digital advertising as a percentage of total advertising is continuing to grow, which highlights the need for increasing the analytics around the sector, especially in the United States.[13]

The Digital Industrial Economy

It is imperative as a business leader to understand the digital space and marketing within it. "By the 2020s, every organization will be an IT organization, and every leader will be a digital leader", said Peter Sondergaard, Gartner SVP and head of research, at the opening of the annual Gartner Symposium. By 2020, he predicts, "digital is the business; the business is digital". Sondergaard creates the analogy in the argument that businesses will be synonymous to their online counterparts. It could be concluded that his beliefs are a product of observing globalization in the Digital Age where businesses strive to compete with their competition and establish market share through online conversions. By increasing digital efforts, businesses may have the opportunity to tap into new segments, create greater brand awareness, or defend their business against competitors.

Other points from Sondergaard at the Gartner Symposium include

- The Internet is changing how business is conducted. It is also vastly increasing the opportunities and precision of business communications and operations.
- Marketing communications have become more complex and streamlined, with many more touchpoints, as well as opportunities to acquire, retain, and convert customers.
- Technological advancement is constant, making it necessary and challenging to keep pace with these changes.
- Business models and their economics are rapidly changing and evolving.[14]

Review Questions

1. What are the main differences between Web 1.0, 2.0, and 3.0?
2. Explain the difference between Web clients and Web servers.
3. What is cloud computing?
4. What are the seven stages of the OSI model?

Summary

In this chapter, we introduced the reader to some of the essential constructs that make digital analytics possible, such as the development of the Internet and World Wide Web. The technology that powers our digital experience is invisible to us until it breaks. At that point, we are painfully aware of the mechanisms for communicating information, such as clients and servers, Internet routing protocols, and so on. The technology becomes useful to us when we run applications such as search engines, that help us organize and find information on the Web. As new technologies, such as search engines and social media, evolved, analytics have developed to help us understand the data and optimize our efforts. Through the effective use of technology, we improve marketing, which sets the stage for the rest of this book.

Chapter 3 Citations

1. "Is the Web dead? 'No,' says Tim Berners-Lee, but native apps are 'boring'." December 10, 2014. http://venturebeat.com/2014/12/10/is-the-web-dead-no-says-tim-berners-lee-but-native-apps-are-boring/. Accessed May 30, 2023.

2. "Would you like to know how the web works?" *BusinessProgrammer.com*. April 16, 2015. www.businessprogrammer.com/how-the-web-works. Accessed May 30, 2023.

3. "Hacker lexicon: What is the Dark Web?" *WIRED*. November 19, 2014. www.wired.com/2014/11/hacker-lexicon-whats-dark-web. Accessed April Access May 30, 2023.

4. "Invisible Web: What it is, why it exists, how to find it, and its inherent ambiguity." August 1, 2006. http://yunus.hacettepe.edu.tr/~soydal/bby216_2011/4/InvisibleWebWhatitis.htm. Accessed May 30, 2023.

5. O'Reilly, T. (2007). "What is Web 2.0: Design patterns and business models for the next generation of software." *Communications & Strategies 1*: 17. www.oreilly.com/pub/a/web2/archive/what-is-web-20.html. Accessed May 30, 2023; Kaplan, A.M. and M. Haenlein (2010). "Users of the world, unite! The challenges and opportunities of social media." *Business Horizons 53(1)*: 59–68; Kietzmann, J.H., K. Hermkens, I.P. McCarthy and B.S. Silvestre (2011). "Social media? Get serious! Understanding the functional building blocks of social media." *Business Horizons 54(3)*: 241–251.

6. "Data." *W3C*. www.w3.org/standards/semanticweb/data. Accessed May 30, 2023.

7. "IBM buys Weather Company's digital assets, expanding move into data crunching." October 28, 2015. www.wsj.com/articles/ibm-buys-weather-companys-digtal-assets-expanding-move-into-data-crunching-I446069911. Accessed May 30, 2023.

8. "How Verizon's Yahoo buy will reshape the digital ad marketplace." August 8, 2016. http://marketingland.com/verizon-yahoo-reshape-digital-ad-marketplace-186713. Accessed May 30, 2023.

9. "Web 4.0: The ultra-intelligent electronic agent is coming" *Big Think*. http://bigthink.com/big-think-tv/web-40-the-ultra-intelligent-electronic-agent-is-coming. Accessed May 30, 2023.

10. "Uniform resource locator – Wikipedia." https://en.wikipedia.org/wiki/Uniform_Resource_Locator, Accessed May 30, 2023.

11. "Who coined 'cloud computing'?" *MIT Technology Review*. October 31, 2011. https://www.technologyreview.com/2011/10/31/257406/who-coined-cloud-computing/. Accessed May 30, 2023.

12. "History of data science (infographic): What's the Big Data?" February 17, 2015. https://whatsthebigdata.com/2015/02/17/history-of-data-science-infographic. Accessed May 30, 2023.

13. "Digital Ad spending, worldwide to hit $137.53 billion in 2014– eMarketer." April 3, 2014. www.emarketer.com/Article/Digital-Ad-Spending-Worldwide-Hit-3613753-Billlon-2014/1010736. Accessed May 30, 2023.

14. "Gartner: Get ready for 2020's 'Digital Industrial Economy'." *PCMag. com*. October 7, 2013. http://forwardthinking.pcmag.com/show-reports/316608-gartner-get-ready-for-2020-s-digital-industrial-economy. Accessed May 30, 2023.

The Growth and Relevance of Social Media in Analytics and Digital Marketing

> **CHAPTER OBJECTIVES**
>
> After reading this chapter, readers should understand the following:
>
> - Common uses of social media in digital marketing
> - The history of the most commonly used social media channels
> - The short history of influence and influencers as used in digital marketing today
> - Network Analysis in Social Media for Digital Marketing

Social Media in Digital Marketing

Social media is a critical component of digital marketing and plays a significant role in the success of businesses and organizations. Here are a few reasons why social media is so essential:

- With billions of active users, social media offers a broad reach and audience engagement. Businesses can target specific demographics, interests, and behaviors, allowing them to tailor their marketing efforts and effectively engage with their target audience.
- Social media provides a powerful platform for building and enhancing brand presence. Consistently sharing valuable content, engaging with followers, and promoting products or services can increase brand awareness and visibility among the target audience.
- Social media allows businesses to establish and nurture customer relationships. Regular interaction and providing customer support build trust and loyalty, leading to long-term customer relationships.
- Social media platforms serve as channels for distributing and promoting content, such as blog posts, videos, infographics, and more. Sharing valuable and relevant content helps businesses attract and engage their target audience, driving traffic to their website and increasing the chances of conversions.
- Partnering with relevant influencers allows businesses to leverage their reach and credibility, reaching a wider audience and potentially driving conversions.
- Social media platforms offer robust advertising capabilities, allowing businesses to create highly targeted ad campaigns. Businesses can specify their target

DOI: 10.4324/9781003025351-4

audience based on demographics, interests, behavior, and more, ensuring their ads are shown to the most relevant users, and maximizing the impact of their advertising budget.

- Social media platforms provide valuable insights and analytics tools that enable businesses to measure the effectiveness of their marketing efforts. Businesses can track engagement, reach, click-through rates, conversions, and more, allowing them to optimize their strategies, refine their targeting, and make data-driven decisions.
- Many social media platforms now offer integrated shopping features, enabling businesses to sell their products or services directly through social media. This seamless shopping experience reduces friction and enhances customer convenience, increasing sales and revenue.

It's important to note that social media should be integrated into a comprehensive marketing strategy that considers other channels, such as email marketing, search engine optimization (SEO), content marketing, and more. An effective digital marketing strategy leverages the strengths of different channels to achieve overarching marketing goals.

In the early 2000s, social media platforms like MySpace and Friendster provided individuals with a unique opportunity to create personal profiles, connect with friends, and showcase their skills to attract a following.

YouTube, which emerged in the mid-2000s, revolutionized content creation and consumption by allowing anyone to upload videos. This gave rise to viral sensations like Justin Bieber and Psy and created a platform for aspiring artists, comedians, and performers to showcase their talents to a global audience.

In the late 2000s, Twitter allowed celebrities to communicate directly with their fans. This gave fans a sense of closeness and accessibility to their favorite celebrities and allowed for more personal insights into their lives and thoughts.

The emergence of Instagram in the 2010s emphasized visual content. This made it a powerful platform for celebrities to curate their image and share glimpses of their glamorous lifestyles. Celebrities used the platform to shape their personal brands, cultivate fan bases, and promote various aspects of their lives, including their work, products, and philanthropic efforts.

The 2010s also saw the rise of influencer culture, which created a new type of celebrity. Influencers built large followings and used their influence to promote products and lifestyles. They often specialized in specific niches and became powerful marketing channels for brands.

Social media platforms introduced verified badges in the 2010s to authenticate the accounts of public figures, establishing trust and providing a means for celebrities to differentiate themselves from impersonators or fan accounts.

TikTok's short-form video format, which emerged in the 2010s and continues to be popular in the 2020s, has led to the rapid rise of new stars. This is facilitated by its algorithmic discoverability and viral challenges (note, there are privacy issues with TikTok, which is ultimately operated out of China, and at the time of publication there is still an open debate on its use and potential banning in parts of the United States).

Live streaming platforms like Instagram Live, Facebook Live, and Twitch have given fans an intimate and behind-the-scenes look into celebrities' lives. This has fostered a sense of connection and increased engagement.

Today, a celebrity's social media presence plays a significant role in shaping their public image and career trajectory. Traditional media outlets have also incorporated social media metrics, trends, and personalities into their coverage. It's important to note, however, that social media has democratized fame to some extent. At the same time, it has presented challenges such as privacy invasion, online harassment, and pressure to maintain an always-on presence. The influence of social media on celebrity and fame continues to evolve, shaping the way we perceive and interact with public figures.

Through these examples, we see how malleable social media is to the needs of the population, whether it is political or entertaining by nature. Since social media is reliant on the content generated by users, users are encouraged to share their interests, passion, and insights within social media. With posts from specific users, marketers can peer into consumer behavior at an individual or group level, but they are not limited to passive research. When users are engaged, marketers can use these connections to build and collaborate with the users on subjects they are passionate about. The use of social media and the impact of its diffusion in contemporary society have reached epic proportions. Billions of people flock to social media platforms such as Facebook, Twitter, and YouTube, where they share, tweet, like, and post content. Social media analytics is based on the underlying tools, measures, and technologies of a social media platform. Average time spent per day with digital media in the United States from 2011 to 2024 is projected to increase.[1]

Society has shifted from viewing smartphones as a luxury to owning them being the new standard of living. Mobile apps dominate due to the rapid growth of iOS and Android mobile devices. By replacing the personal computer with a smartphone, a user had the freedom to document what is happening around them and share it in real time. Beyond devices, the evolution of deep learning systems opens new capabilities for content creators and social media users. Stanford University and Google researchers are building neural networks or computer systems that function like the human brain. The neural nets are used to analyze footage from live webcams and mobile camera devices. Deep learning systems are powered by text and image-based algorithms and used to curate our social media news feeds. In layman's terms, while using social media, the platform learns and adapts to what users post, watch, or like, and provides additional content, advertisements, people to follow, or content that the platform believes will appeal to the individual.

Social Media and Web 2.0

Built on the Web 2.0 philosophy (i.e., to give more control to the user over the content), social media can be defined as an Internet-based platform with capabilities to allow users to upload text, videos, audio, and graphics. Social media and Web 2.0 are often used interchangeably, but they can be slightly differentiated by their "back to the roots of the Web" or "forward-looking, futuristic" direction.[2]

Social Media Timeline and Brief History

Social media is not limited to the most common platforms, such as Facebook, Twitter, YouTube, and blogs. In this book we consider social media to be any online platform (proprietary or purpose built, public or private) that enables users to participate, collaborate, create, and share content in a many-to-many context.

While it is impossible to present a comprehensive timeline of social media's evolution over the last 25 years. Here are the most noteworthy milestones:

- 1997: The first recognizable social media platform, Six Degrees, is launched, allowing users to create profiles and make friends.
- 2002: The introduction of Friendster gains popularity, introducing the concept of social networking to a broader audience.
- 2004: Facebook is founded, initially limited to Harvard University students but later expanded to other universities and eventually the general public.
- 2005: YouTube revolutionizes the way people create, share, and view video content.
- 2006: Twitter is introduced, allowing users to share short messages, or tweets, with their followers.
- 2007: The first iPhone is released, setting the stage for the widespread adoption of mobile social media.
- 2010: Instagram is launched, focusing on photo sharing and offering various filters to enhance images.
- 2011: Snapchat is released, introducing disappearing photos and videos that quickly gained popularity, particularly among younger users.
- 2012: Pinterest gains traction as a platform for discovering and saving visual inspiration and ideas.
- 2013: Vine, a short-form video platform, is introduced, enabling users to create looping six-second videos.
- 2016: TikTok, a social media platform focused on short-form videos, is launched by the Chinese company ByteDance.
- 2016: Instagram introduces Stories, allowing users to share photos and videos that disappear after 24 hours, similar to Snapchat's feature.
- 2018: The Cambridge Analytica scandal brings attention to data privacy and the impact of social media on elections and user information.
- 2020: The COVID-19 pandemic leads to a surge in social media usage as people seek connection, entertainment, and information during lockdowns.
- 2021: Clubhouse, an audio-based social networking app, gains popularity, allowing users to participate in voice chat rooms on various topics.
- 2022: Facebook rebrands as Meta, signaling a shift towards the metaverse and expanding beyond traditional social media platforms.

The social media landscape continues to evolve, with new platforms, features, and trends emerging regularly.

Network Analysis of Social Media for Digital Marketing

Networks are the building blocks of social media and can carry useful business insights. Network analysis consists of constructing, analyzing, and understanding social media networks. Social media analytics can be used for a variety of purposes, and it includes network analysis (i.e., the interrelationship of nodes within a network). The idea behind network analysis is that the structure and interrelationships of a network are as important as who is on the network, perhaps even more important. It is not so far-fetched that the positions of nodes within a network predetermines the quality and tenor of the relationships in that network, and this the main reason to study social media and network analysis in this chapter. Once we understand the type of network we are dealing with, the interrelationships of the nodes gain meaning. Network analysis can be employed to identify influential nodes (e.g., people and organizations) or their position in the network; it can also be used understand the overall structure of a network. Businesses can use network analysis for digital marketing. For example, they can use it to explore their Twitter or Facebook followers and identify influential members on those networks.

This type of analysis shortens the amount of time it takes to research prospective customers and industry influencers, and provides valuable insights to gauge marketing effectiveness within the networks being examined. Some people on social media are more influential, from a marketing perspective, as they can share information with a large audience of followers, subscribers, and friends, and are considered opinion leaders. For example,

- Celebrities such as Kim Kardashian are paid a substantial amount of money to advertise products on social media because their followers look up to them.
- The Humans of New York Facebook page has been very influential, with more than 18 million followers and over 100,000 people talking about the page at a time.
- Athletes like LeBron James post products on their social media accounts; as followers view the product being used by the celebrity or athlete, they are more likely to use it.
- A tweet by politicians such as Barack Obama or Donald Trump can instantly reach several million followers on Twitter (especially in Trump's case).

However, it is important to highlight that not only famous people are considered influencers nowadays. A lot of everyday people are now attracting millions of followers on Instagram, Twitter, YouTube, and other platforms and are chosen as brand ambassadors/influencers. A researcher may be interested in the overall structure of networks to see how certain networks differ or converge. Overall, the purpose of network analysis is to do the following:[3]

- Understand overall network structure, for example, the number of nodes, the number of links, density, clustering coefficient, and diameter.
- Find influential nodes and their rankings, for example, degree, betweenness, and closeness centralities.
- Find relevant links and their rankings, for example, weight, betweenness, and centrality.
- Find cohesive subgroups, for example, pinpointing communities within a network.

Common Social Network Terms

Network

At a very basic level, a network is a group of nodes that are linked together.[4] Nodes (also known as vertices) can represent anything, including individuals, organizations, countries, computers, websites, or any other entities. Links (also known as ties, edges, or arcs) represent the relationship among the nodes in a network.

Social Networks

A social network is a group of nodes, representing social entities such as people or organizations, and links formed by these social entities. For example, links can represent relationships, friendships, and trade relations. Social networks can exist both in the real and online worlds and supplement each other. The online world helps create better connections in our world. A network among classmates is an example of a real-world social network. Moreover, a Twitter follow-following network is an example of an online social media network. In a Twitter follow-following network, nodes are the Twitter users, and links among the nodes represent the follower-following relationship (i.e., who is following whom) among the users.

Social Network Site

A social network site is a special-purpose software (or social media tool) designed to facilitate social or professional relationships. Facebook, and LinkedIn are examples of social network sites.

Social Networking

The act of forming, expanding, and maintaining social relations is called social networking. Using social network sites, users can, for example, form, expand, and maintain online social ties with family, friends, colleagues, and sometimes strangers.

Social Network Analysis

Social Network Analysis is the science of studying and understanding social networks[5] and social networking. It is a well-established field with roots in a variety of disciplines, including graph theory, sociology, information science, and communication science.

Common Social Media Network Types

The following are some common types of social media networks that we come across, and that can be subject to network analytics.

Friendship Networks

The most common type of social media networks are the friendship networks, such as Instagram, Twitter, and Snapchat. Friendship networks let people maintain social ties and share content with people they closely associate with, such as family and friends. Nodes in these networks are people, and links are social relationships (e.g., friendship, family, and activities).

Follower-Following Networks

In the follower-following network, users follow (or keep track of) other users of interest. Twitter is an excellent example of a follow-following network, where users follow influential people, brands, and organizations. Nodes in these networks are, for example, people, brands, and organizations, and links represent follow-following relations (e.g., who is following whom). Below are two common Twitter terminologies.

Following are the people whom you follow on Twitter. Following someone on Twitter means

- You are subscribing to their tweets as a follower.
- Their updates will appear on your home screen or dashboard.
- That person can send you direct messages.
- You are able to subscribe to tweets to be notified when the account tweets (although you cannot send a direct message unless that person follows you back).

Followers are people who follow you on Twitter. If someone follows you, it means that

- They will show up in your "Followers" list.
- They will see your tweets in their home timeline whenever they login to Twitter.
- You can send them direct messages.

Fan Network

A fan network is formed by social media fans or supporters of someone or something, such as a product, service, person, brand, business, or other entity. The network formed by the social media users subscribed to your Facebook fan page is an example of a fan network. Nodes in these networks are fans, and links represent co-likes, co-comments, and co-shares. A fan network can be passive (via bought subscribers) or active (an organically generated follower who actively engages with your posts).

Co-Occurrence Network

Co-occurrence networks are formed when two more entities (e.g., keywords, people, ideas, and brands) co-occur over social media outlets. For example, one can construct a co-occurrence network of brand names (or people) to investigate how often certain brands (or people) co-occur over social media outlets. In such networks, nodes will be the brand names, and the links will represent the co-occurrence relationships among the brands.

Group Network

Group networks are formed by people who share common interests and agendas. Most social media platforms allow the creation of groups where a member can post, comment, and manage in-group activities. Examples of social media groups are Twitter professional groups, Yahoo groups, and Facebook groups. Nodes in these networks are group members, and links can represent co-commenting, co-liking, and co-shares.

Professional Networks

LinkedIn is a good example of a professional network where people manage their professional identity by creating a profile that lists their achievements, education, work history, and interests. LinkedIn members can also search profiles or jobs by specific keywords (i.e., "sports management"). Nodes in these networks can represent people, brands, or organizations. Links are professional relations and in LinkedIn are called "connections" (such as a co-worker, employee, or collaborator). An important feature of professional networks is the endorsement feature, where people who know you can endorse your skills and qualifications. Also, the recommendation feature, where unconnected members of a social network are suggested to a user, is another important characteristic.

Content Networks

Content networks are formed by the content posted by social media users. A network of YouTube videos is an example of a content network. In such a network, nodes are social media content (such as videos, tags, and photos) and links can represent, for example, similarity (content belonging to the same categories that can be linked together).

Dating Networks

Dating networks (such as Match.com and Tinder) are focused on matching and arranging a dating partner based on personal information (such as age, gender, hobbies, common interests, and location) provided by a user. Nodes in these networks are people, and links represent social relations (such as romantic relations).

Co-Authorship Networks

Co-authorship networks are two or more people working together to collaborate on a project. Wikipedia (an online encyclopedia) is a good example of a social media-based co-authorship network created by millions of authors from around the world.[6] A more explicit example of the co-authorship network is the ResearchGate platform: a social networking site for researchers to share articles, ask and respond to questions, and find collaborators. In these networks, nodes are, for example, researchers, and links represent the co-authorship relationship.

Co-Commenter Networks

Co-commenter networks are formed when two or more people comment on social media content (e.g., a Facebook status update, blog post, Yelp restaurant reviews, or YouTube video). A co-commenter network can, for example, be constructed from the comments posted by users in response to a video posted on YouTube or a Facebook fan page. In these networks, nodes represent users, and a link represents the co-commenting relationship.

Co-Like Networks

Co-like networks are formed when two or more people like the same social media content. Using NodeXL (a social network analysis tool), one can construct a network that is based on co-likes (two or more people liking a similar content) of the Facebook fan page. In such network, nodes will be Facebook users/fans and links will be the co-like relationship. Facebook also uses co-likes to suggest other members that they have not yet connected with as a suggested friend. The co-like relationship can be seen on Facebook when people share other's posts.

Geo Co-Existence Network

Geo co-existence networks are formed when two or more entities (e.g., people, devices, and addresses) coexist in a geographic location. In such a network, the node represents entities (e.g., people), while links among them represent co-existence.
   Examples of geo co-existence networking:

- Visitors to a museum (or any location) use social media applications on their mobile devices to check-in using Facebook or Swarm (Foursquare); other members who have recently checked in to the museum are shown to the member via the app.
- Shoppers visit brick-and-mortar stores and shop there using a Bluetooth-enabled app that connects to an iBeacon network installed in the location.

Hyperlink Networks

In simple words, a *hyperlink* is a way to connect documents (such as websites). Hyperlinks can be thought of as being in-links (i.e., hyperlinks originating in other websites,[7] bringing traffic/users to your site), or out-links (i.e., links originating in your site and going out).[8]

Core Characteristics of Social Media

The best way to understand social media is through the core features that set it apart from other forms of communication.

Peer-to-Peer

Social media enables interaction among the users in a peer-to-peer fashion, unlike conventional media, such as print, radio, telephone, and television that use a top-down, broadcast communications model. The effect of a peer-to-peer medium is the exchange is provided to all users so that every voice has a platform.

Participatory

Unlike conventional technologies, social media enables and encourages users to participate in it and provide feedback. Users can engage in online discourse through blogging, commenting, tagging, and sharing content, etc.

User-Generated Content

Users generate social media content that is published on various social media platforms.

Conversational

People can freely express their views and opinions on an equal footing in social media due to its built-in peer-to-peer conversation capabilities. Conversations often take place between celebrities, politicians, companies, and individuals in real time. The peer-to-peer conversation characteristics of social media make it possible for members to communicate and collaborate in real time, regardless of their location, wealth, occupation, or beliefs.

Relationship Oriented

Most social media tools allow users to establish and maintain social and professional relationships easily. For instance, LinkedIn members can leverage their profile page to forge new business relationships and expand their professional connections. Facebook page administrators can use their pages to gain traffic and spread the word about their personal or business project. As the same time, users can share what is going on or how they feel.

Review Questions

1. What is social media? Moreover, what makes it different from the traditional media?
2. What are some core characteristics of social media?
3. Briefly explain different social media types with examples.
4. Briefly explain how businesses can leverage Facebook, YouTube, Twitter, blogs, and wikis?
5. Differentiate among social media, Web 2.0, and social network sites.

Chapter 4 Citations

1. "Average time spent per day with digital media in the United States from 2011 to 2024." https://www.statista.com/statistics/262340/daily-time-spent-with-digital-media-according-to-us-consumsers/. Accessed April 15, 2023.

2. "Eras of the web – Web 0.0 through web 5.0." https://www. business2community.com/tech-gadgets/eras-of-the-web-web-0-0-through-web-5-0-02239654. Accessed May 28, 2023.

3. Perer, A. and B. Shneiderman (2008) *Systematic Yet Flexible Discover: Guiding Domain Experts through Exploratory Data Analysis*. 13th International Conference on Intelligent User Interfaces, New York.

4. Wasserman, S. and K. Faust (1994) *Social Networks Analysis: Methods and Applications*. Cambridge: Cambridge University Press.

5. Hanneman, R.A. and M. Riddle. "Introduction to social network methods." http:// taculty.ucr.edu/~hanneman. Accessed April 15, 2017.

6. Biuk-Aghai, R.P. (2006) *Visualizing Co-Authorship Networks in Online Wikipedia. Communications and Information Technologies, 2006*. International Symposium.

7. Björneborn, L. and P. Ingwersen (2004) "Toward a basic framework for webometrics." *Journal of the American Society for Information Science and Technology 55(14)*: 1216–1227.

8. Björneborn, L. (2001) *Necessary Data Filtering and Editing in Webometric Link Structure Analysis*. Copenhagen: Royal School of Library and Information Science, University of Copenhagen.

Data for Digital Marketing Analytics

CHAPTER OBJECTIVES

After reading this chapter, readers should understand the following:

- Importance of data for digital marketing
- Three types of data
- Digital data ecosystems and third-party data
- Data lakes and big data
- Web analytics maturity models
- Additional third-party market research tools available at university libraries for student use
- Introduction to programmatic advertising

The Importance of Data

Data is the essential raw material for digital marketing analytics. It is crucial for understanding customer behavior, identifying trends, optimizing strategies, and achieving marketing goals. It comes in numbers, text, images, audio, video, or any other digital representation. In the modern era of technology, data is an exceptionally valuable resource, almost as precious as gold. It can provide valuable insights, facilitate informed decision-making, enhance customer experiences, and drive innovation to new heights. Businesses that expertly collect, manage, and apply data to their operations can gain an in-depth understanding of their customers, optimize their processes, personalize their offerings, and improve their performance across the board. However, it is critical to adhere to responsible data practices, ethical values, and privacy regulations to maintain trust and comply with legal requirements. Data is a dynamic and evolving resource that demands careful handling, analysis, and ethical considerations to make the most of its benefits.

Customer data may be the most precious thing that organizations have, especially when the capabilities are in place to leverage data.[1] For example,

- "The vast majority of data never gets used. Only 0.5% of all data is ever analysed".[2]
- "Banks have goldmines of data available to them. However, it is not just about the data they collect. It is how they mine it, interpret it and draw insights to provide: personal customer experiences, which is deployed across the organization".[3]

DOI: 10.4324/9781003025351-5

While technological improvements allow organizations to collect vast amounts of information, they have not learned how to analyze or use most of it. While the approach any given organization takes with big data is unique, they should expect to see increased revenue as an outcome. To gauge success, organizations should be able to drive business decisions with the data and reap the benefits.

Three Types of Data

We look at three types of data in terms of their availability. Organizations use web analytics to collect first-party data on their digital properties. Below, we describe the characteristics of first-, second, and third-party data.

First-Party Data

First-party data has become more valuable to businesses in recent years due to increasing privacy concerns and restrictions on third-party data. As a result, companies rely more on their own first-party data to personalize marketing efforts, enhance customer experiences, and make data-driven decisions. By analyzing and leveraging first-party data, businesses can improve customer segmentation, develop targeted marketing campaigns, and enhance overall customer engagement. It is collected by issuing the first-party cookie to the Web browser of a visitor to a website running web analytics software. Other applications are running on a site serving first-party cookies as well. Most websites issue first-party cookies for applications and login information that takes place on their website. It is also directly obtained from a company's customers or audience through various interactions with the company's website, mobile apps, CRM systems, and other direct sources. It includes customer demographics, purchase history, website behavior, preferences, and contact information.

Second-Party Data

Second-party data refers to the first-party data of another organization or business, which is shared or purchased through a mutually beneficial partnership or arrangement. It allows businesses to access valuable insights and reach a broader audience beyond their own customer base. For example, many online banking and credit card customers provide first-party data that is then provided to their business partners (the terms of this arrangement are usually appear in terms of service of the website). Note: there is no such thing as a second-party cookie, although, as explained, second-party data exists and is always shared with trusted partners – that is how it becomes second-party information. In recent years, second-party data has gained prominence as businesses seek to expand their reach and improve their targeting capabilities. It enables companies to leverage the data of trusted partners or relevant organizations to gain deeper insights into their target audience and improve their marketing strategies.

Third-Party Data

Third-party data refers to data collected by external sources not directly affiliated with a particular business or organization. It includes information about consumer behaviors, interests, demographics, and online activities. Over the past 25 years, third-party data has been widely used for audience targeting and ad personalization. However, privacy concerns, regulations, and changes to browser policies limiting third-party cookie tracking have impacted its availability and usage. The industry has shifted towards more privacy-centric practices and a focus on first-party data.

This chapter will focus on the uses of third-party data along with a few third-party market research platforms that are popular with many digital marketers.

Current Perspectives of the use and Intermix of First-, Second-, and Third-Party Data

Nowadays, marketers prioritize the collection and analysis of first-party data. Building direct relationships with customers and obtaining consent for data usage allows businesses to understand their audience better, personalize experiences, and comply with privacy regulations. The emphasis is on creating customer value, maintaining transparency, and using data responsibly. Moreover, there is a focus on data integration and creating a unified view of the customer across various channels and touchpoints. By combining first-party data with other data sources, businesses can gain a more comprehensive understanding of their target audience and optimize their marketing efforts accordingly. Overall, the evolution of data usage in marketing has shifted towards greater reliance on first-party data, increased emphasis on privacy and consent, and the integration of various data sources to create more meaningful and personalized customer experiences.

Stories About Converging First-, Second-, and Third-Party Data

Here are some general insights and trends regarding the convergence of data types in recent years.

In recent years, companies have formed data partnerships and alliances to understand their target audience better and improve their advertising efforts. This approach combines first-, second-, and third-party data resources, allowing organizations to leverage identity resolution technologies to create a unified view of their customers. By doing so, businesses can better comprehend customer behavior, preferences, and interactions across various touchpoints.

With the rise of privacy regulations like GDPR and CCPA, companies prioritize responsible data usage practices, first-party data collection, and consent management. They focus on obtaining explicit consent and using their data sources in compliance with regulations while still delivering personalized experiences to their customers. Companies are turning to contextual targeting and AI-driven solutions to cope with the limitations of third-party cookies and data tracking. By merging first-party data with contextual data such as website content and user behavior, businesses can deliver relevant and personalized advertising without relying heavily on third-party data.

These trends reflect an evolution and convergence of first-, second-, and third-party data in response to changing privacy landscapes, consumer expectations, and regulatory requirements. Businesses can drive marketing effectiveness and customer engagement by leveraging multiple data types in a privacy-conscious manner. Here's a hypothetical example of the use of first, second- and third-party data by a fashion brand. Fashion retailer Brand ABCD implements a data convergence strategy that involves leveraging first-, second-, and third-party data. The company collects data directly from its website and mobile app and partners with a lifestyle magazine to share anonymized reader interest and engagement data. It utilizes third-party demographic data and consumer behavior insights. This strategy enables the business to personalize product recommendations, optimize marketing strategies, and deliver targeted advertising, resulting in improved customer engagement, increased conversions, and a more effective overall marketing approach.

In conclusion, combining various data sources allows businesses to gain valuable insights into their target audience, enhance personalization efforts, and make more informed marketing decisions.

Organizations Successfully Using First-, Second-, and Third-Party Data

In response to growing concerns around consumer privacy and tighter restrictions on data collection, brands are re-evaluating their data-driven marketing approaches. Notably, industry leaders like Apple and Google are implementing privacy-focused measures, which limit third-party access to data and make ad targeting and attribution more challenging for advertisers. To incentivize customers to share their personal information, brands are leveraging gamified rewards programs, exclusive product offers, and virtual experiences.

By gathering first-party and even zero-party data, brands can establish direct customer relationships and gain valuable insights. While this shift presents its challenges, it is anticipated to ultimately benefit brands by enhancing customer experiences and fostering trust.

- For example, during January 2023, Jimmy John's unveiled a new feature called "Achievement Badges" for its Freaky Fast Rewards Members, which adds a playful and interactive gamification element to the app.[4] The badges were created with the goal of encouraging members to visit the restaurant more frequently. In 2022, the restaurant introduced The Gauntlet badge, which rewarded the first 100 members who ordered every sandwich on the menu with a special limited-edition beanbag chair.
- Halo Top has effectively boosted conversions and gathered valuable first-party data by employing gamification techniques in their low-calorie ice cream product. Their latest initiative at the time of this writing was, "No Work Workouts", has been launched in hand-picked gyms to encourage effortless activities, ensuring more effective data collection and higher conversions.
- Doritos and Netflix teamed up during June 2022 to promote Stranger Things Season four with a creative campaign. They turned Doritos bags into tickets for a fictional music festival called "Live From the Upside Down" set in the show's 1980s universe. The festival featured contemporary and '80s artists and generated buzz for both Doritos and Netflix.

Data Collection Ecosystem

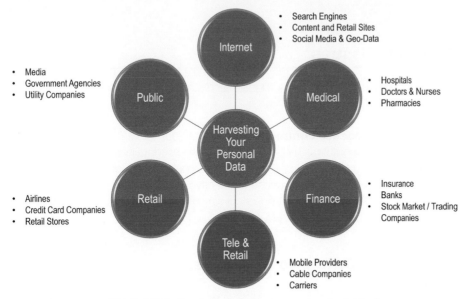

Collectors of Digital Data that is routinely harvested on Individuals

Figure 5.1 Data That Is Routinely Harvested on Individuals
Source: Marshall Sponder

There are so many ways to gather audience data that it is mind boggling – and it continues to get faster and more sophisticated every year. Figure 5.1 shows the collectors of digital data that is routinely harvested on individuals. The data that is collected by consumers is then anonymized, normalized, de-duplicated, aggregated, repackaged, and sold to advertisers and publishers (and pretty much anyone else willing to purchase it).

Data Lakes

Data lakes are a customizable, general-purpose data store where information is saved in its original format. By placing data into the Lake, it becomes available for analysis by everyone in the organization. The Data Lake is usually formed with a Hadoop cluster with several nodes that holds all the information that populates Salesforce, Marketo, and Adobe Analytics. Marketing data is often trapped in the applications that collect the data. Data lakes solve this problem by leaving the information intact in Hadoop in an unstructured (or minimally structured) state, ready and waiting to be analyzed. The Data Lake can live in an in-house cloud or a public cloud depends on what best suits the organization of where to house the data.

Data Lake Governance

- The data must be clean, reliable, and available when it is needed.
- Updated campaign codes are required.

- Attribution models in web analytics need to be chosen with care. "Lookback window" that is long enough to capture enough of the customer lifecycle to provide meaningful marketing attribution.
- The right team is required that has the combination of skills, talents, and a love for data and problem-solving.

Data Lake Issues

While data lakes solve some data collection and storage issues, its utility creates other problems.

- **Security and access control:** Captured data goes into the data lake with no oversight of the contents. The security capabilities of data lakes are still immature.
- **Data quality:** There is an inability to determine data quality, or annotate the findings by other analysts or users that have found value from the same information in the lake. Without descriptive metadata and a way to maintain it, the data lake risks becoming a data swamp.[5]

Third-Party Data and Analytics

Web analytics, an example of first-party data, provides data on what is happening in the organization or business website by placing cookies into a visitor's browser. Web analytics often lacks competitive or industry data outside of the tracked website. Most organizations would like to know how well they are competing in the major areas connected to their business goals and revenue with a few exceptions (see what follows). Taking competitive analysis information into consideration, Google Analytics provides anonymous benchmark data collected that can be useful to provide some idea of how well a website is performing against others in similar industries and locations. It also provides second- and third-party data from the DoubleClick Ad Network. Other platforms, such as IBM Coremetrics and Adobe Analytics, include industry-wide metrics gathered from customers running the analytics platform. Third-Party audience data from ComScore and Nielsen has been combined with Adobe Analytics in some customer implementations.

Digital Analytics Maturity Model

Several proposed models have been put forward for years as the right way to conceptualize the development of this marketing discipline such as the digital analytics maturity model (see Table 5.1).[6]

Everything encountered in within Web/data analytics falls into one of these columns and slots.

Third-Party Data Ecosystem

To provide more depth, Table 5.2 introduces the new concepts before going into detail regarding what is necessary to understand and utilize the information.

Table 5.1 Digital Analytics Maturity Model

Phase 1 Planning & Research	Phase 2 Web Analytics & KPI Formulation	Phase 3 Behavioral Analytics	Phase 4 Digital Marketing	Phase 5 Enterprise Strategy
Select analytics platform	Visitor acquisition reporting	Funnel/clickstream analysis	E-commerce reporting	Analytics powered content servers
Infrastructure planning	Top level dashboard reporting	Visitor and behavioral segmentation	Automated alerts	Omnichannel marketing
Center for excellence consulting	Entry and exit page reporting	Digital campaign measurement	Visitor tracking via web analytics	Enterprise governance and data democratization
Train stakeholder on web analytics reporting	Basic reporting for line of business and stakeholders	Search engine optimization and Search engine marketing	Customer lifetime value optimization	Determining return on investment
Defining requirements for analytics implementation	Customized reporting and instrumentation	Personalized and customized content	Persona generation and scoring models	Participation scoring and activity-based costing
Define and lockdown business goals/objectives	Finalize enterprise dashboards	A/B and MVT Testing	Multichannel tracking/call tracking	Predictive analytics
Define and lock down KPIs	Set up/configure tag management systems	Social media analytics	Email/CRM/web analytics integration	Prescriptive analytics and strategic planning

Source: Marshall Sponder

Table 5.2 Digital Data Landscape

Digital Ecosystem	Role
Publishers	Attract visitors to a site by providing relevant content marketing to a target audience. Site owners can monetize their website through selling advertising and providing anonymous user profiles to data brokers.
Data Owners	Have a direct relationship with digital consumers based on their own first-party data, perhaps using third-party data from Acxiom and Experian
Data Aggregators	Set up and sign deals with publishers and other data providers that allows customized data segmentation and targeting, via advertising
Data Exchanges	Platform for storing, purchasing and combining first-, second-, and third-party data from multiple sources. Use the combined data for precise targeting and programmatic/retargeting
Networks	Identify and purchase audience segments as part of a media buy (typically using programmatic advertising/ retargeting)

Source: Marshall Sponder

Third-Party Data Aggregators – What They Do

1. Aggregate behavioral data of audience members from online publishers, such as *The New York Times*, and Web portals, such as Yahoo, that repackage and resell them to other organizations
2. Provide data collection scripts for publishers to run on their sites, allowing third-party data aggregators to collect data from publishers and portals as part of an ad network (e.g., Audience Science) or revenue share agreement (e.g., Oracle BlueKai)
3. Provide third-party cookie lists for sale to advertisers and agencies that are used for ad targeting. The cookie list is available for bidding within minutes (particularly for in-market audiences) and has a shelf life of up to two months.

Every third-party data aggregator has their way of combining data – that is why it is better to assemble the data side by side *but not intermix it,* which will degrade data quality. Third-party data collection is similar to an uncontrolled laboratory, where platform vendors are mixing up their formulations of data, interpretations, and context with no regulation authority to monitor them, and there is no way to cover the cornucopia in any textbook. Rather, we present an experience of connecting the dots using third-party data and leave the cornucopia conundrum to other writers.

This book provides a combination of digital marketing concepts, definitions, case studies, examples, peer-reviewed research, and exercises or assignments that foster personal observation of data, ideation, and connecting the dots.

As the data can be modeled and interpreted in many ways, it is hard to separate opinion from fact in what vendors want to highlight about their platforms (and for readers to see) versus the business value delivered by the platform. What big data offers is the process of separating the collection from the use of it. Collecting data for one purpose can be reused for another (creating network effects – much as we have seen in the last decade with certain aspects of social media), looking for patterns, clustering, and correlations in near real time that we might otherwise miss. However, in the rest of this chapter, it becomes clear that it is almost impossible to take the data out of the data collection platform without losing its context, validity, and exposing all kinds of bias in the collection and data shaping process that usually remain unseen. Perhaps data curation is what we need to be investing time in exploring and limiting our discussion here to a few platforms that are known to be more reliable. In this book we examine a limited number of data platforms we have used, as authors and practitioners, considering their strengths and limitations as representative of the overall first- and third-party data ecosystem. From the information we covered, readers can generalize the insights and apply them across several industry use cases along with a much larger platform collection.

Third-Party Data Tools Useful for Digital Analytics

University students have access to the many additional resources. Here are some the authors have found to be useful for Digital Analytics:

- **ABI/INFORM Global:** Find articles from trade journals and magazines, scholarly journals, and general interest magazines covering accounting, advertising, business, company information, industry information, management, marketing, real estate, economics, finance, human resources, and international business.
- **Academic OneFile:** Articles from magazines and scholarly journals from a wide range of subjects.
- **Business Monitor Online (now called BMI Research):** Might be useful to find out about a market in each area.
- **eMarketer:** eMarketer takes data from all over the digital marketing world, recharts and organizes it for reference and publication.
- **Gartner:** Analysis of IT markets for hardware, software, IT services, semiconductors and communications. Reports on IT issues in ten industries, including education, banking, retail, healthcare, and manufacturing.
- **Grolier Online:** Useful for definitions of topics along with building citations.
- **IBISWorld:** Reports on more than 700 industries plus specialized analyst reporting.
- **Kanopy:** Might be useful as a source of stock educational videos.
- **American Fact Finder:** Find out details about demographics in a ZIP code in the US.
- **Business Insights: Essentials**: Good for SWOT analysis of companies, perhaps of industries, also allows keyword search. Provides industry reports that might be useful.
- **Mintel Academic:** Provides overall sector studies and trend analysis.
- **PrivCo**: Information of the filings and financials, of private companies.
- **Simmons OneView:** Useful for demographic planning.
- **Statista:** Like eMarketer but has more search capability and numerical data.
- **Warc:** Resource with DATA for many marketing data, trends, and projections.

Web Data Collection Issues

There are some problems with web data collection such as

- Users in web analytics platforms are not identical to people. Users are cookie value (first-party data), and an accurate count of Web users is not the same as actual users – as the same user might be accessing the website through multiple devices (each having its own IP address and cookies). The remedy for this problem is to have users log in to the site, so it is counted accurately, but that is not always possible.[7]
- Web analytics can no longer capture the variety of traffic produced by the customer's journey.[8] In fact, no single, piece of software does it all in one place.
- Meaningful information is hard to isolate due to excessive amounts of generated data (refer to the Metropolitan Museum example earlier in this chapter). It is also tempting to use the wrong key performance indicators, such as likes, shares, and followers because they are easier to gather than others – which might be better suited but are harder to collect.[9]
- To reinforce the confusion about which metrics to use, there is no consensus on the right metrics for consumer activities on the Web.[10]

Combining First- and Third-Party Data Case Study: The Informatica.com Data Lake

A data lake is a storage repository holding vast amounts of raw data in its native format until it is needed. While a hierarchical data warehouse stores data in files or folders, a data lake uses a flat architecture to store data.[11] It is not hard to understand why data lakes are so attractive to organizations. Building a modern data warehouse is a very expensive undertaking that doesn't have a high success rate.[12]

Informatica Business Questions

- Which channels are driving the most net new names that eventually convert into customers and revenue?
- Who are all the members of a buying team we need to influence to have the deal go our way?
- What is the value of the different marketing touches eventually leading to not just an opportunity or pipeline but revenue, booked and banked?

Before beginning to improve the quality of analytics to uncover actionable insights, the data and marketing automation in place should be re-examined and, perhaps, reconsidered and replaced when needed. Next, website and web analytics need to be set up to connect with the data lake, according to Informatica, as quoted here.

> Thus, we switched to the **Adobe Experience Manager** for our whole web stack and ramped up the analytics to where we needed them to be. We looked at lots of web platforms and "marketing clouds" and felt that Adobe was way out ahead in integrating the stack – with high personalization, responsive/mobile capabilities, and all the stuff we would need (metadata capabilities for a robust taxonomy, tag management).

Then we ramped up the analytics to do great visitor tracking, advanced analysis, and track down conversions and affinities. Now we can map visitors to actual product interests on the web, leveraging our product taxonomy in the digital asset management system behind Adobe Experience Manager (visiting web pages and downloading assets for a product like MDM accrues to MDM product interest in the affinity matrix).[13]

The marketing stacks that Adobe and Google have assembled for digital marketing analytics have become crucial – but they are still not very well implemented. Most organizations are learning as they go, and often must redo a lot of the work. When web analytics collaborates with the rest of the marketing technology stack then you get

- Tight tracking of all (anonymous and known) visitor journeys
- Hard-core web analytics to page flows, referrers, repeat traffic, conversions
- Integration with other third-party platforms such as Demandbase for reverse IP mapping, tracking of firmographics like industry, company size

Once visitors arrive at a website, their visitor session can be categorized using advanced segmentation. Web analytics provides the information to stakeholders of where the visitor came from (and where they go to on the site). Behavioral signatures can further categorize visitors based on what they do on the site, then automate the learning to rule-based segmentations (note that web analytics is not alone in setting up and utilizing customer segmentation – other platforms can further segment visitor traffic).

Two examples of successful visitor mapping using Web/data analytics are as follows:

- A large online retailer transformed their website clickstream data, collected with Adobe Analytics, into more simple analytics readouts that support their strategies for planning, budgeting, product selections offerings, and paid search traffic. The visitor pathing information was copied into an enterprise data warehouse to create a rich data inventory of customer-centric information, transactions, and site activity.[14]
- A global financial services company performed clickstream analysis on five billion digital ads each month using Datameer (a big data visualization platform). The goal was to improve ad targeting and conversion while avoiding over-targeting certain consumer segments. The analysis determined they were focusing 60% of the ad budget on just 4% of their potential customers! Thus, they reallocated their advertising budget to broaden its reach; this led to a 20% increase in conversions.[15] Efficient tracking of campaigns in web analytics requires that campaign codes for all marketing activities be in place. Otherwise, the monitoring will be flawed, uneven, and not that useful. Once the web analytics and customer segmentation are in place, organizations can build scalable pad media and SEQ programs to attract new visitors, (and track them in an actionable way).

They can create issues-based content that potential customers would care about and distribute the content in multichannel advertising and social media programs (paid search, content display, remarketing, and pad marketing programs on social channels, such as LinkedIn Lead Accelerator).[16] The next evolution past web analytics is predictive analytics to score visitors as potential leads and then acting on the information (scoring) – here's where the data lake comes in.

Add-on platforms like Lattice Engines, acquired by Apple in 2017, to do predictive scoring can now be added (using the Data Lake). Lattice analyses people/companies who buy an organization's product. Lattice examines many hundreds of data points, from the job title, company data, including credit ratings, hiring profile, technology profiles, and location, to behavioral data and so on with leads scored as A, B, C, and D, with A being the highest propensity to buy. Informatica used Lattice as part of their data lake and reported that "A" scored leads were six times more likely to buy their product than leads they used to get from their sales teams. Lattice was trained (assisted learning) on 70,000 leads that Informatica had in its customer database. Once trained, Lattice rated each lead, allowing Informatica to focus on the highest rated leads, increasing sales of their products.

Three Pillars of the Digital Marketing at Informatica

Data lakes support the rest of Informatica's marketing operations stack, but they do not solve all of the issues similar organizations face with their digital marketing and acquisition. Since they are separate applications, data lakes just add to the data fragmentation that ends up requiring yet more applications floating in the lake.

- **Pillar 1: Adobe Analytics** which is part of the Adobe Marketing Cloud (Google Analytics now has a similar cloud offering connected to Google Analytics, but it was not available at the time of this case study in fate 2015).
- **Pillar 2: Marketo Marketing Automation** used for tracking known visitors, email, and automating our nurture flows, (we chose Marketo).
- **Pillar 3: Salesforce CRM** for tracking the sales opportunities all the way through to revenue, which is a vital part of any big data marketing program.

Additional Pillar Support Applications

- **Dynamic Tag Management via a DTM:** DTM is a CMS for JavaScript, tags, and tracking codes using Adobe Tag Manager (or Google Tag Manager). Adobe's and Google's Tag Managers are powerful (and free) tools, Adobe Tag Manager comes with Adobe Experience Manager and integrates with Adobe Analytics. Google has a similar catering and integrations with Google Analytics and other parts of its cloud marketing stack. DTM is used to determine when to fire a tag and what data to collect and where to send it (in Informatica's case from Marketo and Adobe Analytics to Rio SEO, Demandbase, D&B, and Lattice Engines), and it streamlines and automates what would otherwise be a hugely repetitive and manual process.
- **EDW (Enterprise Data Warehouse):** The data lake hosts all the unstructured data. There needs to be another place where the output of the three pillars (Salesforce, DTM, and Adobe Analytics) resides – the data from the three pillars is structured data. Putting structured data directly into the data lake might be ideal, but at the time of this writing the data lake construct does not have a fast-enough response time to serve up data in real time.
- **Data Management Tools:** Informatica used its data management tools to make sure all the information in the data lake is properly cleaned (cleaning, up information that is incorrect, incomplete or duplicated). Master data management (MDM) acts to streamline and automate data management and ensure data quality. The data management tools include Informatica PowerCenter for

combining data many different sources, Informatica data quality monitoring and automation tools, and big data relationship management for exposing relationships in the data lake, such as various accounts, contacts, and DUNS numbers from Dun & Bradstreet.

- **Demandbase** (Data Enrichment): Used for reverse IP-lookup to see which companies are visiting Informatica.com along with the company size, and industry segments that are fed to pre-fili firms or to personalize the appearance of the website based on industry. Once the forms are populated and submitted, they are fed into Adobe Analytics, Marketo, and ultimately, flow back into the data lake.
- **Dun & Bradstreet** (Data Enrichments): Enrich and validate the data, with filmographies from Dun & Bradstreet – using the DUNS standard.
- **Rio SEO** (Data Enrichment): Used to identify buying teams within accounts and to track word-of-mouth influencers for Informatica. When a visitor is browsing the site, each page URL has a Rio code. Rio SEO copies the URL of when a visitor visits the page and makes It available to be used in an email to a friend or co-worker with a code goes with the link. When an email recipient clicks on the link and arrives on the website, Informatica can tell who the influencer is who sent the email which brought the visitor to Informatica.com.
- **Lattice** (Predictive Analytics/Lead Scoring): Every prospect and account have 300–400. variables attached, used to analyze the companies and prospects of purchasers then, generalize the attributes of the buyers to the wider prospect universe for lookalikes (lookalikes are commonly employed on Facebook, LinkedIn, Twitter). Informatica uses two models: one for buyers of their licensed products and the other for purchasers of their cloud products (with slightly different models for North America and Rest of World, so there are four in total). Lattice assigns each lead with two scores depending on how likely they are to purchase each kind of product.
- **Tableau Data Visualization Platform:** Data visualization is the last mile of big data marketing. Tableau makes it easy to bring together data from different sources into one dashboard.

Programmatic Advertising

Programmatic advertising is automating most of the manual aspects of digital advertising that used to be done more slowly and expensively, such as insertion orders to publisher's websites (both direct and open-auction). According to Digiday, programmatic ad buying typically refers to the use of software to purchase digital advertising, as opposed to the traditional process that involves RFPs, human negotiations, and manual insertion orders. It is using machines to buy ads.[17] Programmatic technology is one more innovation of the digitization of things. It automates processes, eliminates costs, and allows for more time to be spent on the strategy and the analysis of the data.

Applying Third-Party Data with Programmatic Advertising

Most marketers are still trying to figure out what the term programmatic means to a marketer; after all, the term is ambiguous, implying something about building or running a program or creating programming – and that is not a good definition of what programmatic advertising is.

Buy Side vs. Sell Side

This is confusing since buyers can also be sellers and vice versa!

- **Buyers/demand side:** Advertisers are trying to deliver the right message in front (eyeballs) of the right person at the right time (targeting) for the best price (return on investment).
- **Sellers/supply side:** Publishers are trying to maximize the money they can make selling advertising space (inventory) to advertisers.

The Buying/Purchase Cycle

The author is not a fan of canned models of buying activity – not everyone goes through the same process in the same way; we are not all the same in the way we process information. On the other hand, having a model of how consumers behave online when they decide to purchase a product or service is useful because we can make plans and optimize marketing (or so it was thought). As we saw in previous chapters, the consumer buying cycle is not a funnel (except, perhaps, the part of it that happens on a website). However, nothing in this world is perfect. Just because the traditional consumer buying cycle model is deeply flawed, we can still use it at least to get started because digital marketing and programmatic advertising (especially) needs a plan, a model to base our advertising on; otherwise, how are we supposed to know that someone is getting closer to making a purchase decision?

Media Planning

To run a lot of effective programmatic advertising, marketers need to have the creative ready and know when and where to run it – that was always true of any advertising, but even more so of programmatic. Again, the model is oversimplified but can serve us better than the last one as this model helps to explain why some mediums work better for certain things than others.

Why Programmatic Advertising Is Used

Modern technology has changed the way consumers purchase products and services online. Zillions of websites now are on the Web – a lot to wade through (no one can) and/or place advertising on.

- In the past 25 years, we have developed e-commerce – the ease of buying and selling online (just look at Amazon and eBay!).
- The development of precision targeting along with self-service advertising (like Google AdWords) has turned many into digital marketers (whether they realize it or not), although they need to become more sophisticated to take full advantage of what technologies such as programmatic advertising offers.
- Digital and social media platforms have all included sophisticated and powerful analytics (and in some cases, customizable attribution models).

Digital Advertising Types

- **Digital:** Graphic ads appearing next to content on webpages, IM applications, email
- **Video:** Ads appear in the video before, during, or after the video plays. One of the fastest-growing opportunities online today.
- **Mobile:** Ads used on mobile devices, such as cell phones or tablets are growing quickly.
- **Search:** Ads are placed and ranked by search engines on webpages that show associated results from the user's search engine queries (can be combined with display networks-such as Google's).
- **Social:** Produce content that users will share with their social network.
- **Native:** A form of social media advertising Bat matches the shape and function of the platform on which it appears – looks similar to user's post or newsfeed item but is an ad.
- Programmatic can run advertising on any of the channels above (and in some cases on linear television).

Programmatic Advertising Issues

- Requires more expertise from marketers to employ the platform effectively
- Lack of transparency on where the ads appear (in some cases)
- Not enough creative content to take advantage of the inventory that programmatic allows advertisers to run
- The cost of an impression can be higher when targeting accuracy is greater
- Lack of engagement between clients, publishers, and advertisers

Review Questions

1. What is the difference between first-party data and third-party data?
2. Is there such a thing as a second-party cookie?
3. What are the five main elements of the third-party data ecosystem?
4. What are the most common web analytics roles?
5. What are the main data collection issues covered in this chapter?

Chapter 5 Citations

1. "Five business functions expect to reap the biggest benefit from Big Data." October 14, 2013. www.slideshare.net/SAPanalytics/five-business-functions-expect-to-reap-the-biggest-benefit-from-big-data-at-consumer-products-companies-infographic. Accessed May 30, 2023.
2. Bansal, M. "Big Data: Creating the power to move heaven and earth." September 2, 2014. www.technologyreview.com/s/530371/big-data-creating-the-power-to-move-heaven-and-earth. Accessed May 30, 2023.

3. "2015 banking trends slideshare." March 10, 2015. www.mx.com/resources/resources/2015-banking-trends-slides. Accessed May 30, 2023.

4. https://www.thedrum.com/news/2023/05/10/doritos-jimmy-john-s-others-are-capturing-first-zero-party-data-with-clever-tactics. Accessed May 30, 2023.

5. "immeria: Review of maturity models." September 1, 2009. http://blog.immeria.net/2009/09/review-of-maturity-models.html. Accessed May 30, 2023.

6. "LUMAscapes: LUMA partners." www.lumapartners.com/resource-center/lumascapes-2. Accessed May 30, 2023.

7. Cushing, A. "Why Google analytics' user metrics are BS (for most sites)." September 12, 2016. www.annielytics.com/blog/analytics/google-analytics-usermetrics-bs-sites. Accessed May 30, 2023.

8. Seomoz. "Why visitor analytics aren't enough for modern marketers." October 16, 2013. www.olmblog.com/2013/10/search-engine-optimization/why-visitor-analytics-arent-enough-for-modern-marketers. Accessed May 30, 2023.

9. Ingram, M. "When it comes to media, not everything that counts can be counted." January 6, 2015. https://gigaom.com/2015/01/06/when-it-comes-to-media-not-everything-that-counts-can-be-counted. Accessed May 30, 2023.

10. Ingram, M. "We are drowning in data about readers and attention, but which metrics really matter? You won't like the answer." May 30, 2023. https://gigaom.com/2014/04/15/we-are-drowning-in-data-about-readers-and-attention-but-which-metrics-really-matter-you-wont-like-the-answer. Accessed May 30, 2023.

11. Rouse, M. "What is Data Lake? Definition from WhatIs.com." http://searchaws.techtarget.com/definition/data-lake. Accessed May 30, 2023.

12. Merrick, C. "9 Reasons data warehouse projects fail." December 4, 2014. https://blog.rjmetrics.com/2014/12/04/10-common-mistakes-when-building-a-data-warehouse. Accessed May 30, 2023.

13. "The informatica blog." http://blogs.informatica.com. Accessed May 30, 2023.

14. Benesh, P. "Case study: Clickstream analytics in a competitive world." *TDWI*. May 6, 2010. https://tdwi.org/articles/2010/05/06/clickstream-analytics-in-a-competitive-world.aspx. Accessed May 30, 2023.

15. "Understanding your customer journey by extending Adobe Analytics." www.datameer.com/wp-content/uploads/2015/09/Multi-Channel-Customer-Journey-Analytics.pdf. Accessed April 15, 2017.

16. "The informatica blog." http://blogs.informatica.com. Accessed April 15, 2017.

17. "WTF is programmatic advertising?" *Digiday*. February 20, 2014. http://digiday.com/platforms/what-is-programmatic-advertising. Accessed April 15, 2017.

Social Media Analytics for Digital Marketing

CHAPTER OBJECTIVES

After reading this chapter, readers should understand the following:

- Social media analytics for digital marketing
- Composition of the seven layers of social media analytics
- Common goals, KPIs, and use cases for social media analytics
- Descriptive, prescriptive, and predictive analytics for social media
- Differences between business analytics and social media analytics
- Challenges to the efficient use of social media analytics
- How to use the social analytics vendor assessment

The Rise of Social Media in Marketing

Social media is such a big part of the fabric of society today that it is almost impossible to imagine our lives without it. To succeed on social media and accomplish your goals, there are several effective strategies and opportunities one can follow:

- First and foremost, establish your objectives and determine exactly what you aim to achieve through social media. Whether it's to increase brand awareness, drive website traffic, generate leads, or boost sales, having a clear idea of your goals will guide your entire social media strategy.
- Conduct thorough research to really understand your target audience's demographics, preferences, and behaviors. Armed with this knowledge, you can tailor your content and engage with them in a more meaningful way.
- Identify the social media platforms where your target audience is most active and focus your efforts there. It's better to excel on a few platforms than to spread yourself too thin across all of them.
- Produce high-quality content that is both relevant and appealing to your target audience. Utilize a variety of mediums such as text, images, videos, and interactive elements to capture attention and encourage sharing.
- Partner with influencers or micro-influencers with a large following that aligns with your target audience to promote your products or services, expanding your reach and credibility.

DOI: 10.4324/9781003025351-6

- Create and share videos that offer value, entertainment, or education to your audience, as video continues to dominate social media. Consider using live streaming, stories, and short-form videos to engage with your followers in real time.
- Motivate your audience to create content related to your brand and products. User-generated content helps build trust, increases engagement, and expands your reach. Repost and give credit to users who create relevant content.
- Use chatbots to automate tasks such as responding to common inquiries or sending personalized messages. They can enhance customer service and streamline interactions, saving time and effort.
- Stay up-to-date and experiment with new features and formats like stories, reels, polls, and interactive stickers. These additions often receive priority in platform algorithms and can help increase visibility.
- Regularly review your social media analytics to measure the performance of your posts, campaigns, and overall strategy. Identify what's working and what needs improvement. Adjust your approach accordingly to optimize your results.

Remember, social media is a constantly evolving landscape, so stay informed about trends, algorithm changes, and emerging platforms. Adapt your strategy as needed and continue to connect with your audience in an authentic and engaging way. With these strategies, you can confidently and effectively navigate social media to achieve your goals.

There Is Wide Social Media Adoption by Age and Gender

Social media usage worldwide has dramatically increased, with 4.9 billion users as of March 2023, expected to reach 5.85 billion by 2027. Facebook dominates with 2.958 billion users. Eastern Asia has the most social media users, and 85% of mobile phone users are active on social media. Millennials and Gen Z are the most frequent users, and TikTok has experienced significant growth with a 105% increase in the US over the last two years.[1]

The Complex and Fragmented Ecosystem of Social Media Analytics

Measuring and analyzing social media data there are numerous tools, platforms, and metrics available. To simplify social media analytics, define clear objectives, focus on essential metrics, choose the right tools, automate and report, use data visualization, regularly analyze and adjust, and stay informed and adapt. By implementing these strategies, you can focus on the metrics that matter most to your goals and achieve optimal results.

- To successfully analyze social media data, it is essential to establish your objectives and key performance indicators (KPIs) upfront (which we cover in other chapters of this book). Identify the metrics that are most relevant to your goals and focus on tracking and analyzing those specific data points.

- It is crucial to prioritize the social media platforms that are most pertinent to your target audience and business objectives. By doing so, you can concentrate your efforts and resources on these platforms to gain deeper insights.
- Streamlining the process with social media management tools or analytics platforms can consolidate your data sources and provide a unified view of your social media performance. Furthermore, automated reporting systems that gather and present key metrics clearly and concisely can save you time and deliver timely and relevant data.
- Rather than being overwhelmed by excessive data, look for patterns, trends, and correlations to extract actionable insights that can inform your social media strategy and decision-making process.
- Investing in training or hiring individuals with expertise in social media analytics can simplify the process and maximize its value. Continuously reviewing your analytics strategy, based on new insights or changes in your business goals, is also crucial.
- By implementing these strategies, you can simplify the complex ecosystem of social media analytics and focus on the data that truly matters for your business. This allows you to gain meaningful insights and make informed decisions to optimize your social media performance and achieve your goals.

Introducing the Seven Layers of Social Media Analytics

Social media analytics is a science as it requires systematically identifying, extracting, and analyzing various social media data using a variety of sophisticated tools and techniques (this book will examine some of the tools and technology to extract and use social media data). However, social media analytics is also an art, which requires analysts, stakeholders, and business owners to align the insights gained via the analytics with business goals and objectives. We should master both the art and science of social media analytics to get full value from it for digital marketing.

In this book, we have posited that the analytics of social media is best understood as a series of data layers. Determining the best social data layer(s) to utilize for business issues is where the art and science of social media analytics merge.

The science part of social media analytics requires a combination of skilled data analysts, sophisticated tools and technologies, and reliable/cleaned data. Getting the science right, however, is not enough. To effectively consume the results and put them into action, the business must master the other half of analytics; that is, the art of interpreting and aligning analytics with business objectives and goals.

Each layer of social media carries valuable information and insights that can be harvested for business intelligence purposes by using layer-specific social/text analytics platforms as covered in this book. Out of the seven layers (see Figure 6.1), some are visible or easily identifiable (e.g., text and actions), and others are mostly invisible (e.g., social media and hyperlink networks).

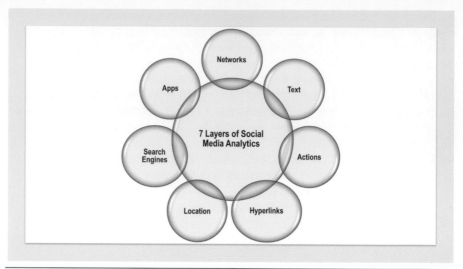

Figure 6.1 Seven Layers of Social Media Analytics
Source: Gohar F. Khan

The following are seven social media layers that will be discussed in detail in the subsequent chapters.

1. Text
2. Networks
3. Actions (referred to as intermediate metrics elsewhere in this book)
4. Hyperlinks
5. Mobile
6. Location
7. Search engines

Definition of the Seven Layers

Layer One: Text

Social media text analytics deals with the extraction and analysis of business insights from textual elements of social media content, such as comments, tweets, blog posts, and Facebook status updates. Text analytics is mostly used to understand social media users' sentiments or identify emerging themes and topics.

Layer Two: Networks

Social media network analytics extract, analyze, and interpret personal and professional social networks, for example, Facebook, and Twitter. Network analytics seeks to identify influential nodes (e.g., people and organizations) and their position in the network.

Layer Three: Actions

Social media actions (intermediate metrics) analytics deals with extracting, analyzing, and interpreting the actions performed by social media users, including likes, shares, mentions, and endorsement. Actions analytics are mostly used to measure popularity, influence, and prediction in social media. The case study included at the end of the chapter demonstrates how social media actions (e.g., Twitter mentions) can be used for business intelligence purposes.

Layer Four: Hyperlinks

Hyperlink analytics is about extracting, analyzing, and interpreting social media hyperlinks (e.g., in-links and out-links). Hyperlink analysis can reveal sources of incoming or outgoing web traffic to and from a webpage or website.

Layer Five: Mobile

Mobile analytics is the next frontier in the social business landscape. Mobile analytics deals with measuring and optimizing user engagement through mobile applications (or apps for short).

Layer Six: Location

Location analytics, also known as spatial analysis or geospatial analytics, is concerned with mining and mapping the locations of social media users, contents, and data.

Layer Seven: Search Engine Analytics

Search engines analytics focuses on analyzing search engine data to gain valuable insights into a range of areas, including trends analysis, keyword monitoring, keyword research, search results, and search engine marketing (text ads, etc.).

Emergence of Social Media Analytics

Based on Google Trends data, the term *social media analytics* appeared over the Internet horizon during 2008, and interest in it (based on Internet searches for the term) has steadily increased since then. Social media analytics was present as a cottage industry, or a business or manufacturing activity carried on in a person's home, as early as 2003 based on the authors' personal experience. In 2008, Google Trends began to detect enough usage of the term "social media analytics" to show up in its trend reporting, and the subject is becoming ever-more popular as we move towards 2020. No doubt, the growth in the development and usage of various social media channels spawned social media analytics, as the means to better understand and harness social data.

Social media has become one of the main ways people express themselves. Because of this activity, social media analytics is gaining prominence among both the research and business communities.

Some Popular Reasons for Using Social Media Analytics

- Measure brand loyalty
- Generate business leads
- Drive traffic to owned media (Facebook pages, corporate blogs, company webpages, organizational microsites, specific mobile applications, etc.)
- Predictive business forecasting
- Demographics and psychographics around specific audiences and topics
- Business intelligence and market research
- Business decision-making

However, it is hard to put a dollar value on the data without accurately tracking every step in the process of acquiring customers. One of the co-authors was recently interviewed on the issue of social media return on investment (ROI) – to read more refer to http://oursocialtimes.com/how-to-measure-social-media-roi/.

Goals of Social Media Analytics

The main purpose of social media analytics is to enable informed and insightful decision-making by leveraging social media data.[2]

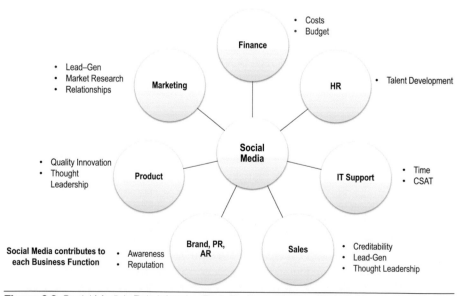

Figure 6.2 Social Media's Role Informing Each Business Function/Stakeholder
Source: Authors

Social media plays a significant role in every aspect of business functions as shown in Figure 6.2. The following are some sample questions that can be answered with social media analytics:

- What are customers using social media saying about our brand or a new product launch?
- Which content posted over social media is resonating more with clients or customers?
- How can we harness social media data (e.g., tweets and Facebook comments) to improve our product/services?
- Is the social media conversation about our company, product, or service positive, negative, or neutral?
- How can we leverage social media to promote brand awareness?
- Who are our influential social media followers, fans, and friends?
- Who are our influential social media nodes (e.g., people and organizations) and what is their position in the network?
- Which are the social media platforms driving the most traffic to our corporate website?
- Where is the geographical location of our social media customers?
- What are the keywords and terms trending over social media?
- How current is our business with social media, and how many people are connected with us?
- Which websites are linked to our corporate website?
- How are my competitors doing on social media?

Social Media Analytics KPIs

The questions, use cases, and goals that inform social media can be measured using key performance indicators such as share of voice and sentiment score (see a list of suggested KPIs matched to business goals in Table 6.1).

Social Media vs. Traditional Business Analytics

While the premise of both social media and traditional business analytics is to produce actionable business, they do however slightly differ in scope and nature. Table 6.2 provides a comparison of social media analytics with traditional business analytics.

The most visible difference between the two types of information comes from the source, type, and nature of the data that is being mined. Unlike the traditional business analytics of structured and historical data, social media analytics involves the collection, analysis, and interpretation of semi-structured and unstructured social media data to gain an insight into the contemporary issues while supporting effective decision-making.[3] Social media data is highly diverse, high volume, real time, and stored in third-party databases in a semi-structured and unstructured format.

Structured business data, on the other hand, is mostly stored in databases and spreadsheets in machine-readable format (e.g., rows and columns). Thus, it can be easily searched, computed, and mined. Unstructured and semi-structured social media data is not machine readable and can take a variety of forms, such as the contents of this book, Facebook comments, emails, tweets, hyperlinks, PowerPoint presentations, images, emoticons, videos, etc. Thus, it is not analytics-friendly and

Table 6.1 Social Media Key Performance Indicators Matched to Key Business Goals

Aligning Business Goals & KPIs (usually Intermediate Metrics, in the case of Social Media) for Business Success					
Business Goals	KPI 1	KPI 2	KPI 3	KPI 4	KPI 5
Awareness	Share of voice	Social community growth	Reach, volume of conversations	Sentiment analysis (+/- neutral)	Unique commenters
Engagement	Interactions per follower	Daily active users	% of community interacting	Viral content spread	Hashtag/meme use
Lead Gen	Cost to acquire leads from social	Web referrals via social media	Qualified sales leads via social	Growth of reach in targeted audiences	Number of downloads of select content
Conversion	Downloads via tracked links	Revenue via tracked links	Cost per acquisition (CPA)	Increase % of social conversions	Revenue attribution via Influences
Customer Support	Cost savings	Decreased time of issue resolution	Sentiment change on support issues	Number of issues resolved	Resolution rate per issue/agent
Advocacy	Number of active advocates	Volume of advocate conversations	Volume of brand advocates conversations	Influence score and reach of advocates	Revenue attributed to advocates
Innovation	Number of ideas submitted related to products or services	Number of ideas that are developed into products or services	Number of bugs that are fixed in developed products or services	Community feedback from development of products or services	Engagement rate in product development forums

Source: Authors

Table 6.2 Social Media Analytics vs. Business Analytics

Social Media Analytics	Business Analytics
Semi-structured and unstructured data	Structured data
Data is not analytically friendly	Data is analytical friendly
Real-time data	Mostly historical data
Public data	Private data
Stored in third-party databases	Stored in business-owned databases
Boundary-less data (i.e., boundary within the Internet)	Bound within the business intranet
Data is high volume	Data is medium to high volume
Highly diverse data	Uniform data
Data is widely shared over the Internet	Data is only shared within organizations
More sharing creates greater value/impact	Less sharing creates more value
No business control over data	Tightly controlled by business
Socialized data	Bureaucratic data
Data is informal in nature	Data is formal in nature

Source: Gohar F. Khan

needs a lot of cleaning and transformation. Another visible difference comes from the way the information (i.e., text, photographs, videos, audio, etc.) is created and consumed. Social media data originates from the public Internet and is socialized in nature. Socialized data is provided for the benefit of humanity; it is created and consumed using various social media platforms and social technologies to maintain social and professional ties (e.g., Facebook, LinkedIn, etc.), to facilitate knowledge sharing and management (Wikipedia, blogs, etc.). Socialized data creates awareness (i.e., Twitter), or to exchange information in the form of text, audio, video, documents, graphics, to name a few.[4]

Social media data is generated by people communicating with each other through social media. Social media is not like the common business analytics data, which is structured and formal in nature and is often controlled by organizations and bound within an organizational network or intranet. The value of socialized data is determined by the extent to which it is shared with other social media accounts (e.g., people or organizations): the more it that is shared (i.e., socialized), the greater its overall value. However, it is important to point out that most social media metrics/KPIs are engagement-based and do not yield a tangible return on investment (ROI); instead, social media produces intermediate, activity-based metrics that support traditional business metrics (but do not replace them). For example, the value/effect of information can be considered an intermediate metric and is measured by the growth of followers (e.g., on Twitter or Facebook). On the other hand, most of the common business data and metrics are confined within an organization's databases for use within the organization, and can serve as a source of competitive advantage for that organization.

Types of Social Media Analytics

Like any business analytics, social media analytics can take three forms:

- Descriptive analytics
- Predictive analytics
- Prescriptive analytics

Descriptive Analytics

Descriptive analytics is mostly focused on gathering and describing social media data in the form of reports, visualizations, and clustering to understand a business problem. Actions analytics (e.g., number of likes, tweets, and views) and certain aspects of text analytics are examples of descriptive analytics. Social media text (e.g., user comments), for instance, can be used to understand users' sentiments or identify emerging trends by clustering themes and topics. Currently, descriptive analytics accounts for most social media analytics.

Predictive Analytics

Predictive analytics involves analyzing large amounts of accumulated social media data to predict a future event. For example, an intention expressed over social media (such as buy, sell, recommend, quit, desire, or wish) can be mined to predict a future event (such as a purchase). Alternatively, a business manager can predict sales figures based on past visits (or in-links) to a corporate website. The Tweepsmap tool, for example, can help users determine the right time to tweet for maximum alignment with the right audience time zone (for more information see https://tweepsmap.com).

Prescriptive Analytics

While predictive analytics help to predict the future, prescriptive analytics suggest the best action to take when handling a situation or scenario.[5] For example, if you have groups of social media users that display certain patterns of buying behavior, how can you optimize your offering to each group? Like predictive analytics, prescriptive analytics has not yet found its way into social media data.

Social Media Analytics Cycle

Social media analytics is a six-step irrelative process (involving both the science and art) of mining the desired business insights from social media data (see Figure 6.3). At the center of the analytics is the company. We want objectives that will inform each

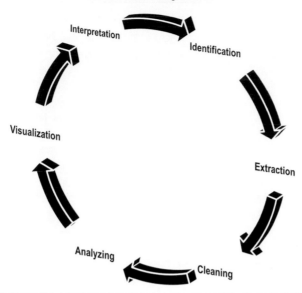

Figure 6.3 The Social Media Analytics Cycle
Source: Gohar F. Khan

step of the social media analytics journal. Business goals are defined at the initial stage, and the analytics process will continue until the stated business objectives are fully satisfied. The steps may vary considerably based on the layers of social media data-mined (and the type of the tool employed). The following are the six general steps, at the highest level of abstraction, that involve both the science and art of achieving business insights from social media data. Interestingly, the steps of the social media analytics cycle are like processes that are used to manage corporations, such as setting goals and objectives that are aligned with the business' vision. Managing a business, which often involves identifying risks and controls, is like performing the same thing with data.

Step 1: Identification

The identification stage is the art part of social media analytics and is concerned with searching and identifying the right source of information for analytical purposes. The numbers and types of users and information (such as text, conversation, and networks) available over social media are huge, diverse, multilingual, and noisy. Thus, framing the right question and knowing what data to analyze is extremely crucial in gaining useful business insights. The source and type of data to be analyzed should be aligned with business objectives. Most of the data for analytics will come from business-owned social media platforms, such as an official Twitter account, Facebook fan pages, blogs, and YouTube channels. Some data for analytics, however, will also be harvested from non-official social media platforms, such as Google search engine trends data or Twitter search stream data. The business objectives that need to be achieved will play a major role in identifying the sources and type of data to be mined. Aligning social media analytics with business objectives is discussed in a later chapter.

Step 2: Extraction

The type (e.g., text, numerical, or network) and size of data will determine the best method and platform tools that are suitable for the extraction. Small-size numerical information, for example, can be extracted manually (e.g., going to your Facebook fan page and counting likes and copying comments), and a large-scale automated extraction is done through an application programming interface (API). Manual data extraction may be practical for small-scale data, but it is the API-based extraction tools that will help us get most out of various social media platforms. Mostly, the social media analytics tools use API-based data mining.

APIs, in simple words, are sets of routines/protocols that social media platforms (e.g., Twitter and Facebook) have developed to allow users to access small portions of data hosted in their databases. The greatest benefit of using APIs is that it allows other entities (e.g., customers, programmers, and other organizations) to build apps, widgets, websites, and other tools based on open social media data. Some data, such as social networks and hyperlink networks, can only be extracted through specialized tools from platforms like Brandwatch and Crimson Hexagon (for social media analytics data), and several Web scrappers that can extract hyperlinks on webpages.

Privacy and Ethical Issues with Social Media Analytics Data

Two important issues to bear in mind are privacy and ethical issues related to mining data from social media platforms. Privacy advocacy groups have long raised serious concerns regarding large-scale mining of social media data and warned against transforming social spaces into behavioral laboratories. The social media privacy issue first came into the spotlight particularly due to the large-scale "Facebook Experiment" carried out in 2012. In this experiment, Facebook manipulated the news feeds feature of thousands of people to see if emotion contagion occurs without face-to-face interaction (and absence of nonverbal cues) between people in social networks.[6] Although the experiment was consistent with Facebook's Data Use Policy[7] and helped promote our understanding of online social behavior, it does, however, raise serious concerns regarding obtaining informed consent from participants and allowing them to opt out.

The bottom line here is that data extraction practices should not violate a user's privacy and the data extracted should be handled carefully, and the policies should explicitly detail social media ownership regarding both accounts and activities such as individual and page profiles, platform content, posting, activity, data handling, and extraction, etc.

Step 3: Cleaning

This step involves removing the unwanted data from the automatically extracted data. Some data may need cleaning, while other data can go directly into analysis. In the case of the text analytics cleaning, coding, clustering, and filtering of the text data may be needed to get rid of unrelated text using natural language processing (NLP).[8]

Note that coding and filtering can be done automatically using machines or manually done by humans. In the later chapters, we also cover text analytics in detail, including the process of text cleaning. Coding and filtering can be performed by machines (i.e., automated) or it can be carried out manually by humans. For example, Discovertext combines machine learning and human coding techniques to code, cluster, and classify social media data.[9]

Step 4: Analyzing

At this stage, the clean data is analyzed for business insights. Depending on the layer of social media analytics under consideration and the tools and algorithm employed, the steps and approach to take will vary greatly. For example, nodes in a social media network can be clustered and visualized in a variety of ways depending on the algorithm employed. The overall objective at this stage is to extract meaningful insights without the data losing its integrity. Most of the analytics tools lay out a step-by-step procedure to analyze social data; having background knowledge and an understanding of the tools and its capabilities are crucial in arriving at the right answers.

Step 5: Visualization

In addition to numerical results, most of the seven layers of social media analytics will also result in visual outcomes. The science of effective visualization known as visual analytics is becoming an important part of interactive decision-making facilitated by visualization.[10] Effective visualization is particularly helpful with complex and large datasets because it can reveal hidden patterns, relationships, and trends. It is the effective visualization of the results that will demonstrate the value of social media data to top management. Depending on the layer, the analysis part will lead to relevant visualizations for effective communication of results. Text analytics, for instance, can result in a word co-occurrence cloud; hyperlink analytics will provide visual hyperlink networks, and location analytics can produce interactive maps. Depending on the type of data, different types of visualization are possible, including the following.

- **Network Data (with whom):** Network data visualizations can show who is connected to whom. For example, a Twitter "following-following" network chart can show who is following whom. Different types of networks are discussed in a later chapter.
- **Topical Data *(what):*** Topical data visualizations are mostly focused on what aspect of a phenomenon is under investigation. A text cloud generated from social media comments can show what topics/themes are occurring more frequently in the discussion.
- **Temporal Data *(when):*** Temporal data visualizations slice-and-dice data on a time horizon and can reveal longitudinal trends, patterns, and relationships hidden in the data. Google Trends data, for example, can visually investigate longitudinal search engine trends.
- **Geospatial Data *(where):*** Geospatial data visualization is used to map and locate data, people, and resources. Location analytics chapter provides more details on mapping.
- Other forms of visualizations include trees, hierarchical, multidimensional (chart, graphs, tag clouds), 3D (dimension), computer simulation, infographics, flows, tables, heat maps, plots, etc.

Step 6: Interpretation

This step relies on human judgments to interpret valuable knowledge from the visual data. The data should be presented in the right form for the person who is going to read it. It can be as dashboards, for example. Meaningful interpretation is of particular importance when we are dealing with social media data that leave room for different interpretations. Having domain knowledge and expertise are crucial in consuming the obtained results correctly.

Two strategies or approaches used here can be summarized as follows:

1. Producing easily understandable analytical results
2. Improving analytics analysis and insights capabilities[11]

The first approach requires training data scientists and analysts to produce interactive and easy to use visual results. Moreover, the second strategy focuses on improving management analytics consumption capabilities.[12]

Challenges to Social Media Analytics

Social media data is high-volume, high-velocity, and highly diverse, which, in a sense, is a blessing regarding the insights it carries; however, analyzing and interpreting it presents several challenges. Analyzing unstructured data requires new metrics, tools, and capabilities, particularly for real-time analytics that most businesses do not possess.

Big Data Volume and Velocity as a Challenge

Managing and processing social media data can be a daunting task due to its vast volume, diverse range of formats, and real-time nature. The sheer amount of data generated every second makes it challenging to analyze effectively. Furthermore, different formats require specific tools and techniques to analyze, and the lack of standardization across platforms makes it difficult to compare and consolidate information from different sources. Social media data is large and generated swiftly. Capturing and analyzing millions of records that appear every second is a real challenge. Capturing all this information may not be feasible. Knowing what to focus on is crucial for narrowing down the scope and size of the data. Luckily, sophisticated tools are being developed to handle high-volume and high-velocity data.

In addition, the dynamic and real-time nature of social media data presents challenges for timely data collection, analysis, and response. Ensuring data quality and filtering out irrelevant or misleading information is essential for accurate analysis. Furthermore, organizations must address privacy and ethics concerns to conform to regulations and ensure the ethical use of data while extracting valuable insights.

To extract actionable insights from the complexity of social media data, organizations need to invest in robust data strategies, data governance, and skilled professionals. Sophisticated analysis techniques are required to understand the impact of social media activities across different channels and attribute conversions or actions to specific social media interactions. By addressing these complexities, organizations can effectively leverage social media data for informed decision-making.

The first point we want to make is that the growth of social media and its proliferation makes it imperative to study its analytics. Businesses and individuals now accept the notion that social media is measurable and have even used it to gain an advantage over their competitors. However, many of the intermediate metrics such as likes, shares, posts, and pins have turned out to be poor proxies for return on investment (ROI) unless they are used to measure audience engagement or campaign effectiveness.[13] Unlike web analytics and text analytics that depend more on the capabilities of specific platforms for data and metrics, social media analytics evolved to focus on online audiences and their activities. Thus, the creation and analysis of digital data need to be considered together, as one unit. Content creation today utilizes a combination of these tools and disciplines that should not be glossed over.

Activities in social media differ somewhat, based on the channel. What we have found is a fragmentation has evolved where we cannot understand the activity in a social media channel without the analytics created just for that channel. Much of the data from one channel is incompatible with the others, and even when it has the same terminology (i.e., shares, likes, friends, etc.) this doesn't always mean the same thing and cannot be added together with integrity. When data is gathered through APIs and rolled up into a dashboard platform, the information is useful just for trend correlation and directional purposes, perhaps nothing more. From a business analytics perspective, the latter is a challenging situation to be in as we are working with platform tools and metrics that don't add up to a clear return on investment. And yet, that is the challenge we face as marketers and students. How does one make sense of all this data? It comes down to what we want to achieve in the first place (our goals). We need to understand the capabilities, technologies as well the digital transformation strategies of organizations.

Social Media Analytics Tools

Social media analytics tools are being constantly developed to keep up with the growing need to extract, clean, and analyze the vast number of social media data. Social media analytics tools come in a variety of forms and functionalities. Table 6.3 lists some example tools on each layer of social media analytics. These tools are briefly discussed in several of the following chapters. These tools can be used to measure different layers of social media data, especially when aligned with an organization's business strategy.

Data Diversity Challenges

Social media users and the content they generate are extremely diverse, multilingual, and vary across time and space. Not every tweet, like, or user is worth looking at. Due to the noisy and diverse nature of social media data, separating relevant content from noise is challenging and time-consuming.

Unstructured Data Challenges

Unlike the data stored in corporate databases, which are mostly numbers, social media data is highly unstructured and consists of text, graphics, actions, and

Table 6.3 Examples of Social Media Analytics Tools

Text	Actions (Intermediate Metrics)	Network	Mobile	Location	Hyperlinks	Research Engines
Discovertext	Lithium	NodeXL	Countly	Google Fusion Table	Webometrics Analyst	Google Trends
Lexalytics	Twitonomy	UCINET	Mixpanel	Tweepsmap	VOSON	
Tweet Archivist	Google Analytics	Pajek	Google Mobile Analytics	Trendsmap		
Twitonomy	SocialMediaMineR	Netminer		Followerwonk		
Netlytic	Brandwatch	Flocker		Esri Maps		
LIWC	Crimson Hexagon	Netlytic		Agos		
Voyant		Reach		Geofeedia		
		Mentionmapp		Picodash		

Source: Gohar F. Khan

relations. Short social media text, such as tweets and comments, has dubious grammatical structure and is laden with abbreviations, acronyms, and emoticons (a symbol or combination of symbols used to convey emotional expressions in text messages), thus representing a significant challenge for extracting actionable business intelligence.

Case Study: The Underground Campaign that Scored Big[14]

Background

ESPN is a digital sports leader in the UK, operating websites and apps that deliver a range of multimedia content to sports fans. ESPN.co.uk, the brand's central offering in the region, covers most sports, including football, cricket, rugby, tennis, golf, boxing, F1, and others. Other sport-specific websites under ESPN's stewardship include ESPN FC, which is available in app form, as is the award-winning ESPN UK app.

With a mandate to serve sports fans wherever they are, whenever they want, ESPN's websites and apps carry the latest news, live scores, video, tables, fantasy games, and more. Featuring ESPN's global roster of talents from across the entire sporting spectrum, the brand has enjoyed significant growth in the past 12 months in the primary user engagement metrics and continued to do so. ESPN is a sports television channel in the United Kingdom and Ireland owned by the BT Group under license from American sports broadcaster ESPN Inc. The channel was operated by ESPN from 2009 to 2013 when it was sold to BT and became part of its BT Sports package that focused on international sporting events, predominantly American sports. Programming is available in standard definition and high definition formats.

ESPN FC is the football-dedicated division of ESPN, providing rolling coverage of the world's most popular sport. Formerly ESPN Soccernet, ESPN FC is a multimedia football website that currently has global, UK, US, and Spanish editions. The site offers news, live scores, fantasy football, blogs, stats, interactive polls and more; ESPN FC showcases the best in world football coverage. Through ESPN FC TV, the website hosts football-related video, utilizing the brand's roster of global football experts, journalists, and contributors, providing insight, analysis, and reaction to football around the globe.

The Goal

The World Cup is the most widely viewed and followed sporting event in the world. The 2014 event, held in Brazil, was eagerly anticipated, with major sponsorship from some of the largest organizations on the planet, including Adidas, Coca-Cola, and Visa. Teams – and fans – from all corners of the earth traveled to the country. The world's spotlight was on Brazil. ESPN FC wanted to capitalize on the excitement, enjoyment, and enthusiasm of people all over the planet to hear about the matches taking place in Brazil.

ESPN FC's main goal over the period of the World Cup was to increase awareness of ESPN FC and to drive football fans to www.espnfc.co.uk for the latest news, scores, and team information, helping build the profile of the brand across the globe.

The Challenge

ESPN FC likes to go the extra mile to serve sports fans, anytime and anywhere. With the World Cup being held outside the UK, many of the games were being played at inconvenient times for sports fans in the UK to watch them live on TV, as the matches were being played while people were still at work, traveling home, or very late in the evening. ESPN FC wanted to find a way to get the games to sports fans wherever they were during the World Cup.

The Solution

During the World Cup 2014, ESPN FC estimated that 100 million people would travel on the London Underground. Most Underground stations do not have Internet access, meaning fans were kept in the dark with no access to the scores during vital points in the tournament. With their mantra of "serving sports fans anytime and anywhere", ESPN FC had the ingenious idea of bringing the results of World Cup games to those traveling on the London Underground. Transport for London (TFL) is a local government body responsible for most aspects of the transport system in Greater London. ESPN FC partnered with TFL to display game results on announcement boards at 150 stations across London – a media first. No brand had ever displayed messages on TFL's boards before.

Influencing the Right Demographic

The ESPN FC and TFL World Cup campaign was aimed at the commuting masses. However, ESPN FC wanted to ensure that they were also reaching the specific demographic segments relevant to their brand. Using the Brandwatch (one of the world's leading social media listening and analytics technology platforms) demographic feature, ESPN FC could identify which mentions about the campaign were from sales, marketing, and PR professionals, a key audience they were attempting to target. Regarding all positive sentiment about the campaign, 18% came from sales, marketing, and PR professionals, and just 0.4% of negative sentiment came from that industry. Those tweets went on to help influence five other influential people in that sector, each with more than 1,000 followers. Using Brandwatch, ESPN FC could measure that those five tweets alone reached nearly 15,000 followers.

Underground Results

Searching for the online reception of a campaign when there is no Internet reception can be tricky. Using Brandwatch, ESPN FC tracked 3,438 online mentions of the campaign in the first seven days. However, most commuters have no access to Wi-Fi or Internet while on the London Underground, so many remained excited enough about the campaign when returning to street level to share it online. Of the mentions relating to the live coverage, more than 60% of them were positive, a figure much higher than for most marketing campaigns according to Charles Boss, Head of Marketing at ESPN FC UK. To truly understand the effectiveness of this campaign, ESPN FC used Brandwatch analytics to measure how many mentions other London

Underground-based projects received over a similar timeframe. Remarkably, the recent decision to introduce euro cashpoints in London Tube stations generated only 218 mentions in the first week, while commuters mentioning Virgin Media's new London Underground Wi-Fi was only slightly better with 473 mentions over seven days. When placed in this context, ESPN FC's World Cup updates were mentioned more than seven times more than these similar campaigns, proving they had the loudest fans and that the campaign was well-received.

The Right Line

Finding out *where* commuters are tweeting can be just as important as *what* they are tweeting. ESPN FC utilized Brandwatch's advanced Boolean queries to listen to conversations specifically from each Tube line during the campaign. The Central Line proved to generate the largest volume of conversation of ESPN FC's World Cup updates, with 40% of tweets coming from that line, whereas the Northern and Jubilee lines followed with 27% and 23% of the chat. These insights could prove to be invaluable to ESPN FC when planning future social media advertising campaigns on the London Underground. As Charles Boss put it, "Brandwatch was able to demonstrate that the campaign reached a potential 2,363,921 people on Twitter".

Commentating to Commuters

During the campaign, London commuters traveling during the World Cup Final could follow Germany's 1–0 win over Argentina thanks to ESPN FC's live commentary and analysis at Waterloo Station. The game was relayed over the public-address system at London's busiest train station by ex-Chelsea defender Scott Minto and Tottenham Hotspur Assistant Head Coach Steffen Freund. Using Brandwatch's sentiment analysis, ESPN FC could gauge public reaction to the commentary. Of the mentions relating to the live coverage, again more than 60% of them were positive. More significantly, ESPN FC did not receive a single negative mention for their World Cup Final commentary: impressive considering many of those commuting during football's signature game are not the biggest fans of the sport.

Connecting the Dots: The Social Analytics Vendor Assessment

We discussed some of the many tools that are used to understand data from the seven layers of social media analytics. However, deciding which platform best suits our needs is another matter entirely. While the narrative around social media is to consider social data as fuel, as a public commodity that is mined by platforms for us, it is not that simple. One issue that arises with social media analytics is that the tools we use shape the data we get. Each platform captures and stores data in its own way; even when the same information is requested from analogous platforms, the results will often differ. Choosing the right tools and frameworks to work within our organization is crucial to creating successful outcomes.

Filling Out the Social Analytics Vendor Assessment

We are presenting readers with a social analytics vendor assessment created by Demand Metric to help them choose the vendor that best fits an organization's need.[15] The authors call it a "soft-assessment", as results depend on how the assessment is conducted. The assessment does not provide the right answer; it simply helps the user or reader organize their questions so they can be answered and acted on if desired. Use the accompanying Microsoft Excel matrix to compare social analytics vendor solutions based on the requirements of an organization. For each requirement, rank vendors based on their ability to deliver on the organization's needs along the criteria detailed in what follows. At the time this manuscript went to press, we are trying to get permission from Demand Metric to include this assessment spreadsheet in the instructor's guide and supplemental material.

Vendor Evaluation Criteria

- Does not support
- Meets requirement
- Ideal solution

What the Assessment Does

- Logical apples-to-apples comparison between up to three vendors
- Documents requirements and necessity for each vendor
- Provides visual report for results in the resulting radar diagram
- Helps the reader cut through marketing hype and negotiate with various vendors
- Saves several hours on research and formatting and is reusable in several contexts
- Focuses vendor demo presentations

Conducting the Assessment

Use the vendor evaluation tab to do the following:

- For each parameter, rank each of the vendors based on the information that the organization or reader currently has. As every organization has different requirements, the questions can be modified to fit most decision-making criteria.
- In the "Vendor Evaluation" tab, rate each vendor based on your requirements (1– Does not support, 2– Meets requirement, 3– Ideal solution).
- View the "Scorecard" tab to see how the scores translate into a vendor's rating (percentage of total requirements that are ideal solutions).
- Use the data to evaluate which social analytics vendor is the best fit for an organization.

The authors are familiar with the social media analytics space and filled out the assessment to give readers an example of how to fill it out – but the example we used should not be taken literally and is just a way of answering the questions the assessment posed based on one's opinion. There is no perfect solution or ultimate right answer. The assessment presented in this chapter is a way to foster dialogue between stakeholders and users; out of the dialogue, the best answer often emerges.

Hypothetical Situation

Here is a situation that mirrors are a real occurrence that one of the co-authors had. A large computer hardware manufacturer needed to understand how their brand and products were perceived by their target audiences around the world. Which platform best fulfills the organization's various needs?

Stakeholder Requirements

- They need to know about conversations about their products, locations, languages.
- Which conversations are positive, neutral, or negative to their brand?
- Who are the brand's influencers and advocates? The platform chosen should be able to identify and track the influencers.
- Collect problems or issues around specific products or use cases (such as pricing resistance and what to charge for their products).
- Use social data to come up with new products (market research).
- Use social data for customer service.
- Wide coverage of social media platforms that the organizations use to communicate with clients or potential customers.
- The readout from the chosen platform should be as close as possible to real-time data, actionable to employees and analysts in several lines of business (LOBs) within corporate marketing.
- The brand would also like to know what is going on at retailers' locations where their products are being sold. As the brand sells most of its products through affiliate sales channels such as Target, K-Mart, Staples, Office Depot, and Amazon.com, they do not get as clear a picture as they would like in regard to what is going on at the point of sale.
- How is the brand doing in their online marketing compared to competitors in social media?
- The brand has a significant amount of textual and image data, both internal and on the Web, and they want to understand the patterns within the data by using text analytics.
- The brand uses coupons and social applications to sell their products across various channels; they would like to track the return on investment of these initiatives.
- The brand would like to understand the unique opportunities to market their products in specific locations in the main metropolitan centers throughout the world (at the neighborhood and block level).
- The brand owns several analytics platforms that are internally developed or bought, that are used internally to measure various use cases and desires the best integration so the data collected can be reused, if needed, in other applications.
- The brand wants the best platform and the lowest price.

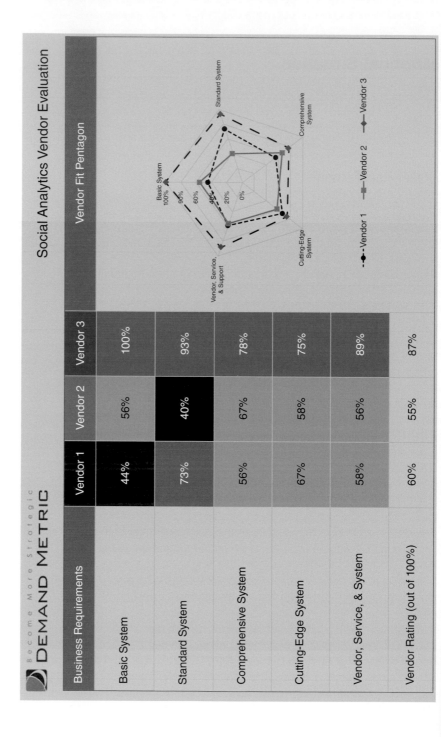

Figure 6.4 Sample Social Analytics Vendor Assessment Example

Note: The grading of this example is hypothetical and was done simply as a quick exercise by one of the authors.

Source: Demand Metric

The list of stakeholder requirements is not their entire list of needs! In fact, the organization may have additional requirements that have not been identified yet, and might not be unless a rigorous discovery process occurs before a choice is made, and continues as the platform is deployed. What is already evident is that no platform is going to be able to meet all the identified needs that the stakeholders have. While there are several platforms to choose from, and they each have their strengths and weaknesses, there are also several things that need to be tracked and understood (making it problematic to choose the best platform). Also, most vendors have invested in marketing that tends to obscure their platform's actual capabilities and utility as it pertains to particular organizations needs and data (See Figure 6.4), and we believe that this is common in the social media analytics space.[16]

Vendors Under Consideration

Note: We left the default questions in place for this example, but in many situations, customizing the assessment questions to match the stakeholders' exact requirements will provide better results.[17]

- Platform 1
- Platform 2
- Platform 3

First, stakeholders need to examine each platform by performing research on the Web and speaking to sales and technical support staff at each vendor. Assuming all of that has been done, then the assessment should be relatively easy to fill out.

Using our example, we ranked each vendor based on our understanding and experience of what the platform offers; each platform has its interface and methods for collecting, processing, and storing data.

Review Questions

1. Why is it important for business managers to understand and data-mine social media data?
2. What is social media analytics, and how it is different from traditional business analytics?
3. Briefly explain the seven layers of social media data. Support the answer with examples.
4. Explain the social media analytics cycle.
5. What ethical issues should be considered when mining social media data?
6. What are some main challenges to social media analytics?
7. Compare different social media analytics tools available in the market and explain their strengths and weakness.

Chapter 6 Citations

1. See (https://www.demandsage.com/social-media-users/). Accessed May 30, 2023.

2. Chen, H., R.H.L. Chiang, and V.C. Storey (2012) "Business Intelligence and Analytics: From Big Data to Big Impact." *MIS Quarterly 36(4)*: 1165–1188.

3. Bekmamedova, N. and G. Shanks (2014) *Social Media Analytics and Business Value: A Theoretical Framework and Case Study*. The 47th Annual Hawaii International Conference on System Sciences, IEEE Explore.

4. Khan, G. (2013) "Social Media-Based Systems: An Emerging. Area of Information. Systems Research and Practice." *Scientometrics 95(1)*: 159–190.

5. https://www.ibm.com/prescriptive-analytics Accessed: May 30, 2023.

6. Kramer, A.D.I., J.E. Guillory, and J.T. Hancock (2014) "Experimental Evidence of Massive-Scale Emotional Contagion through Social Networks." *Proceeding of the National Academy of Sciences 111(24)*: 8788–8790.

7. Editorial (2014) "Editorial Expression of Concern: Experimental Evidence of Massive-Scale Emotional Contagion through Social Networks." *Proceedings of the National Academy of Sciences 111(29)*: 10779.

8. For more details on this process, visit www.linkedin.com/p.ulse/making-datasclence-accessible-text-minlng-dan-kellett. Accessed April 15, 2017.

9. Qhulrran, S.W. "Five Pillars of Text Analytics." *Screencast.com*. www.screencast.com/t/J1P7R6thJUFR. Accessed April 20, 2017.

10. Wong, P.C. and J. Thomas (2004) "Visual Analytics." *IEEE Computer Graphics and Applications 24(5)*: 20–21.

11. Kielman, J. and J. Thomas (2009). "Special Issue: Foundations and Frontiers of Visual Analytics." *Information Visualization 8(4)*: 239–314.

12. RansPotham, S. "Once You Align the Analytical Starts, What's Next?" March 31, 2015. http://sloanreview.mit.edu/artlcle/once-pu-align-fte-analytical-stars-whats-next. Accessed April 15, 2017.

13. See www.Prandwatch.com/case-studies/espn-fc – the original case study is referenced and summarized here. Accessed April 15, 2017.

14. "5 Social Media Metrics You Can Stop Tracking Yesterday." https://blog.loginradius.com/2015/05/social-media-metrics-stop-tracking. Accessed April 15, 2017.

15. Refer to the Demand Metric website for overall information about the assessment methodology, and specifically to www.demandmetric.com/content/website-vendor-selection-tool. Note: To download this Excel Assessment one must be a member of the Demand Metric site (however, we may be able to provide university students with a copy of the assessment, based on Demand Metric academic use policy – currently under consideration). We adapted the methodology to focus on Social Media Analytics, which the authors, as members: of Demand Metric site, can do.

16. "Social Media Analytics: Effective Tools for Building, Interpreting, and Using Metrics." www.amazon.com/Social-Media-Analytics-EffectiveInterpreting/dp/0071824499. Accessed April 15, 2017.

17. Refer to www.lumapartners.com/lumascapes/marketing-technology-lumascape. Accessed April 15, 2017.

7

Actions, Hyperlink, and Mobile Analytics in Digital Marketing

---

CHAPTER OBJECTIVES

After reading this chapter, readers should understand the following:

- Action analytics
- How social media metrics fit in with other intermediate metrics produced by Web and search analytics
- Various free and paid social media analytics platforms that collect intermediate (Action) metrics
- Hyperlink analytics for digital marketing
- Mobile analytics for digital marketing

What Are Actions Analytics?

Actions analytics deals with extraction, analysis, and interpretation of the insights contained in the actions performed by social media users. In social media, platforms actions are a way to express symbolic reactions. For example, Facebook allows users to select emoticons that express certain specific emotions, such as love, related to a Facebook post. Symbolic actions are an easy and fast way to express feelings, unlike written reactions in the form of textual comments. Actions are not just typical responses; they carry emotions and behaviors that can be used in a variety of ways. More importantly, social media actions are social expressions that can be understood as a user's action (e.g., liking certain content) is visible to (or shared with) other social media users, with their friends. This shareable nature of social media actions makes them very attractive to social media marketers and businesses.

Take as an example Moviefone (an American-based movie listing and information service company), which enabled logins with Facebook and Twitter credentials. Enabling such login services not only allow users to use the Moviefone service conveniently but also lets them connect with their social media friends and share content over the Moviefone site. Enabling social logins led to a 300% increase in site traffic, a 40,000–250,000 increase in referrals per month, and a 40% growth in click-

DOI: 10.4324/9781003025351-7

Figure 7.1 Business Metrics Pyramid of ROI
Source: Authors

through rate.[1] Also, social logins enable analysts to build better customer profiles by matching precise social actions to specific individuals via their logins.

Social media actions are of great value to social media marketers because of their role in increasing revenue, brand value, and loyalty. Organizations can employ actions analytics to measure the popularity and influence of a product, service, or idea over social media. However, actions analytics are not effective proxies for return on investment (ROI), as depicted in Figure 7.1, and they are better suited to measuring the engagement that an audience has with the organization's product or service.

For example, as illustrated in Figure 7.1, a brand marketer can analyze the popularity of their new product among social media users by analyzing engagement data from social media. By analyzing the Facebook likes and Twitter mentions, they can discern specific answers to their marketing questions.

Common Social Media Actions

Below, we briefly discuss some of the most common social media actions; social media users performed all of them and they are used as social media metrics. Metrics, in simple words, are anything users or stakeholders want to measure. Social media users can be described as followers, fans, and subscribers.

Like Buttons

Like buttons are a feature of most social media sites (e.g., social networks, blogs, and websites) that allow users to express their feelings of liking certain products, services, people, ideas, information, places, or content. These actions are performed by social media users to express a typical positive reaction to the content. Also, the number of likes that a person, product, or feature gets gauges their popularity in social media. Facebook's like button enables users to voice their feelings easily and give your product or service a virtual thumbs-up. In addition to the like button, Facebook implemented reaction buttons so that users can express their feelings with the click of a button rather than commenting.

These reaction buttons serve as emotional faces, for lack of a better term, indicating how people express specific emotions, such as shock or humor, related to the specific post they appear on. Incorporating a "like" button in social media platforms and websites is becoming the norm. Social media platforms display accumulated likes received by content over time. Facebook's like button is the most famous one, but the like button can also be incorporated into a company website or blog. Recently, Facebook has introduced a range of other buttons, including love, sad, and angry, to allow people to express a variety of emotions; and Facebook users have sometimes wished there was a dislike button provided by the platform. Instead, they can react with an angry or sad type of emoji that Facebook offers. One could argue social media creates more negativity than positivity.[2] However, most social media platforms do not want their members to dislike user content, instead preferring to promote a positive image of the product/services offered by users and advertisers.

Share Buttons

Share buttons or sharing is a feature that allows social media users to distribute the content posted over social media to other users.

For example, the Facebook share button lets users add a personal message and customize whom they share the content with. The share button on WordPress (a blogging platform) allows users to share their blog content across a range of social media platforms. Companies incorporate share buttons into their website to boost their website traffic by channeling visitors from social media sites. Also, social media share buttons can be used to raise awareness for events or causes.

Dislike Buttons

Dislike buttons are included in some social media platforms (e.g., YouTube) and allow users to express their negative feelings of disliking certain content (e.g., products, services, people, ideas, information, or places) posted over social media. Similar to like buttons, they are visible to others and accumulated over time. The dislike button, when it is present, is not as prevalent as the like button. Perhaps social media companies do not want people to dislike the content posted on their platforms. Such a practice may go against the core philosophy of advertising, which is used to create a positive mental image of product/services offered by companies and convince them to buy it.

Visitors, Visits, Revisits (Web Analytics Data)

Visitors are a metric that is reported on by web analytics platforms. Visitors are measured based on first-party cookies that are captured through a script executed on the Web browser of the visitor; the raw data is sent to a collection server that processes the information into, a visitor and visits metrics of the site being measured, as covered in previous chapters. A visitor is a person who visits a website or blog. A single visitor may visit a page or content one or more times (revisits). Visits are also known as sessions. Other related concepts related to a visitor's visit to a website are:

- **Unique User:** A person who arrives at the website page for the first time.
- **Average Bounce Rate:** The percentage of visitors who visit a website and leave the site quickly without viewing other pages.
- **Session Duration:** The average length of a visitor's visit or session.

View

Views are the number of times users view social media content (a post, video, graphic, etc.). For example, YouTube measures video views based on a unique cookie/IP address combination. Once a visitor views a video during a visit, viewing the video again does not count as a second view. A slightly different but related concept is the pageview, which is a count of each time a visitor views a page on a company website or blog. Instagram allows members to see how many views they receive on a video or image. Although members cannot see the names of all the people who viewed their Instagram content, they can still see the names of everyone who liked it.

Clicks

Clicks are the actions performed by users by pressing or clicking on the hyperlinked content of a website, image, click-ad, or blog. Through clicks, users navigate the web. Click data can be collected for business intelligence purposes and serve as key performance indicators (KPIs). One of the main reasons to measure clicks is to improve specific website metrics, such as bounce rate, time spent on a site, and the conversion rate, to name a few of the more common metrics that are measured in this manner. Business managers use a technique called clickstream analysis for a variety of business intelligence purposes, including website activity, website design analysis, path optimization, market research, and finding ways to improve visitor experience on the site. The clickstream is the semi-structured data trail/log (such as date and time stamp, IP address, and the URLs of the pages visited) a user leaves while visiting a website. The clickstream includes every click, download, link in/out, search, keyword, time spent, and much more that is recorded using programs such as Google Analytics 4 or Adobe Analytics.

Tagging

Tagging is the act of assigning or linking extra pieces of information to social media content (such as photographs and bookmarks, among others) for identification, classification, and search purposes. Tagging has assumed additional uses, such as tagging individuals (usually friends or connections) within a photo, tweet, or post by adding the metadata of their social media account name (which does not always correspond to their real name). Tagging can be used to raise users' popularity by letting users classify social media content as they see fit. Tagging may take a variety of forms. For example, bloggers can attach descriptive keywords (tags) to their posts to facilitate classification and searching of content, and Facebook users can add tags to anything they post on their status, including photos and comments. Social bookmarking services (such as Pinboard) let users organize their bookmarks by adding descriptive tags. This practice of collaborative tagging is commonly known as *folksonomy* – a term coined by Thomas Vander Wal.[3] These days, almost all prominent companies (e.g., Facebook and Flickr) provide tagging services to their users. Because the contents are tagged with useful keywords, social tagging speeds up searching and finding relevant content. Tagging is also used to share interpersonal relationships and showing a user's followers who they are via tagging pictures. In fact, Instagram users can tag an Instagram company site, friend, follower, or Instagram public page; doing so makes it easier to generate attention and user interaction on the platform.

Mentions

Social mentions are the occurrences of a person, place, or thing over social media by name. For example, a brand name may be referred to in a Facebook comment, blog post, YouTube video, or tweet. Mentions are significant and can indicate the popularity of person, place, or thing. For example, a social marketer may be able to gauge the popularity of a product/service/campaign by mining Twitter mentions data. A Twitter mention is the inclusion of an "@username" in a tweet.

Hovering

Hovering is the act of moving a cursor over social media content. Capturing users' cursor movement data can help understand user behavior on a social media site. Cursor movement/hovering over an ad, for example, can be considered as a proxy for attention. Most people who view an ad do not click on it, thus if we are relying on clicks analytics only, we may lose a vital piece of information (i.e., attention). Traditionally, hovering data has been used in website design and for improvement of user experience. However hovering activity may be useful to marketers for consumer intelligence, but it also presents serious issues regarding a user's privacy.

Two Examples of Issues Surrounding Hovering and Privacy
- Collecting the hovering data of users can infringe on their online privacy even when a user "knows" their online behavior is being tracked. For example, the online learning programs run by many universities are using software to verify the identity of students who are taking an online test or quiz.[4] The verification tracks a student's cursor movement, typing pattern, and gaze to build a profile of the student (via a computer cam) for test-taking purposes, but it is done for regulatory reasons, aid to strengthen the reputation and competitiveness of the university program. However, the adoption of such programs has turned out to be very repugnant to many people because of the privacy issue. However; as time goes on people have become more accepting of the monitoring activity, even though they may still hold their own reservations about it.

- Third-party data providers such as comScore and Nielsen employ millions of panelists that traverse the Web during their work or leisure, with their precise clickstream tracked with intricate detail. However, concerns about privacy violations led thousands of individuals to sue comScore claiming they were secretly surveilled through its proprietary tracking software. The lawsuit claimed comScore sold panelists' private information to other parties without their knowledge or consent.[5]

Check-Ins

Check-ins have been covered in previous chapters; they are a social media feature that allows users to announce and share their arrivals in certain locations, such as a hotel, airport, city, or store. Check-ins are also an action analytics metric used to gauge a user's engagement with a location or activity. Many social media services, including Facebook, provide check-in features. The location of the user is determined using GPS (global positioning system) technology. Check-in data can, for example, be mined to offer location-based services/products. However, there are privacy issues with sharing location data. For example, when a user of a geo-location app such as Foursquare is checking into a location on the other side of the country, it tells friends and followers that the person is on vacation, which could be dangerous – especially if the information gets into the wrong hands.

In other instances, location tracking may be even more invasive, such as police surveillance of public activities around protests, employee movement, and activities both on the job and off the job. While location tracking is usually not illegal, many consider it unethical with many legal challenges that are yet to be resolved. These days, most of the check-in activity is now passive; mobile devices automatically register their location via GPS coordinates (often translating to a designated location, such as specific restaurant or museum). This information is collected by various apps and Internet service providers that are connected to the mobile device by wireless, cellular, or Bluetooth networks.

Thus, certain applications can reconstruct a clickstream of a mobile users' movements over a given period, even when they do not check-in to any locations with their mobile devices, and most people are unaware this happening. Google, Facebook, TripAdvisor, Foursquare, and Yelp, to name a few, are collecting information on passive check-ins and our clickstream movements over time. The passive check-in data is used to predict where users are most likely to go next, or where they are likely to have been in the recent past. Passive check-ins have also been used to measure the boundaries of a location, similar to the concept of the "aura" of a landmark such as a restaurant or a museum, etc.

Pinning

Pinning is an action performed by social media users to pin and share interesting content (such as ideas, products, services, and information) using a virtual pinboard platform. Some popular pinning platforms include Pinterest and Tumblr. Businesses can use these virtual pinboards to share information while connecting with and inspiring their customers. Four Seasons Hotels and Resorts, for example, use Pinterest to curate travel, food, and luxury lifestyle content to inspire customers.

Embeds

Embedding is the act of incorporating social media content (e.g., a link, video, or presentation) into a website or blog. An embed feature lets users embed interesting content into their personal social media outlets.

Endorsements

The endorsement is a feature of social media that lets people share their approval of other people, products, and services. For example:

- LinkedIn lets users endorse the skills and qualifications of other people in their network.
- Celebrities, like Kim and Khloe Kardashian, command large sums of money to endorse specific products or services. Also, platforms such as Yelp provide endorsements via a like or a positive review on a product or service.
- Twitter retweets are a form of endorsement; when a Twitter user retweets content that appears in their news stream, it can be considered a tacit form of approval of the tweet.

Uploading and Downloading

Uploading is the act of adding new content (e.g., texts, photos, and videos) to a social media platform. The opposite of uploading is downloading; that is, the act of receiving data from a social media platform. Almost all social media content is created and uploaded by users, which is better known as user-generated content. For some companies, uploading and downloading are the most significant actions to measure. For Instagram and Flickr, which are both photo sharing platforms, the number of photos uploaded daily matters more than anything else.

Actions Analytics Tools

Currently, no single platform can capture all the actions discussed in this chapter. Certain platforms can be employed to measure social media actions across platforms. Here is a list of popular actions analytics tools.

- **Hootsuite**: Hootsuite is an easy to use online platform that enables users to manage their social media presence across the most popular social networks. Hootsuite offers different plans depending on business needs and budget: free, pro, or enterprise. In the tutorial later in this chapter, we will employ the free version, which supports up to five social media profiles and has limited analytics information.
- **Rdrr.io:** Rdrr is a social media analytics tool that takes one or multiple URLs and returns the information about the popularity and reach of the URL(S) on social media. The reports include the number of shares, likes, tweets, pins, and hits on Facebook, Twitter, Pinterest, StumbleUpon, LinkedIn, and Reddlt.[6]

- **Khoros:** Khoros (https://khoros.com/platform/social-media-management) is social media management tool that provides a variety of products and services, including social media analytics, marking, crowdsourcing, and social media marketing.
- **Google Analytics 4:** Google Analytics 4 (www.google.com/analytics) is an analytical tool offered by Google to track and analyze website traffic. It can also be used for blogs and wiki analytics.
- **Facebook Page Insights:** (https://www.facebook.com/help/794890670645072#) it helps Facebook page owners understand and analyze trends within user growth and demographics.
- **Kred:** Kred (www.home.kred) helps measure the influence of a Twitter account.
- **Hashtagify.me:** This tool measures the influence of hashtags: http://hashtagify.me.
- **DiscoverCloud:** (https://www.discovercloud.com/products/twtrland) it is a social intelligence research tool for analyzing and visualizing our social footprints and is a form of competitive analysis.

Case Study: Cover-More Group[7]

Visualizing Social Media ROI

The heart of travel insurance provider Cover-More's social efforts is its social media command center, a unique way to provide customer feedback and performance metrics in an easy-to-understand visual display. Here's how the social media team took control of the cumbersome task of presenting analytics and came out looking like stars.

Cover-More Group

Cover-More Group is an Australian-owned global travel insurance and assistance group with offices in Australia, the United Kingdom, China, India, New Zealand, and Malaysia. Each year, Cover-More provides insurance policies for more than 1.6 million travelers, manages more than 70,000 insurance claims, and helps more than 42,000 customers with emergency assistance.

Goals

Cover-More had three main objectives in building a social media command center:

- To prove the ROI on social media efforts to stakeholders
- To provide a snapshot of Cover-More's social media presence to the board of directors
- To give a real-time feel to reporting and automate the process

At the board level, Cover-More needed to be able to show a snapshot of how the company's social strategy was progressing, particularly in comparison with competitors. They were also keen to show executives how social media could benefit the business and not just be a risk. However, the social media and e-commerce teams wanted to know how their activities were tracking on a day-to-day basis. Reconciling the reporting needs of executives and practitioners was proving difficult.

Once a month, Lynton Manuel, Cover-More's Social Media Manager, would populate a spreadsheet with data from each of the company's social network profiles, to put the various channels and results in context with one another. The process was inefficient and labor-intensive: dedicating half a day each month to compile a pseudo dashboard became the norm. Manuel presented an overview of status, successes, and challenges to the board of directors monthly, but the board was most interested in a visual snapshot. Realizing that executives – or anyone within the business that doesn't have knowledge of different platforms – needed a more simplified, visually attractive way to interact with the data, the social media team decided that Hootsuite's Social Media Command Center could be the solution.

Outcomes

The Cover-More social media team needed to bring social media intelligence into the company's nerve center via a large display to inform and impress viewers. So, with the help of the IT department, they set up a 60-inch television in a prominent location where employees, executives, and potential clients could see it. The team decided on what they wanted to display and set up the command center using some adjustable Hootsuite widgets via a simple drag-and-drop process. From there, it was just a matter of adjusting the Hootsuite Analytics, Streams, and Monitoring features to customize the display. The team picked specific widgets like Mentions, Sentiment, Exposure, and Sharing, making it quick and easy to choose what information meant the most to them, to the executives, and to prospective and current clients.

By integrating the Social Media Command Center, the social media team could

- **Show the positive impact of the social media team's efforts to executives**. After the Command Center went live, a senior executive saw the most recent tweets and remarked, "I did not know we had people saying thanks on Twitter. This looks fantastic".
- **Increase employee engagement and morale**. Employees could quickly understand the real-time data, which demonstrated the company's leadership in the social media sphere.
- **Customize the Command Center screen for maximum brand visibility**. The company's graphic designer created a custom background image and style incorporated elements to make sure the command center was visually appealing and on-brand.

The Results

The Social Media Command Center was a success, attracted new customers, and helped Cover-More's team to monitor its social media much more efficiently than before.

Tutorial: Analyzing Social Media Actions with Hootsuite

The tutorial assumes that the reader already has their social media profiles configured (such as a Twitter account and Facebook fan page). Below are the step-by-step guidelines to configure and use Hootsuite.

- **Step 1:** To start using the free version, go to http://signup.hootsuite.com/plans-cc/ and click on the "Get Started Now" button available under the free version.
- **Step 2:** Next, provide an email address and name, choose a strong password, and then click on the "Create Account" button.
- **Step 3:** Click on the "Twitter" button available under the "Connect Your Social Network" section. Note that users can choose several social media accounts to manage using Hootsuite. For now, we will only configure Twitter and Facebook.
- **Step 4:** A pop-up window will open asking users to authorize Hootsuite to access the Twitter account. A Twitter username (or email) and password need to be entered, then click on the "Authorize App" button.
- **Step 5:** After authorization, the Twitter account will appear in the added accounts. Next, click the "Continue" button. Note that each user can monitor multiple Twitter accounts using Hootsuite.
- **Step 6:** Click on the "Get Started" button to complete the three simple steps (i.e., adding streams, creating a tab, and scheduling a message) suggested by Hootsuite.

Adding Streams
- **Step 7:** To monitor conversations and actions over Twitter, add additional streams. To do so, click on all the streams to be added for monitoring (e.g., tweets, mentions, and retweets).
- **Step 8:** Streams will start appearing on the Hootsuite dashboard for the user, creating a Tab.
- **Step 9:** Tabs are used to group stream-based interests or similarities. To add a tab, click on the "+" icon.
- **Step 10:** Name the new tab (e.g., "Followers") and click "Next".

Scheduling a Message
- **Step 11:** With Hootsuite, one can post messages to several social media platforms (e.g., Twitter and Facebook) either instantly or for later. To write a message, click to select the social profile(s) that will post your message (in this case Twitter). Click "Compose Message", and then type message. After writing the message, either click the "Send Now" button or the "Calendar" icon to schedule it for later. This step will complete the initial configuration of Hootsuite.

Hootsuite Analytics

Hootsuite provides two ways to generate analytics reports:

1. Using premade templates
2. Creating custom-made analytics reports

Note that the free version has limited analytics abilities and the user will be able to use only a small number of templates.

To use Hootsuite's premade templates, go through the following steps:

- **Step 1:** Click the bar graph icon on the left-aligned launch menu.
- **Step 2:** Choose from several report templates. For example, click on the "Twitter Profile Overview" template.
- **Step 3:** Click on the "Create Report" button. Note that there can be multiple social media accounts configured and then chosen them from the drop-down list. Next, the report will be generated.
- **Step 4:** A report can be printed, saved as a PDF or CSV, and shared with others by using the toolbar available at the top-right corner of the report.

Creating Custom Reports

- **Step I:** Click the bar graph icon on the left-aligned launch menu.
- **Step 2:** Click "Build Custom Report".
- **Step 3:** Click "Custom Report".
- **Step 4:** Click "Upload Image" to upload a logo or an image to brand the report. Selecting and applying a logo is done by locating the image file on the computer, or the Web and clicking "Open". One can also edit the details of the organization and type of header for the report.
- **Step 5:** Under "Details" in the top-left corner, enter the title of your report and a brief description. Moreover, under "Email and Scheduling", click the drop-down menu and select the frequency of distribution.

Tip: Users can also have this report emailed to the members sharing this report by clicking on the box, making a check.

- **Step 6:** Next, click on "Add Report Modules" and then click to select the module, adding it to your report. Modules with ENT and PRO are only available to enterprise users.

Note: Modules added to reports can be removed by clicking "Remove" in the top-right corner of the module on the report.

- **Step 7:** Complete the information requested by that module to achieve the best results.
- **Step 8:** Click on the "Create Report" button available at the top-right of the page. Alternatively, users can click "Save as Draft".

Monitoring and Analyzing Facebook Data with Hootsuite

- **Step 1:** First, add a new tab for the Facebook network. To do so, click the home (Streams) icon on the left-aligned launch menu, and then click on the "+" icon.
- **Step 2:** Name the new tab (e.g., Facebook).
- **Step 3:** Click on the "Add Social Network" button.
- **Step 4:** Select Facebook from the list, and click on the "Connect with Facebook" button.

- **Step 5:** Type the Facebook email (or mobile phone number) and password, and then click "Log In".
- **Step 6:** Next, read Hootsuite's access to the Facebook account message; click to read "App Terms and: Privacy Policy" on the bottom left corner, and then click "OK".
- **Step 7:** Read posting permission note, click to select who can see the content being; posted to Facebook from Hootsuite, and then click "OK".

Note: Clicking "Skip" will prevent you from being able to post to Facebook from Hootsuite.

- **Step 8:** Read the page permission note, and then click "OK".

Note: Clicking "Skip" will prevent you from being able to manage your Facebook pages from Hootsuite.

- **Step 9:** Click to select the timeline, pages, and groups to import. A check mark indicates that the content will be imported; a plus icon indicates the content will not be imported. When done, click "Finished Importing".

Adding a Facebook Stream

Now that Facebook is added to Hootsuite, it is time to add streams to measure.

- **Step 1:** Click the home (Streams) icon on the left-aligned launch menu, then click the tab hosting your Facebook content.
- **Step 2:** Next, click "Add Stream".
- **Step 3:** Select Facebook and then select a profile that will stream content.
- **Step 4:** Click the "+" button across from the social media stream to add. This process can be repeated for multiple Facebook streams.

Similar steps can be repeated for configuring Twitter, WordPress, and LinkedIn streams for analytical purposes.

Hyperlinking

Hyperlinks embedded elements in digital content of social media and other online pages that allow users to navigate from one web page or document to another by simply clicking or tapping on the linked text, image, or other interactive element. Hyperlinks act as bridges for linking resources on the Internet by enabling navigation between web pages, websites, and online resources.

Here are some examples:

- Hyperlinks (usually shortened URLs) within a tweet that links to other resources (e.g., websites) available over the Internet
- Hyperlinks within a site that link to internal resources, such as the homepage, contact us page, about us page, etc.
- Graphics that have embedded hyperlinks
- QR codes that contain a link to a website page

Hyperlinks are not merely links between two websites, but serve a more symbolic means.[8] As a website is an official and unique entity representing an organization itself,[9] embedding hyperlinks in an organization's website can be considered an official act of communication between two organizations. Hyperlinks to websites represent not only a reasonable approximation of a social relationship[10] but also serve as a validation or endorsement of the linked organization.[11] Also, incoming links serve to increase the page authority, which helps SEO page rankings.

In conjunction with this, hyperlinks that exist between two organizational websites reflect a sense of validation, trust, bonding, authority, and legitimacy.[12] Websites mostly connect or link to other websites of a similar nature, so hyperlinks can also serve as indicators of content similarity.[11]

Hyperlink Analysis

Hyperlink analysis is still widely used and a valuable tool in various contexts, and that is why we have kept it as part of the second edition. Hyperlink analysis involves examining the links between web pages to understand their relationships and derive meaningful insights. Here are a few areas where hyperlink analysis is applied:

- Search Engine Optimization (SEO): Hyperlink analysis helps search engines determine the relevance and authority of web pages. By analyzing the links pointing to a page, search engines can assess its importance and rank it accordingly in search results.
- Web Crawling and Indexing: Search engines utilize hyperlink analysis to discover and index web pages. Crawlers follow links to navigate the web, identifying new pages and updating existing ones. Hyperlink analysis assists in building comprehensive indexes of web content.
- Social Network Analysis: Hyperlink analysis is employed to study the structure and dynamics of social networks. Researchers can understand a network's influence, relationships, and information flow by examining links between individuals or entities.
- Spam Detection: Hyperlink analysis can be used to identify spam or malicious websites. Patterns of excessive or manipulative linking behavior can signal low-quality or deceptive content, aiding in spam detection and web security.
- Recommender Systems: Hyperlink analysis is sometimes employed in recommender systems to suggest related or relevant content. By analyzing the linking patterns of users or documents, someone can make recommendations can be made based on the interconnectedness of web resources.

While newer methods and algorithms have emerged to complement hyperlink analysis, it is still a relevant and valuable technique. Its applications extend beyond the web and into network analysis, information retrieval, and knowledge discovery.

Types of Hyperlinks

From a hyperlink analytics point of view, there are three types of hyperlinks, as shown in Figure 7.2:

- In-links (incoming links)
- Out-links (outgoing links)
- Co-links and co-citations

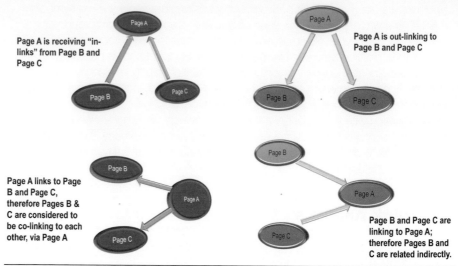

Figure 7.2 Different Types of Hyperlinks
Source: Gohar F. Khan

In-Links

Incoming hyperlinks are links directed towards a website originating from other websites.[13] For example, consider the top-left of Figure 7.2: page A is receiving two in-links from pages B and C. Internet marketers want to get more in-links to their websites because they correlate with higher Web traffic and popularity of the websites. In-links also play a major role in website analytics, as both the quality and number of in-links can impact the search engine ranking of the site.

In-links impact the popularity of social media content. In-links are a measure of site popularity, and the Google PageRank algorithm has been the main mechanism employed to measure this. A study on YouTube viral videos, for instance, found that among other things, in-links play crucial roles in the viral phenomenon, particularly in increasing views of videos posted on YouTube.[14] Studies have also shown that in-link counts strongly correlate with measures describing business performance.[15]

Out-Links

Out-links are hyperlinks generated out of a website.[16] As shown in the top-right image in Figure 7.2, page A is sending two out-links: one to page B and one to page C. Website out-links are tracked in the same way as in-links. A website's out-links become the in-links of the websites they point to. Out-links attract relevant and valuable eyeballs.[17]

In the past, out-links (outbound links) were not considered an important factor in SEO ranking, but that position has changed; the consensus is that out-links may count for search engine ranking almost as much as in-links. For example, when a website or page out-links to an authoritative site, it has a positive impact on rankings.[18]

Out-links can damage a site's reputation, drop their search engine rankings, and create exit portals, where customers will drop off.[19] However, when out-links are used strategically, organizations may benefit from the outbound links in many ways. Regardless of the quality of a website, it is impractical to include all the valuable information people seek on the site. Providing out-links to valuable content that aligns with a site's business objectives is an excellent way to improve a visitor's experience on the site.

Co-Links and Co-Citations

Co-links are the relationship created by two or more websites or webpages that link to the same website or webpage. Co-links are similar in concept to the idea of "co-citation". Essentially, co-links and co-citations are used by search engines to relate and rank pages on various topics, based on the words they contain (and the words they do not contain but are related to or based on other common webpages the pages link to).

Co-links and co-citations are difficult for humans to keep track of, but search engine algorithms do a good job of topic relationships and rank search result pages based on this information. In fact, co-links have been used to compare and map competitive similarity among organizations.[19]

Examples of co-linking and co-citations:

- When *The New York Times* and *The Wall Street Journal* both link to the Wikipedia Twitter account page in various articles being published, the Wikipedia Twitter page becomes a co-link to both websites.
- ConsumerReports.com gets a first page ranking on Google with the search engine query "cell phone ratings", although it does not contain the term "cell phone" or the word "ratings", except in some of the text on the website. Cell phone ratings are not even in the page title, yet they rank well on a competitive query.

Search engines have evolved, via co-linking and co-citations, to rank websites for highly competitive keywords regardless of the presence of website copy containing these keywords anywhere in the title tags, metadata, or the content of the page. Because of the evolution in the application of search engine algorithms, optimizing Web copy for optimal search ranking has become much more complicated to achieve than it once was.

The Importance of User Design (UX) in Search Engine Rankings

Search engines have become more focused on the "searcher experience", resulting in the improved design and execution of webpages. Moreover, web-based apps are simply mobile-friendly HTML5 code that is executed by a Web server. Thus, they are not distributed in an app store, and it is hard to monetize them, but they are among the main UX drivers of an improved searcher experience.

The end goal of UX improvements is to attract visitors to specific websites and convert them into customers. That is not going to happen when website visitors experience technical and aesthetic issues arising on the websites they are visiting.

With the broad adoption of web analytics platforms, particularly Google Analytics 4, search engines determine a visitor's aesthetic satisfaction with the websites they visited using a variety of signals (being fed to highly tuned algorithms) provided by the analytics. Search engines determine a user's satisfaction with a website or page visitor by determining the searcher's intent. A search engine may combine a user's search query with specific web analytics metrics such as page load speed, the time spent during a visit to the website, or the bounce rate (to name a few of the more popular "Intermediate Metrics") to determine the search ranking for the user's query.[20]

Search Engines Algorithms Reward Great Website User Design (UX) With Higher Search Engine Rankings

Great websites link to other great websites, and search engines know this. Search engines developed algorithms that reward searcher/user behavior. There are hundreds of ranking factors that search engines use to determine the quality of website/page for a searcher's query or search terms, such as keywords, links, and content (to name a few). Most of these factors are based on the way people process text and images, attention span, and clickstream behavior.[21]

Ranking factor examples:

- By placing keywords near the beginning of the title tag of a page, content creators are practicing good SEO, better known as "white hat SEO". White hat SEO refers to the optimization strategies focusing on a human audience, as opposed to search engines, and that completely follow stated search engine rules and policies. Conversely, "black hat SEO" refers to the use of aggressive SEO strategies that focus only on search engines and not on a human audience, and usually do not obey search engine guidelines.
- Search engines are believed to reward websites owners who employ white hat SEO strategies and practices, as people tend to read content at the beginning of a sentence and the end, but not so much all the words in the middle of sentences; the algorithms that rank page quality are based on average user behaviors. Websites using black hat SEO technologies, such as website cloaking and keyword stuffing, tend to have their search engine ranking drop drastically over a period of a few months. However, certain languages such as Hebrew are read from left to right while others are symbol-based (such as Chinese, Korean, Japanese, and Arabic), requiring modifications to search engine algorithms for various countries, languages, dialects, and localities.
- Search engines examine the keywords within the first 250 words of a document as part of a ranking algorithm. The selected keywords have more weight for search engine ranking when used with a white hat SEO strategy than if the content is placed in the middle of a document page (again, based on user behavior). The authors believe the search engine algorithms involved in ranking content are trying to emulate the way people read and process content regarding titles and the first paragraph of a news article. Search algorithms are emulating and automating what people do naturally, which is why the keywords located in the first part of the document are weighted more highly. Eye-tracking studies have confirmed the optimal placements for text and images within a webpage; algorithms have been created to determine and score how page content based on these placements.

- Images are favored by search engines when they have ALT text that details the subject of the image. Search engines favor Images that have snippet text next to the image that explains the image subject to the reader. Until recently, search engines did not know how to read images and needed the snippet text to determine page content quality. Again, search algorithms are simply approximate the way humans process images but not being sentient, often depend on a written snippet of text to understand the subject and meaning of the image, making it a search ranking factor.
- Many websites run a form of web analytics called Google Analytics; Google Analytics provides raw data to Google on user and searcher behavior; the data informs search algorithms on page quality and user engagement. Similarly, more website referral traffic, as measured by web analytics platforms, originates from mobile devices than desktop computers. Thus, search algorithms rank mobile-friendly websites higher in search results than websites that are not search friendly. Even page load speed is now a ranking factor. The reason for this is obvious and rooted in good UI, or user interface, design; a slow loading web page frustrates searchers and users – people have a shortage of time and patience, it is best not to aggravate potential or actual customers/users.[22]
- Link anchor text (the actual "link text") is more highly rated by search engine algorithms when it matches the content of the webpages it points to. The use and evaluation of link anchor text are based on the searcher's intent to find relevant information.

The examples provided earlier confirm that search engines have built their search algorithms around searcher behavior and experience. After all, search engines exist to assist searchers in finding the best content based on their search.[23]

Hyperlink Analytics

Hyperlink analytics deal with extracting, analyzing, and interpreting hyperlinks (e.g., in-links, out-links, and co-links). Hyperlink analytics reveal the Internet traffic patterns and sources of the incoming or outgoing traffic to and from a website.

Hyperlink Analysis Has Been Used to Study a Variety of Topics

The case study included in this chapter demonstrates the importance of hyperlinks in viral phenomena and shows the valuable insights they carry for viral marketers in formulating viral marketing strategies. By studying hyperlinks, researchers have been able to observe linking patterns and gain new insights in several areas.

Link analysis examples:

- University rankings, blogosphere interconnections, scholarly websites[18]
- Political networks[24]
- Business competitiveness[25]
- Influencer networks[20]

Hyperlink Analysis Limitations

- Fails to provide any real insight into the type or amount of web traffic flowing among sites[20]
- Does not measure the effectiveness of navigation within a website
- Ignores or gives low importance to internal linking within a website[26]

Types of Hyperlink Analytics

Hyperlink analytics can take several forms, including the following:

1. Hyperlink website analysis
2. Link impact analysis
3. Social media hyperlink analysis

1. Hyperlink Website Analysis

Hyperlink website analysis examines the in-links and out-links of a site or set of websites. Hyperlinks (i.e., out-links, in-links, and co-links) of a website are extracted and analyzed to identify the sources of Internet traffic.[27]

Hyperlinked website networks take two forms:

- Co-links networks
- In-links and out-links networks

Co-Links Networks

In co-links environment networks, nodes are websites and links that represent a similarity between websites, as measured by co-link counts. With the Webometric Analyst tool, one can construct a co-link network diagram among a set of websites.[28]

In-Links and Out-Links Networks

In-links and out-links hyperlink networks are built based on in-links and out-links from a website or set of websites. In such a network, websites are represented as circular nodes, and the inbound and outbound links show how websites are connected/interconnected. The VOSON tutorial provided in this chapter demonstrates constructs such as a network using the VOSON hyperlink analysis tool.

2. Link Impact Analysis

Link impact analysis investigates the popularity of a website address (or URL) regarding citations or mentions it receives over the Internet. In a link impact analysis, statistics about webpages that mention the URL of a given website are collected and analyzed.[29] URLs that are frequently cited on the Web are more popular and topical. Thus, measuring the popularity of URLs is a measure of the importance of a website, page, hashtag, or social media account.

3. Social Media Hyperlink Analysis

Social media hyperlink analysis deals with the extraction and analysis of hyperlinks embedded within social media texts (e.g., tweets and comments). These hyperlinks can be extracted and studied to identify the sources and destination of social media traffic. However, within social media, both the sources and destinations of social media traffic are visible to most members of a social network that desire to see them (especially on Twitter; most of its data is open to everyone). For example, a Twitter hashtag could be considered a destination of social media traffic.

A good example of the usefulness of the hyperlink embedded in the social media text is the 2014 study by Khan et al.,[29] in which they extracted out-links from Korean and US government agencies' tweets. By extracting out-links and tracing them back to their sender, the authors could construct a map of the out-link structure. According to a comparison of out-links between tweets of the South Korean and US governments, there were some differences in citation (i.e., out-link) patterns. The Korean government tended to cite domestic portals' news services and their blogs (i.e., self-citation).

Although there were social networking services and newspaper sites, most of the related out-links were for portals. On the other hand, the US government showed a more diverse pattern regarding out-link destinations. US out-links were not concentrated in specific sites and tended to go directly to news agencies, not to secondary sources such as portals. These comparisons between the US and Korean governments suggest that social media out-links can carry valuable information and can help explain real-world phenomena and shed light on the disparities in social media use among different cultures.[30]

Hyperlink Analytics Tools

The following are some popular hyperlink analytics tools:

- **Webometric Analyst** (http://lexiurl.wlv.ac.uk) is a Web impact analysis tool and can conduct variety of analysis on social media platforms, including hyperlink network analysis and web mentions.
- **VOSON** (www.uberlink.com) is a hyperlink analytics tools for constructing and analyzing hyperlink networks. This chapter includes a tutorial on using VOSON for Hyperlink Analysis.
- **Open Site Explorer** (https://moz.com/researchtools/ose) is a link analysis tool to research and compare competitor backlinks, identify top pages, view social activity data, and analyze anchor text.
- **Link Diagnosis** (www.linkdiagnosis.com) is a free online tool for analyzing and diagnosing links.
- **Advanced Link Manager** (www.advancedlinkmanager.com). provides a variety of link analysis capabilities, including the ability to track link-building progress over time, quality domain analysis, backlinks evolution, and website-crawling abilities.
- **Majestic** (https://majestic.com) provides a variety of link analysis tools, including link explorer, backlinks history, and link mapping tools.
- **Backlink Watch** (http://backlinkwatch.com) is a free fool for checking the quality and quantity of in-links pointing to a website.

Case Study: Hyperlinks and Viral YouTube Videos

Background

Do hyperlinks play a role in the popularity of a video posted on YouTube? YouTube popularity was one of the questions that a research team at Social Listening (a social media consulting company: https://www.sociallistening.co.nz/) set out to explore. The research team knew that the answer lay in extracting and visualizing hyperlinks (particularly in links pointing to a video) network and was looking for ways to get hands on YouTube videos data.

What They Did

At the first stage of the quest, the research team identified the 100 most viewed YouTube videos. Every video posted on YouTube was automatically assigned a unique ID embedded within the URL of the video.[31]

At the second stage, to explore the effects of hyperlinks on the viral phenomenon, the team used the Webometrics Analyst platform (http://lexiurl.wlv.ac.uk) – a well-established tool for measuring different aspects of the Web, such as Web impact analysis, hyperlinks analysis, and the Web search engine results.[32] Using the IDs text file as an input, through Webometrics Analyst, the search team determined the number of external links and Internet domains pointing to a video. This data was used to construct a two-mode network diagram for better understanding using UCINET social networking tool.[33]

Results

Most of the videos received URLs from a common set of domains. However, some videos received more links from URLs than others, while other domains sent more links, etc. By studying network maps related to successful viral content, such as a popular video by a celebrity, we can begin to understand the factors and relations that promote the sharing of viral video content.

Conclusion

This analysis shows that apart from the popularity of YouTube network, the most popular videos had a strong in-links network (links received by videos and users) originating from diverse domains over the Internet. This case study demonstrated the importance of hyperlinks and the valuable insights they carry. The study found that in-links may be a factor impacting the viral potential of a video. For example, linking the videos/contents posted on YouTube in several external platforms (e.g., blogs, social network sites, and online discussion communities) may increase the chance of the video going viral.[34]

Other Platforms for Hyperlink Analysis

There are several widely used and popular tools available for network analysis that offer user-friendly interfaces and comprehensive functionalities. Here are a few examples:

- **Gephi:** Gephi is a powerful open source software for visualizing and exploring networks. It provides a user-friendly interface and a range of network analysis algorithms, allowing users to analyze and visualize network data effectively.
- **Cytoscape:** Cytoscape is another widely used open source network analysis and visualization platform. It offers a rich collection of plugins and tools for network analysis tasks, including centrality measures, community detection algorithms, and pathway analysis.
- **NodeXL:** NodeXL is a free and user-friendly Excel add-in for network analysis and visualization. It simplifies importing, analyzing, and visualizing network data, making it accessible to users without extensive programming knowledge.
- **NetworkX:** NetworkX is a Python library that provides tools for creating, manipulating, and analyzing network structures. It offers a wide range of network analysis algorithms and is particularly useful for users comfortable with programming in Python. Besides VOSON, the aforementioned tools have unique features and strengths, and the choice depends on the requirements, dataset characteristics, and user preferences. Exploring their documentation, tutorials, and user communities is recommended to determine which tool aligns best with your needs.

Tutorial: Hyperlinks Analytics with VOSON

VOSON is a web-based tool for hyperlink network analysis. To construct and analyze hyperlink networks, VOSON relies on Web mining, data visualization, and traditional social science techniques, such as social network analysis.[15] VOSON is freely available to academics, researchers, consultants, government entities, and others outside of academia. This tutorial is based on the free version.

Crating an Account on VOSON

- **Step 1:** To access VOSON, create an account by visiting www.uberlink.com and clicking on the "create a new account" option available at the top of the page.
- **Step 2:** Create a username and password by filling in the appropriate form, then log into the system. After the account is approved, start using the tool.

Logging in to VOSON

To avoid confusion, note that there are two identical versions of the VOSON System. The first version is from VOSON@ANU and other is offered from VOSON@Uberlink. Each version is accessed from slightly different locations. So, first, determine the version being subscribed to.

To see which version of VOSON the reader has been granted access to, use the following steps:

- Go to www.uberlink.com and log in with your username and password.
- Click on the "My Account" option available at the top of the website.
- Scroll down to the bottom of the profile to see the version currently subscribed to.
- If it is VOSON@ANU, log in to the VOSON System at http://voson.anu.edu.au/voson-system. If it's VOSON@Uberlink, log in to the VOSON System at https://voson.uberlink.com.au.

VOSON Menus

After logging into VOSON for the first time, users are presented with the following active menu items (many other menus are not active and only become active when they are needed). Details on the description of all menus can be found in the VOSON documentation available at www.uberlink.com/software#voson-system.

Info

User– only gives basic information on the access privileges and the projects that belong to the user.

Data

- *Data browser*– this allows users to see the data, where each row is a webpage.
- *Save database* – use this to save copies of the database.
- *Add seed sites* – use this to add more seed sites to the database (seed sites are used to create hyperlink networks).
- *Download* – use this to access the data for viewing in other software, for example, Excel.
- *Show databases* – this lists all the databases the user has access to. Initially, there are only two databases available: testdb and testdbAN. Users can start with these two databases to get familiar with the tool.

Furthermore, the VOSON System contains two database types:

1. VOSON databases
2. VOSON-analysis databases

VOSON databases are the parent from which VOSON-analysis databases are created. VOSON databases contain the raw network data; whereas, VOSON-analysis databases are used to conduct network analysis such as crosstabs and network visualization.

Create: *VOSON database* – this menu is used to create a VOSON analysis database.
Help: The Help menu provides two submenus for accessing documentation and information about the software.

Creating a Hyperlink Network

Often, by looking at the pattern and interrelationships of inbound and outbound links to a website (and where they interconnect), a better understanding of the value of a site can be derived.

Step 1: After login, the first thing a user needs to do is to build a database. To create a database, click on the "Data" tab, click "Create" and then click on "VOSON database".

Step 2: Provide the requested information (e.g., database name and description). Leave the other options on their default setting. The default options will perform the following tasks:

- The crawler will look for inbound links.
- For each seed, the crawler stops when it discovers 1,000 in-links.
- The crawler will not look for inbound links to each internal page.
- The crawler will look for outbound links.
- For each seed, the crawler will stop, when it discovers 1,000 out-links.
- Then, it will crawl 25 pages without finding a new outbound link (the maximum number of unproductive pages).
- It will crawl only 50 pages (the depth of crawl in pages).
- It will crawl two levels (the depth of crawl, in levels), but the text content will not be parsed for analysis (yet).
- The database is now created.

Step 3: Notice that other submenus within the "Data" menu have become active. To create a network, click on the "Data" menu, click on "Create", and then on "VOSON analysis database".

Step 4: Provide a name for the database. Select "Hyperlinks" in the "Link type" and "Page group" in the "Node type" in the drop-down boxes, then click "Create, database". This database will be used to construct our hyperlink network.

Step 5: Now it is time to add seed sites that will be used to create the hyperlink network. For this tutorial, we used www.uberlink.com as the seed site, but users can use the website address of any website or company URL.

Users can add several additional seed sites, but the total number of seed sites that can be added depends on the subscription plan a user signs up for. To add a new location to the seed list, first click on the newly created database to activate it. Then click on "Data", then on "Add Seed Sites".

A new window will be opened. Type the URL to be analyzed in the box provided. Leave other options on their default settings and click on the "Add" button next to the comment box (which you can use to add comments if you have any). Now, check the "ready to crawl" box. A pop-up window will alert the user about the status of credit and number of credits needed to perform the crawl. Click "OK" to start the process. Note that the sites will not be crawled immediately; the user will receive an email when the crawling has finished.

Step 6: After having received the email from VOSON informing the user that the data set is ready, click on "Data>Show databases". Now the database has been populated with data (e.g., 31 rows).

Step 7: To check the network properties of the hyperlink network, first click on the database (VOSON-analysis type) to make it active. Then, click on the "Analysis" tab and then click on "SNA".

Step 8: A new window will open summarizing in detail the properties of the network, including the following:

Size – the total number of websites (or nodes) in the network

Number of edges – the total number of hyperlinks (in-links and out-links) of the websites

Components – the isolated sub-networks that connect within but are disconnected between networks[26]

Density – the number of links in a network

Number of isolates – the number of nodes that have no connections to other nodes

Inclusiveness – the proportion of the nodes in the network that are connected

Step 9: To visualize the hyperlink network, click on the "Analysis" tab, and then "Maps", and then select one of the three available options:

• Minimum spanning tree
• Complete network
• Hierarchy

Depending on the version of VOSON being used, there may be more options. These are network visualization algorithms, and each one will visualize the network differently. We selected the "Complete network", which shows all links and nodes simultaneously.

Step 10: The hyperlink network will appear in a separate window. Users can easily notice the out-links and in-links by looking at the arrowheads. If the arrowhead points to the seed site, it is an in-link, and if it points away, it is an out-link from the seed site to another website. The countries where the hyperlinks are coming from are shown on the right-hand side.

Users can redraw the network based on several parameters shown in the upper part of the window. For example, we configured the node size based on the in-degree (i.e., the number of incoming hyperlinks). The node size will be bigger when a website has more in-links. Clicking on a specific node will display more details about the node.

Step 11: To save the network diagram, click on "download map PNG" and save it on your computer.

Step 12: Users can also export the network data to be used with other network analysis software (e.g., Pajek and GrapML). To do so, click on "Data", then "Download" and then select the format you want to download the data in.

What is Mobile Analytics?

Mobile data is constantly generated by our mobile devices, and there are two main methods to view and analyze this data:

1. Mobile web analytics
2. Apps analytics

Mobile analytics focuses on characteristics of the mobile devices and the activities that originate on them; whereas, traditional web analytics focuses on the activities that occur on HTML websites. Mobile analytics platforms are designed to track the actions and behaviors of visitors to websites or apps originating from visitors or app users.

Mobile analytics is both similar and different to traditional web analytics in its scope and methodology. However, in some cases, using traditional web analytics to visualize mobile device activity can be misleading. For example,

- A web referral in traditional web analytics is generated from a website domain or page within a domain; whereas, in mobile web analytics, the referral originates from a mobile device, which is not the optimal way to visualize the activity.
- Showing activity from a specific app or mobile web application would be much more helpful, but traditional web analytics was not designed to collect and represent this relationship (although attempts have been made to broaden the scope of web analytics to include more activities than it was originally created to track).

Organizations collect and analyze a variety of mobile user data, including views, clicks, demographic information, and device-specific data (e.g., the type of mobile device used to access the website). However, all websites should be mobile friendly for several reasons.

Reasons to Make Websites Mobile Friendly

1. Search engines rank mobile-compatible websites higher in search results than websites that are not mobile-compatible. Since 2015, mobile compatibility has been a Google search engine ranking factor and, overall, most of the referral traffic arriving on websites originates from mobile devices.[35] Similarly, searches that originate from desktop and laptop computers is also taken into consideration by Google's search ranking algorithms.[36]
2. Many websites have been designed to work on desktops or laptops rather than mobile devices; thus, creating frustration in the user experience while use is attempted on mobile devices.
3. There is evidence that searches performed on a mobile device are highly correlated to customers who are willing to visit a local business and make a purchase the same day.[37] Mobile devices are portable and broadcast their location; they are optimized to take advantage of this information via services such as Yelp, Foursquare, and Google Now. It should come as no surprise that a mobile search engine query or API-issued request from a mobile app such as Yelp provides better conversion results than desktop and laptop searches when it pertains to a local retail purchase.

Thus, when a business fails to create a mobile-friendly website experience for visitors, they are most likely leaving money on the table and losing business.

Mobile App Analytics

Today, most organizations, big or small, are using mobile apps to drive sales, improve brand affinity, and make purchases possible with a few swipes. For instance, Virgin Atlantic allows customers to search, book, and board their flights with swipes on their smartphones. Companies also need to have a thorough understanding of their customers and their characteristics. Mobile app analytics focuses on the understanding and analysis of mobile app users' characteristics, actions, and behaviors.

Purpose of App Analytic

The main purpose of apps analytics is to measure and analyze user behavior, improve user experiences, drive revenue, user engagement, and loyalty. Some sample questions that can be answered with app analytics are provided here:

- Who are our users?
- Which countries are they coming from?
- What actions they are taking?
- How do our customers navigate in the app?
- What are our in-app payments and revenue?
- How long do they stay on our app?
- How many daily active users (DAU) do we have? (Note: DAU is considered an important business metric because it provides better insights related to how well the app is performing.)
- Which operator, operation system, and devices do they use?
- What item is purchased the most?
- Which countries were top performers regarding in-app purchases (IAP)?
- Which application version leads to more sales?
- How often do our users open the app?
- How many users started a specific number of sessions?
- How do our applications versions compare to one another?

Based on the types of questions being asked, the answers will vary depending on what app analytics are being performed.

Types of Apps

Apps can be mainly classified in two ways:

1. App development
2. Type of app

App Development

There are three classification methods[38] that mobile apps are developed and deployed across:

1. Native apps
2. Web-based apps
3. Hybrid apps

Native Apps (Mobile Apps)

Mobile or native apps are specifically created for and installed on mobile devices by downloading them from the iPhone or Android app store. Obviously, as native apps are executable code, run directly by the microprocessors on the mobile device, they can only run on compatible devices that can run that code (hence, the term "executable" is used). For example, apps for Android-based mobile devices are created in the Java programming language, and iOS apps are developed in Objective-C and Cocoa programming (a programming language native to Apple devices).

When a business wants to create an app that can run both on Android and iOS, they need to develop two separate versions of the app. As previously mentioned, native apps are made available for download in app stores (such as Google Play and the Apple Store). One way to distinguish native apps from the other types is that these apps can only be accessed through specific mobile devices. Tinder (a social networking app) and Uber (a taxi-sharing app) are examples of native apps whose program must first be downloaded and installed from the app store. Both Apple and Google run their own app stores and the keep track of the most updated version of the app. App users are notified when a new version of the app is available on the app store. Frequently, updated apps are automatically downloaded and installed on mobile devices where the app is installed.

Web-Based Apps

Web-based apps look like native apps, but are websites that are optimized for mobile access. For example, TouchStyle (a fashion design app) is a web-based app for the iPad that is accessed with Safari. Web-based apps are created using standard web coding techniques (such as JavaScript or HTML5) and are accessed using Internet browsers, and are hence not available in app stores. The advantage of developing web-based apps is that they can be accessed from any mobile device and are less costly to establish and maintain. However, regarding performance, web-based apps are not as fast and usable as native apps. Moreover, web-based apps are simply mobile-friendly HTML5 code that is executed by a web server. Thus, they are not distributed in an app store, and it is hard to monetize them. It should be noted that web-based apps should execute similarly on mobile and desktop devices.

Hybrid Apps

A hybrid app combines the functionalities of both native and web-based apps. Like native apps, they are available in the app stores; and like web apps, they are developed using standard web programming languages (e.g., HTML) and then packaged up into native applications. Packaging or wrapping it into a native container makes it possible for a hybrid app to access native platform features.[39] The Facebook app, for example, was initially a hybrid app, but later was changed to a native app so it could take advantage of features of the various mobile devices it runs on. The advantage of hybrid apps is that they can be used on any mobile device, including Android, iOS, Windows, and BlackBerry. This way, businesses can get the advantages of native applications while keeping the cost of development down.

Classifying Apps by Type

Mobile apps have been created with the purpose to assist users in pursuing many different tasks, and there are dozens of possible categories that apps fall under. For example, the Google Play store lists at least 27 different app categories; only a few of the most common categories are discussed on the following pages.

- **Transaction-oriented apps** are designed to carry out virtual business transactions (such as purchasing a product or depositing money into an account) with customers. For example, eBay's app allows the user to buy, sell, and manage products using their mobile devices. The Venmo app is a digital wallet,[40] which allows users of the app to send and request money from friends, but they must also be a Venmo user to do so. Transaction-enabled apps provide functionality like an electronic commerce website's shopping cart system. Mobile transaction applications such as Vemno and Square fall into this category. Square helps millions of sellers run their business by including secure credit card processing and other point of sale solutions.[41]

- **Ads-oriented apps** are designed to generate revenue using advertising banners that are embedded in the app. Owners provide the app for free with the hope of generating revenue by linking the user to the advertiser's website. However, it should be noted that advertising can appear within any of types of apps listed in this section. For example, the YouTube app requires users trying to watch a video to view several seconds of advertising before proceeding to the content. However, there are ways to ensure users do not see ads or commercials on YouTube Finally, apps such as Pandora and Spotify each have a free version that requires users to view advertising and premium versions that are free of advertising.

- **Information-oriented apps** are designed primarily for providing information. Companies, organizations, and sometimes ordinary people deploy these apps to help users find information about things such as products, services, and facilities. These apps do not have virtual transaction abilities. Examples of information-oriented apps include Find-My-iPhone (locate an iPhone), Toilet-Finder, MyCar (for locating cars), and MapFactor (a navigation app).

- **Networking-oriented apps** such as Instagram, Twitter, and Tinder are designed to make it easier for users to connect with each other. These apps may have a common purpose, but they often appeal to different demographics. Millennials tend to use Instagram, Tinder, and Snapchat while the older population are easier to reach on Twitter and Facebook, etc. Meanwhile, organizations can use these apps to generate more attention by using selected features, such as hashtags.

- **Communication-oriented apps** are used to facilitate communication among users. Users can exchange text messages, pictures, and carry voice and video communication. WhatsApp, Snapchat, Group Me, and Facebook Messenger are examples of communication-oriented apps.

- **Entertainment-oriented apps** such as Netflix and Hulu are created for entertainment purposes, such as watching popular network programming. Gaming apps, such as Angry Birds and Candy Crush are free but are monetized through in-app purchases.

- **Education-oriented apps** many apps are created for educational purposes, such as learning a new skill, language, or subject. For example, Quizlet is an app that allows users to use commercially available study sets or create their own to study with.

- **Self-improvement apps** are used to track their progress for a variety of purposes, including improvement of health, habits, skills, and abilities. Nike+, for example, is an app for tracking users' workouts and fitness progress. Also, My Fitness Pal is a free online calorie counter and diet plan and has millions of users.

Characteristics of Mobile Apps

The best way to differentiate mobile apps from desktop-based applications is through its features. The following are some main features that distinguish mobile apps from desktop-based applications.

- **Always on:** An app is always on and connected to the Internet; this makes it possible to push information and content to users as it becomes available. For example, the Starbucks app sends users promotions when they are near a Starbucks (and, as Starbucks locations are numerous and widespread, there are many opportunities to be alerted by the app). The Weather App and Yahoo's Weather App send alerts to users when there is a high probability that it is about to rain or snow. It should be noted that many apps remain active even when a user closes out of them; however, notifications from the apps can be manually turned on or off.

- **Movable:** Unlike the desktop applications, mobile apps go where the user goes. Thus, it stays with the user 24/7, and users can access it anywhere and anytime.
- **Location Awareness:** Thanks to the GPS (global positioning system) embedded in mobile devices, apps are always aware of the user's location. The location awareness ability of apps is of great interest to social marketers, as it can be used to send target ads and promotions based on users' current locations. For example, Groupon helps users to find the best deals for restaurants and entertainment in their specific locations.
- **Focused:** Being focused on one theme/issue is one of the key features of mobile applications that distinguishes it from desktop-based applications or websites, which have a wider scope. There are always a narrow set of activities that apps are designed to carry out. For example, the Google Maps app is a subset of Google (and is fully integrated into Google's desktop website), but it is presented as a standalone application for mobile devices.
- **Personalized:** Mobile apps can provide personalized experiences based on a user's preferences. Users get to control what content they see and how it is shared. They can also control what exactly the app does, and how it performs (specifics depend on the app).
- **Short-Term Use:** Unlike desktop applications that are used for longer sessions (with some exceptions, such as video-streaming apps such as Netflix or Hulu), mobile app usage is characterized by frequent but short-term use ranging from several seconds to several minutes.
- **Inexpensive:** Most apps cost only a few dollars or are free.
- **Easy To Use:** Last but not least, mobile apps are extremely easy to use and navigate.

Developing Apps

App development is beyond the scope of this book. However, when it comes to developing a mobile app, organizations have three options:

- **Do-It-Yourself:** Hire a programmer/developer to develop one for the user or organization, which is usually very expensive. Google's software development kit (SDK) for mobile analytics is a great place to start.[42] This way the user can cut some of the development expenses; however, it requires a lot of technical resources.
- **Outsource App Development:** If it is beyond the programming skills of an organization or individual to create an app, they can hire a company to develop a custom app for the user. However, by outsourcing app development, users lose control over the app and increase the development costs.
- **Open Source:** Users can create the business app through open source platforms. For example, OpenMEAP™ is a case of an open source application platform that enables businesses with no technical skills to easily create, manage, and deploy mobile apps. Alternatively, business users could deploy the PhoneGap open source platform to create their app for free.[43]

Mobile Analytics Tools

Mobile analytics play a crucial role in digital marketing. With the increasing availability of analytics tools for mobile devices, marketers are now able to measure KPIs and assess the effectiveness of their mobile marketing campaigns. Some leading mobile analytics tools are listed in what follows:

Google Analytics for Mobile

Mobile analytics tools by Google enable organizations to track user interactions within mobile app, such as user acquisition, engagement, and conversion rates. It provides detailed reports and real-time data that can be translated into valuable insights for marketers.

Firebase Analytics

Firebase, a mobile development platform by Google, includes Firebase Analytics, which provides insights into user behavior, demographics, and app performance. It offers event tracking, user segmentation, and conversion tracking.

Flurry Analytics: Flurry Analytics by Yahoo (now Verizon Media) is a comprehensive mobile analytics tool that provides detailed insights into user behavior, retention, and engagement. It supports both iOS and Android platforms and offers real-time reporting.

Mixpanel: Mixpanel is a powerful analytics tool that focuses on user engagement and retention. It provides event tracking, user segmentation, funnel analysis, and A/B testing capabilities. Mixpanel also offers a mobile-specific SDK for easy integration.

Amplitude: Amplitude is a user behavior analytics platform that helps businesses understand how users interact with their mobile apps. It offers features like user segmentation, cohort analysis, funnels, and predictive analytics.

Review Questions

1. Define social media actions analytics.
2. Briefly, list and define different actions performed by social media users.
3. Why it important to measure actions carried out by social media users?
4. What are hyperlinks, and why they are important?
5. Briefly discuss in-links, out-links, and co-links.
6. What is hyperlink analytics, and its underlying assumptions?
7. What is hyperlink website analysis?
8. What is link impact analysis?
9. What is social media hyperlink analysis?
10. Explain the two main categories of mobile analytics.
11. What is the purpose of apps analytics?

Chapter 7 Citations

1. Petersen, R. "166 Case Studies Prove Social Media Marketing ROI." *BarnRaisers*. http://barnraisersllc.com/2014/04/166-case-studies-prove-social-media-roi. Accessed June 2, 2023.

2. Graham, R.F. "Psychologist: Social Media Causing a 'Distancing Phenomena' to Take Place." April 16, 2014. http://washington.cbslocal.com/2014/04/16/psychologist-social-media-causing-a-distancing-phenomena-to-take-place. Accessed June 2, 2023.

3. Wal, T.V. "Off the Top: Folksonomy Entries." www.vanderwal.net/random/category.php?cat=153. Accessed June 2, 2023.

4. Singer, N. "Online Test-takers Feel Anti-cheating Software's Uneasy Glare." *The New York Times*. April 5, 2015. www.nytimes.com/2015/04/06/technology/online-test-takers-feel-anti-cheating-softwares-uneasy-glare.html. Accessed June 2, 2023.

5. Scurria, A. "ComScore Pays $14m to Escape Massive Privacy Class Action." June 4, 2014. www.law360.com/articles/544569/comscore-pays-14m-to-escape-massive-privacy-class-action. Accessed June 2, 2023.

6. "SocialMediaMineR." https://cran.r-project.org/package=SocialMediaMineR.

7. "Transforming Data into Action: Cover-More Group." *Hootsuite*. https://hootsuite.com/resources/case-study/transforming-data-into-action cover-more-group.

8. Kim, D. and Y. Nam (2012) "Corporate Relations with Environmental Organizations Represented by Hyperlinks on the Fortune Global 500 Companies' Websites." *Journal of Business Ethics 105*(4): 475–487.

9. Garrido, M. and A. Halavais (2003) "Mapping Networks of Support for the Zapatista Movement: Applying Social Network Analysis to Study the Contemporary Social Movements." In M.M.M. Ayers (ed.), *Cyberactivism: Online Activism in Theory and Practice*. London: Routledge.

10. Jackson, M.H. (1997) "Assessing the Structure of Communication on the World Wide Web." *Journal of Computer-Mediated Communication 3*(1).

11. Vreeland, R. (2000) "Law Libraries in Cyberspace: A Citation Analysis of World Wide Web Sites." *Law Library Journal 92*: 49–56.

12. Nam, Y., G. Barnet, et al. (2014) "Corporate Hyperlink Network Relationships in Global Corporate Social Responsibility System." *Quality & Quantity 48*(3): 1225–1242.

13. Chakrabarti, S., M.M. Joshi, et al. (2002) "The Structure of Broad Topics on the Web." www2002.org/CDROM/refereed/338.

14. Björneborn, L. and P. Ingwersen (2004) "Toward a Basic Framework for Webometrics." *Journal of the American Society for Information Science and Technology 55*(14): 1216–1227.

15. Khan, G.F. and S. Vong (2014) "Virality over YouTube: An Empirical Analysis." *Internet Research 24*(5): 629–647.

16. Vaughan, L. (2004) "Exploring Website Features for Business Information." *Scientometrics 61*(3): 467–477.

17. Björneborn, L. (2001) *Necessary Data Filtering and Editing in Webometric Link Structure Analysis*. Royal School of Library and Information Science.

18. Fishkin, R. "5 Reasons You Should Link Out to Others from Your Website." *Moz*. February 24, 2009. https://moz.com/blog/5-reasons-you-should-link-out-to-others-from-your-website. Accessed May 30, 2023.

19. Aharony, S. "Study – Outgoing Links Used as Ranking, Signal." *Reboot SEO Company*. February 21, 2016. www.rebootonline.com/blog/long-term-outgoing-link-experiment. Accessed May 30, 2023.

20. Vaughan, L. and J. You (2006) "Comparing Business Competition Positions Based on Web Co-Link Data: The Global Market vs. the Chinese Market." *Scientometrics 68(3)*: 611–628.

21. Thurow, S. "Conversion Optimization: Measuring Usability in the User Experience." April 11, 2014. http://marketingland.com/conversion-optimization-measuring-usability-user-experience-ux-part-1-79557. Accessed May 30, 2023.

22. "The Periodic Table of SEO Success Factors." http://searchengineland.com/seotable. Accessed May 30, 2023.

23. Lohr, S. "For Impatient Web Users, and Eye Blink Is Just Too Long to Wait." *The New York Times*. March 1, 2012. www.nytimes.com/2012/03/01/technology/impatient-web-users-flee-slow-loading-sites.html. Accessed May 30, 2023.

24. Vaughan, L. and M. Thelwall (2003) "Scholarly Use of the Web: What Are the Key Inducers of Links to Journal Web Sites?" *Journal of the American Society for Information Science and Technology 54(1)*: 29–38.

25. Park, H. and M. Thelwall (2008). "Link Analysis: Hyperlink Patterns and Social Structure on Politicians' Web Sites in South Korea." *Quality & Quantity 42(5)*: 687–697.

26. Ackland, R. (2010) "WWW Hyperlink Networks." In D. Hansen, B. Shneiderm and K.H.M. Smith (eds.), *Analyzing Social Media Networks with NodeXL*. New York: Morgan-Kaufmann.

27. Thelwall, M. "Big Data and Social Web Research Methods." www.scit.wlv.ac.uk/~em1993/papers/IntroductionToWebometricsAndSocialWebAnalysis.pdf. Accessed May 30, 2023.

28. "Image Map Example from SocSciBot Network." *Webometric Analyst*. http://lexiurl.wlv.ac.uk/examples/cybermetrics.htm. Accessed May 30, 2023.

29. Thelwall, M. (2005) "Webometrics." In M.A. Drake (ed.), *Encyclopedia of Library and Information Science*. New York: Marcel Dekker, Inc.; Thelwall, M. "Big Data and social Web Research Methods." www.scit.wlv.ac.uk/~cm1993/papers/IntroductionToWebometricsAndSocialWebAnalysis.pdf. Accessed May 30, 2023.

30. Khan, G.F., H.Y. Yoon, et al. (2014) "Social Media Communication Strategies of Government Agencies: Twitter Use in Korea and the USA." *Asian Journal of Communication 24(1)*: 60–78.

31. Khan, G.F., H.Y. Yoon, et al. (2014). "Social Media Communication Strategies of Government Agencies: Twitter Use in Korea and the USA." *Asian Journal of Communication 24(1)*: 60–78.

32. For example, www.youtube.com/watch?v=kffacxfA7G4 was the URL of a video posted by the user "Justin Bieber" having an ID "kffacxfA7G4." *The data was collected for all 100 videos and saved in a text file with one ID per line.*

33. Thelwall, M. (2005) "Webometrics." In M.A. Drake (ed.), *Encyclopedia of Library and Information Science*. New York: Marcel Dekker, Inc.

34. *To see the image being referenced from the source*, refer to http://lexiurl.wlv. ac.uk/images/justin%20bieber%20replies.PNG.

35. "Make Sure Your Site's Ready for Mobile-friendly Google Search Results." https://support.google.com/adsense/answer/6196932?hl=en. Accessed April 10, 2023.

36. "Google and Mobile-friendly Websites 2016." *Search Infuse*. May 17, 2016. www.searchinfuse.co.uk/google-mobile-friendly-websites-2016. Accessed April 15, 2017.

37. Lee, J. "Google: Local Searches Lead 50% of Mobile Users to Visit Stores." May 7, 2014. https://searchenginewatch.com/sew/study/2343577/google-local-searches-lead-50-of-mobile-users-to-visit-stores-study. Accessed April 10, 2023.

38. Korf, M. and E. Oksman. "Native, HTML5, or Hybrid: Understanding Your Mobile Application Development Options." https://developer.salesforce.com/page/Native,_HTML5,_or_Hybrid:_Understanding_Your_Mobile_Application_Development_Options. Accessed April 10, 2023.

39. Korf, M. and E. Oksman. "Native, HTML5, or hybrid: Understanding Your Mobile Application Development Options." https://developer.salesforce.com/page/Native,_HTML5,_or_Hybrid:_Understanding_Your_Mobile_Application_Development_Options. Accessed May 30, 2023.

40. "Venmo." https://venmo.com. Accessed May 30, 2023.

41. "Square." https://squareup.com. Accessed May 30, 2023.

42. "Google Analytics for Mobile Apps." *Google Developers*. https://developers.google.com/analytics/solutions/mobile. Accessed May 30, 2023.

43. "PhoneGap." http://phonegap.com. Accessed May 30, 2023.

Advanced AI and Algorithms

CHAPTER OBJECTIVES

After reading this chapter, readers should understand the following:

- What text analytics is
- AI Generative Communications
- How GPT-3 (and future versions) responds to the questions humans ask
- A note about the algorithms used in text analytics
- Text analytics processing
- The text analytics market through 2020
- Types and use cases of text analytics
- Text analytics use cases
- Future trends in text analytics
- Algorithms use in text analytics
- Issues with using text analytics
- An introduction to specific free and paid text analytics platforms
- Choosing the right text analytics platform

New Developments in Text Analytics

One of the most exciting aspects of text analytics today is the rapid advancement of natural language processing (NLP) techniques powered by deep learning and artificial intelligence. These advancements enable more sophisticated and accurate analysis of text data, leading to exciting possibilities. Here are a few noteworthy aspects:

- **Contextual Understanding:** Modern NLP models, such as transformer-based architectures like BERT, GPT, and their variants, have significantly improved the ability to understand the context and meaning of the text. These models can capture nuanced relationships, contextual clues, and subtle nuances, enabling more accurate sentiment analysis, entity recognition, and language understanding tasks.
- **Multilingual and Cross-Lingual Analysis:** With the advancements in NLP, there has been progress in developing models that can handle multiple languages and perform cross-lingual analysis. The multilingual analysis opens

DOI: 10.4324/9781003025351-8

up opportunities for analyzing and extracting insights from text data in various languages, facilitating global applications and communication.

- **Domain-Specific Text Analytics:** NLP models can be fine-tuned or specialized for specific domains or industries, such as healthcare, finance, legal, or customer service. This domain-specific focus enhances the accuracy and applicability of text analytics techniques in specific contexts, leading to more tailored and meaningful insights.

- **Ethical and Bias Mitigation:** Text analytics researchers and practitioners are increasingly addressing concerns related to bias, fairness, and ethical considerations in NLP models and applications. Efforts are being made to develop methods that reduce biases, promote inclusivity, and ensure the responsible use of text analytics in sensitive domains.

- **Interactive Visualization and Explainability:** As text analytics techniques evolve, so do the tools and platforms that enable interactive visualization and explainability of the results. This visualization allows users to understand better and interpret the outcomes of text analytics models, enhancing transparency, and fostering trust in the analysis.

These advancements in text analytics hold great promise for improving the accuracy, scope, and impact of analyzing text data and they enable deeper understanding, richer insights together with more effective decision-making based on textual information. As the field continues to evolve, it's exciting to see how these developments will further enhance our ability to extract knowledge and value from the text.

AI Generative Communications Is Super-Hot, Today!

Since the first edition was published text analytics came into the world in a very visible way with the rise of AI generative platforms such as ChatGPT chatbot which provide an natural language interface between humans and artificial intelligence. GPT-3. This deep learning model is a powerhouse in natural language processing tasks, boasting an impressive 175 billion parameters. Its capabilities are vast, allowing it to tackle a range of language-related tasks, including text generation, translation, and summarization. We have no doubt that by the time this second edition is published, what we now call ChatGPT will be even more advanced than it is at the current moment. The development of GPT-3 involved training the model using unsupervised learning techniques on a vast corpus of text data. By leveraging this extensive training, GPT-3 learned to understand and generate human-like text, making it a versatile tool for various applications, including chatbots, virtual assistants, and content generation. From a business analytics perspective the chatbots hypercharge both marketing and creative but how much should depend upon such technologies?[1]

According to Gartner "ChatGPT's uniqueness lies not in the creation of cohesive sentences, which many spelling and grammar applications can do, but its ability to do so based on your organization's corpora, or collection of content for AI, against a large language model (LLM)" (ibid). However, when one of the authors used Chat GPT's instructions about a web analytics process, there were some gaps and inaccuracies in the instructions. So, while AI generative technologies are progressing amazingly fast, they aren't yet ready yet to bank on, though they certainly are entertaining! Gartner's recommendations are that ChatGPT technologies can be used to draft informal communications such as sales conversations, marketing and advertising communications tailored to audiences, proposal introductions and job descriptions. However, avoid using ChatGPT for contracts, any type of regulated communications (i.e., broker communications with clients or job offer letters) (ibid).

How GPT-3 (and Future Versions) Responds to the Questions Humans Ask

Communications between humans and these new intelligent chatbots are created and delivered through a web-based interface or API (Application Programming Interface).

When a person interacts with GPT-3 through an interface, the input provided by the user is sent to OpenAI's servers (*OpenAI is the company that first came out with the most popular scalable human/machine text and graphics interface*), where the language model resides. The input can be in the form of text, typically a prompt or a question. It could be a single sentence or a paragraph, depending on the complexity of the desired interaction.

Once the input is received, GPT-3 (or even more powerful later versions) processes it and generates a response based on its understanding of the input and the patterns it has learned from its training data. The generated response is then sent back to the user through the interface, typically as text.

The process of generating a response involves several steps. GPT-3 uses its understanding of the context provided by the input and attempts to generate a coherent and contextually relevant response. It can consider a wide range of factors, including the wording, tone, and intent of the input, as well as any prompts or instructions that may have been given.

It's important to note that GPT-3's responses are generated based on statistical patterns learned from training data and do not have true understanding or consciousness. The model does not have access to real-time information or personal experiences beyond what it has learned during training. It operates solely based on the patterns and information present in the text it was trained on. The delivery of GPT-3's responses to the user is typically near instantaneous, depending on the network connection and server load. The user can then read and interpret the response, continuing the conversation or providing further input as needed.

A Note About the Algorithms Used in Text Analytics

We noted in the first edition that the fundamental algorithms mentioned is this chapter can be and are applied in many other domains besides text analytics and often are. The algorithms haven't changed much at all, the major advances have been in the human/AI interfaces and in processing speeds, which enable real time and personalized communications that mimic two humans communicating with each other.

With all this in mind, it's all the better for us to examine the algorithms and processes that have been associated with text analytics in some depth here. Sometimes, we just generate word clouds and other forms of visualizations, and they are not turned into numbers, but we still describe the activity as text analytics. We found an excellent introductory article that explains text analytics in seven minutes.[2]

We believe that text analytics is now being used more much more widely and more effectively than it ever was before, but for most how it works behind the curtains remain a "niche" activity mostly confined to those specializing in mathematics, computer programming, and advanced linguistics studies.

Reasons for Using Text Analytics

- Hearing from people provides tremendously valuable insights.
- Text can be utilized alongside statistical measures to build predictive models that are stronger than are possible with either the measures alone or text alone.
- Textual data can give us very useful insights in a variety of use cases such as customer sentiment (VOC), healthcare (patient and hospital), financials (stock trading is especially hot), voluntary opinion mining (with and without survey data).
- Text analytics can be used to get customer sentiment in ways customers are reluctant to share voluntarily by mining their textual data.

Process

Most text information is unstructured data for the standpoint of the text analytics process; that is because the processing is done by a software program that is not a sentient, thinking, being, and it cannot understand the world in the way humans do.[3] The text analytics process involves many operations:

1. First, the text analytics application counts the words in the chosen document, calculating the word distance from a word of interest (such as wellness or illness) and choosing word categories (via pre-processing and employing complex algorithms). The goal at this stage of the process is to produce cleaned text data that has had its sentence structure, punctuation, and word groupings eliminated.
2. Second, the raw text is transformed into a set of information and placed in an internal text table for further processing.
3. Finally, the frequency of the words is counted and then normalized by running mathematical operations on table elements.

All this pre-processing seems like a lot of work, and it is.

Purposes of Text Analytics

Sentiment Analysis

Referring to Figure 8.1, one reason to use text analytics is to understand the opinion of others. Sentiment analysis an aspect of text analytics that focuses on opinion

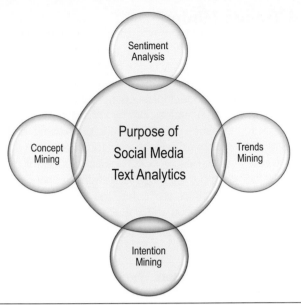

Figure 8.1 Purposes of Text Analytics
Source: Gohar F. Khan

mining. Sentiment analysis uses computational methods to gather sentiment, opinions, appraisals, and emotions from the text. Opinion mining involves building a system to collect and categorize opinions about a product, service, or event. Automated opinion mining uses machine learning, a type of artificial intelligence (AI), to mine text for sentiment.[4] Sentiment analysis uses the following text analytics operations:

- **Polarity Analysis:** Identify if the tone of communications is positive or negative.
- **Entity Identification, Categorization, and Emotion Tracking:** Identify the emotion and subject of the communications.
- **Context Analysis:** Determine the context of social media posts and other forms of customer communication.

Sentiment analysis can be used to understand how others see the world regarding the data being studied. Sentiment analysis works by comparing the words in documents to external tag lists of words (called lexicons) that are classified as positive or negative. However, the meaning and sentiment of the terms can change, depending on the context they are used in. Analysts must make their own determination about text sentiment and meanings, as the software platforms are not able to do this.

- The overall balance of positive to negative words determines the sentiment score of a document (this can be done on the sentence level as well). The type of list (lexicon/dictionary) is often subjective and applied arbitrarily by whoever composes the list; these definitions may or may not work well in every situation.
- There has been a lot of misrepresentation involved with sentiment analysis capabilities and interpretations, but there are still excellent and valid reasons to employ it provided there is a good set of data (sample frame) to work with.

Topic and Trends Mining

Another reason to use text analytics is to understand what the text in the document is about. Use cases span from scholarly analysis of Shakespeare plays to counterterrorism/threat detection, and everything in-between. We could read a document and form an opinion about topics, but someone else could read the same document and come away with an entirely different set of topics and meanings. Besides, when there are thousands of documents to understand, manually reading large swaths of data is not feasible. Consequently, topic and trend mining are usually performed on large sets of data. Researchers can use deep learning to automatically try to make sense of themes and the trends that lie within a document or set of documents, but that doesn't work too well unless the text analytics software is manually trained beforehand on documents that are very close in subject, language, syntax, and form to the documents being analyzed.

Topic and trends analysis use the following text analytics operations:

- **LDA or latent Dirichlet allocation:** Words are automatically clustered into topics, with a mixture of themes in each document.
- **Probabilistic latent semantic indexing:** Given a document, calculates the probability that certain topics are covered within the document. Also, given a certain topic, calculates the likelihood that a word would be used to describe it.
- **Term frequency-inverse document frequency:** TF-IDF counts how frequently a word appears in a document and its importance to the whole set. Frequent words like "the" or "an" are given a much lower weight, but words that show up frequently in certain contexts (say, a story) are given higher weight and used to build classifiers or predictive models, as we will examine shortly.

Examples of Topic and Trends Mining:

- David Rhea, an assistant professor of communication studies at Governors State University, undertook a qualitative project to determine how viewers of these talk shows disseminate the information they hear. The purpose of the study was to explore how the viewer comes to accept humorous information that they watch on late-night talk shows as legitimate political information. Rhea used NVivo 9 text analytics software to process the transcripts of the talk shows and found it easier to organize information than manually coding in a spreadsheet. NVivo helped him code data thematically with just a couple of clicks.[5] However, the method used by Rhea was still manual, and he had to define his topics first (modifying them while he was coding his project in NVivo); this approach works for a small research project, but would not be able to scale to millions of documents.
- In January 2015, Pew Research tested Crimson Hexagon, a text and sentiment analysis platform to analyze Twitter conversations mentioning New Jersey Governor Chris Christie. Crimson Hexagon employs a supervised machine learning approach. Two people trained Crimson Hexagon on more than 250 documents divided into four categories. Each of the four categories in the training set (the categories are manually defined by the people conducting the analysis) had more than 20 posts in them. Finally, once they were happy the training set was accurately categorized for their purposes, Pew Research ran the monitor. Pew used the keyword "Christie" on Twitter posts covering the period between November 4 to December 31, 2014. Crimson Hexagon automatically categorized many thousands of posts with the word "Christie" in it and placed it in one of the

four categories that had been defined. The supervised learning model works well when analysts have a good idea what patterns they are looking for, but Crimson Hexagon requires a human analyst to review the analysis and decide on its meanings.[6] Pew Research also used Crimson Hexagon for sentiment analysis[7] around Chris Christie and the Bridgegate incident, demonstrating that text analytics platforms are usually able to perform multiple types of analysis.

Intention Mining

Intention mining is what the Google search engine does when you enter a search query into Google, and it figures out what you mean based on your query. Google doesn't stop there, it also analyzes queries and webpages for what people did not explicitly say but what they intended to say, to understated the underlying opinions expressed in the document intention mining is a Text analytics operation that is a big part of search engine optimization. Intention mining can be done in several ways and uses some of the following text analytics operations:

- **Topic modeling:** Identify the dominant themes in a vast array of documents or text. The method used to uncover the topics within text include the following:
- **Named entity recognition:** NER looks at recognizing nouns and could be used to extract persons, organizations, geographic locations, dates, monetary amounts, or the like from text, this works by looking at the words surrounding them.
- **Event extraction:** Determines the relationships and the events connected with named entities (NER). Establishes the kinds of inferences that can be made from the text.
- **Latent semantic analysis:** Examines relationships within a set of documents along with the terms they contain; assumes that words that are close in meaning will occur in similar places in the text.
- **Latent Dirichlet allocation:** Topic modeling that is based on the idea that each text document contains a few topics such that each word in the document is attributable to one of its topics.
- We can take what someone has written and access the probability that it falls into one of the several categories (opinions), which is very close to what Crimson Hexagon and other platforms do in the previous example regarding Chris Christie.
- Use latent semantic indexing to disambiguate the words in a document and try to find the most relevant meanings within it.
- Use unsupervised learning to determine topic segments of based on various characteristics. Techniques such as clustering or dimension reduction are types of unsupervised learning techniques that can take raw data and form groups based on certain characteristics.[8]

Examples of intention mining:

- An analysis of the Bible and the Quran has found that violence and destruction are discussed more frequently in Christian scripture than in the Islamic text. The analysis was done with text analytics platform called Odin Text. The Old and New Testaments were studied as well as an English-language version of the Quran dated from 1917. It took just two minutes to complete the analysis and produce a series of data analyzing the words included in the scriptures. The analysis concluded that the Old Testament had more than twice as many violent mentions as the New Testament or the Quran.[9]

- A researcher analyzed 18,000 TripAdvisor reviews from hotels located in Santorini and scored them on cleanliness, value for money, sleep quality, and service and found that mentions of *bathrooms* are commonly found in negative reviews, but mentions containing *service* were found mostly in positive reviews.[10] Text classifiers were employed to find the most common words around *service* and *bathrooms*. By using text analytics, analysts can uncover opinions and feelings about a described experience that are not always explicitly stated.
- Digging down further, the analyst found a clean place, complimentary' champagne, delicious food, nice breakfast, and Greek hospitality are the way to a positive review.
- On the other hand, problems with having a restful night's sleep, a shower that doesn't work as it should, and bad odors from the bathroom are likely to lead to a negative review.

Concept Mining

Text mining is the discipline of extracting information from a document. Concept mining attempts to do the same thing using the concepts in the document. Mapping words to concepts is ambiguous. Each word in a document may relate to several possible concepts. For example, the Google search engine indexes billions of new documents each day; using concept mining, it will automatically group similar documents together, as representative of a specific idea, along with other documents it has already categorized with the same or similar concept. Google can further refine its content classification by clustering the documents its index by topic; it uses this information to rank search results for a searcher's query better. Examples of concept mining include the following:

- The Dutch National Library has made publicly available more than 80 million historical newspaper articles from the past four centuries, and researchers have been able to search the entire corpus. Using custom developed dictionary software, the researchers could develop a custom dictionary based on statistically relevant words, derived from the frequency of particular words in the document collection and the particularity of those words. Since the words that stood out reflected changes taking place over 400 years, researchers could surmise cultural concept changes (as reflected in language charges) spreading across the entire span.[11]
- Google Books' Ngram Viewer can be used to view the usage terms words or terms over time. For example, comparing the terms "digital marketing" and "web analytics" went up sharply beginning with 2003 (around the time the web analytics Association was formed, so the spike in term usage makes perfect sense) while the term "digital marketing" remained relatively flat.[12] Books that cited each term are clustered by decade and can be further searched for occurrences. Google Books' Ngram Viewer covers roughly 200 years.

Text Analytics Market

Text analytics is a growing market and is estimated to reach $6.5 billion by 2020, growing at a rate of as much as 25% per year from 2013 through 2020. Text analytics supplies necessary data to customer relationship management (CRM), predictive analytics, and brand reputation management.[13]

Mining Unstructured Data

While text we read has structure and organization based on language/grammar, it is not well organized for text analysis (as mentioned at the beginning of this chapter) – for this, the text must be transformed and placed in a repository where it can be data-mined (see Figure 10.2). Unstructured data takes much more effort to work with than structured data – it is also much, more expensive (due to the transformations). Often, organizations merge several types of data using ETL (Extract Transfer Load) in a data warehouse. ETL is a dynamic data rewrite process. ETL was designed to consolidate enterprise information that originated before the era of big data.[14]

Once the data is loaded into the data warehouse, it can be queried with other types of information that have been stored there, such as customer records.

Uses of Text Analytics

Table 8.1 shows some of the more common situations where text analytics is likely to be used. Text analytics tools do not exist independently of the need and use cases for them. In every industry, there are different use cases where it makes sense to use text analytics platforms. For example, ETL (Extract, Transform, Load) processes (shown in Figure 8.2) are used across a broad range of industries and business types such as, retail, bankings and E-commerce.

Common situations where text analytics is useful include

- **Tracking customer feelings regarding key topics:** Sentiment regarding a subject within a block of text, scoring it based on the intensity of specific words in the verbatim(s). For example, Facebook analyzed 24,000 confession posts on the social network to find out what millennials thought of their college or university.[15]

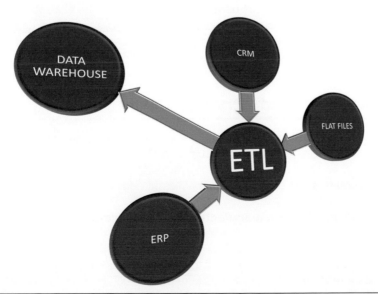

Figure 8.2 Transforming Data Using Enterprise Data Tools and Storing It in a Data Warehouse
Source: Marshall Sponder

Table 8.1 Common Use Cases of Text Analytics

Area	More Common Use Cases
Business	Competitive intelligence, document categorization, HR (voice of the employee), records retention, risk analysis, website navigation
Marketing	Voice of the customer, social media analytics, churn analysis, survey analysis, market research
Analytics	Fraud detection, e-discovery, warranty analysis, medical research
Education	Syllabus classification (compliance analysis), GRE, SAT (writing analysis)
Law Enforcementw	Crime and terrorism detection, psychological assessments based on written data (by suspects), fraud detection

Source: Authors

- **Tracking customer sentiment around a brand or business:** Text analytics has been used in industry verticals quite successfully such as healthcare.[16]
- **Enriching news articles with metadata:** *The New York Times* built a robot to help make article tagging easier. Tags and keywords in articles help readers dig deeper into related stories and topics, and provides another way for readers to discover stories. However, adding tags to news stories is very tedious. Tools to automate content tagging can have a big difference to the bottom line. The *Times'* R&D lab developed the new tagging tool; the Editor tool scans text to suggest article tags in real time.[17]
- **Recognizing works of art using an algorithm:** There is a fascinating study conducted at Rutgers University that identified which paintings have had the greatest influence on later artists and whether they can measure a painting's creativity using only its visual features.[18]

Text Analytics Industry Use Cases

At least 80% of enterprise information and new data generated are in text form. Here are some examples of industry-specific use cases of text analytics.

- **Municipalities** use predictive text analytics around call centers to support public welfare initiatives.[19]
- **Financial institutions, manufacturers, and retailers** use text analytics to support a range of applications including marketing, risk monitoring, staff recruitment, and more. In addition, financial institutions use that data to look out for the next "black swan" – a term used to describe the next debacle.[20]
- **Aviation industry** analyzes reports from pilots, mechanics, and other personnel to identify patterns related to airline safety.[21]

- **Finance industry** incorporates customer feedback in efforts to improve service levels and reduce fraud.[22]

Upcoming Trends

Text analytics has already been widely deployed in enterprise applications for data mining and text extraction.[23] Here's what is coming up next for text analytics:

- Multilingual text analysis will increase.
- Text analysis will gain recognition as a key business solution capability.
- Machine learning, stats, and language engineering will coexist.
- Image analysis will enter the mainstream.
- Speech analytics, with video, will emerge.
- Expanded emotion analytics is arriving soon (already prototyped).
- ISO emoji analytics will be a standard feature on most platforms shortly.

Text Analytics Operations

Turning text into numerical data allows analysts and researchers to run mathematical and statistical operations on the data as shown in Figure 8.3.

Working with Unstructured Information

Structured data is organized into rows, columns, and arrays within databases. The data is structured to be easily retrieved and analyzed using statistical and mathematical operations. Conversely, unstructured data is not organized for statistical or mathematical operations. Usually, unstructured data must be structured first, before it can be operated on. Semi-structured data is information that has a combination of structured and unstructured data (such as an email). Emails have a subject line, to and from fields, and a body of text that is usually comprised of unstructured data.

Figure 8.3 Text Classification Process Engine
Source: Authors

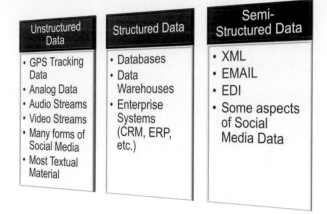

Figure 8.4 Structured, Semi-Structured, and Unstructured Data
Source: Authors

It is extremely complicated to take raw information as shown in Figure 8.4, including raw image data and turn it into usable data. The first part of this chapter gave readers a high-level overview of the text analytics process – now we are doing a second pass to take a more detailed look.

The Text Analytics Process (Detailed)

In the process of transforming text to numbers, there are many manipulations on the data, including tokenization, so we can find named entities in the text – many of these steps are shown in Figure 8.5.

- Stop words (such as "the", "of", "and", "a", "to", and so on) are removed.
- All remaining words are made regular by a process sometimes called stemming. Lemmatization is a stemming operation that regularizes words while trying to figure out their part of speech. Caveat: How words get reduced to a stem may differ depending on how the words are used. For instance, the noun "moped" should not be stemmed into the form "mope", while the verb "moped" should.
- Spelling errors are corrected using a dictionary and plurals must be singularized. Idiomatic expressions are resolved.
- Tenses of words are made uniform so that the same word does not reappear many times with minor variations. Comments, such as "nothing" or "what?" or "no comment" or "mpmpmpmpmp", often appearing in the commentary, especially social media, are removed (however, for sentiment analysis these are retained and analyzed).
- However, word pairs or larger groups of words (e.g. "not good" or "not bad" or "South Gas Works") are noted in sentiment analysis. (Obviously, the kinds of text analysis we do determine if certain words of phrases are retained and analyzed.) Infrequent words are removed, which helps to reduce the overall analytical burden.

Tokenization

Tokens are words taken from a block of text that has been cleaned. This process is called tokenization, and it is often being used to identify people or organizations (named entity extraction). Named entity extraction aims to overcome a problem created when separating words by using blank spaces; IBM SPSS and SAS Data Miner both do this operation.

- For instance, an expression such as "Mr. Sand" contains two tokens (Mr. and Sand), and the computer must recognize that they belong together.

Once we have words cleaned and prepared, we need some further way of reducing the information so it can be analyzed and compared. We should be careful to look at data that can be analyzed easily (into cluster groups, see Figure 8.5).

Turning Text to Numbers, and Numbers into Data

It is very hard to take what people say and turn it into useful information. Humans intrinsically understand many of the structures and meanings of language that computer software does not, making even seemingly simple sentences such as "A dog is chasing a boy on the playground" tough to decode. As text is processed, tagged, entities extracted, sentiment applied, much of the intrinsic meaning we humans take for granted, is lost in translation. Turning text into numbers also involves semantics to derive meaning, involving the ability to disambiguate the meaning of words in various contexts (See the Building a CSV Analyzer example in Figure 8.6). Even very simple sentences can be difficult for sophisticated software programs to extract the right meaning from, as so much of the meaning of words is contextual.

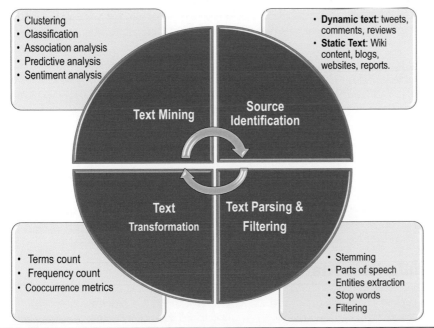

Figure 8.5 How Text Is Transformed into Numbers by Text Analytics
Source: Gohar F. Khan

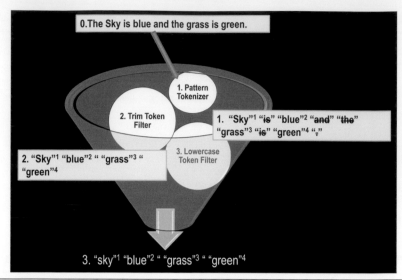

Figure 8.6 Building a CSV Analyzer
Source: Authors

Sliding Windows and N-Grams

While searching for information within a document, an n-gram or sliding window (of varied character lengths) is used to pick up the occurrences of words and to find named entities. Sometimes the simplest models are also the most efficient – take the n-gram; it is a method of scanning information much the way our eyes scan. If we want to see what is around us, we should systematically move our eyes in a zig-zag fashion across the area of view, the point where vision is focused would correspond to the n-gram or the window from which we are looking at details. Text analytics works much the same way, zig-zagging across a text document with a window size (n-gram) of a certain number of characters.

- A sliding window (or as it is sometimes called an n-gram window) is one way to address the question of which words occur together.

Think of the sliding window like a box that is a certain length (say seven characters, as illustrated in Figure 8.7) that moves through the text, one word at a time, and which keeps a count of how many times words fall together in that moving box. An approach like this would be useful for analyzing a collection of documents and looking for the strongest themes expressed across this set. (This might be helpful in looking at a single document if it was a long blog post or article.) The sliding window continues this path until it reaches the end of the block of text. As it moves, it keeps count of how many times words fall together in the box.

Similarities Matrix

Turning text into numbers is hard work, and one step in the process of running equations of the resulting data is to organize it into a similarity matrix. A similarities matrix shows how often words occur together. With a sliding window, the text takes a roundabout route to a table but finally appears in one. This chart, in turn, can lead to other, still more compact forms of data representation.

	N-Gram
Paul Cezanne is a great painter.	'Paul Ce'
Paul Cezanne is a great painter.	'aul Cez'
Paul Cezanne is a great painter.	'ul Ceza'
Paul Cezanne is a great painter.	'l Cezan'

Figure 8.7 N-Gram Sliding Window Text Parsing
Source: Authors

Automated Coding

Statistical platforms such as IBM SPSS and SAS Text Miner can be set up to auto-code verbatim into a table.

Factor Analysis

Factor analysis is a statistical method developed more than 100 years ago to examine responses to questions on intelligence tests that seemed highly related. The factors teased out the ways responses were similar using factor analysis to find common underlying ideas or themes in a set of scaled questions. Factors capture groups of issues around an underlying idea or groups of words that tend to appear together.

Eigenvalue and Factor Analysis

Eigenvalues are the measure of the effectiveness of a factor in a factor analysis. The stronger factor will have a larger eigenvalue (usually a maximum value of 1, but the min/max values can vary). The eigenvalue is used in social media as a way to Identity Influencers within a social graph. It is used to signify the accounts that have the largest number of close connections to other nodes in the social graph (and are more centrally located), which can be calculated mathematically using social Network analysis.

Aspect Analysis

Feature analysis is another term for aspect analysis. Often, when people describe a person, object or event, they mention the distinguishing characteristics such as size, color, texture, price, availability. Text analytics can extract the aspects or features within the text. Analysts and marketer's opinions about an object or experience, then divide it into aspects and evaluate each individually, summing up the combined score.

Deep Learning and Neural Networks

If there is a large enough sample of text, even if the opinion holders are not clearly segmented, it is possible to forecast the sentiment (and opinions) of opinion holders with increasing accuracy, and this is what we will examine in this section. Deep learning neural networks are now being used for sentiment analysis with some interesting results. Socher[24] used deep learning to sort words and phrases into categories using distributional semantics. Neural networks and the math that power them have been around for about 30 years and attempt to replicate human biology in machine processing. To that end, neural nets are evolving very quickly – although they cannot currently understand the meanings behind what they are classifying, some day in the not too distant future they may be able to do this.

Counting Words, Centricity, and Betweenness

Another way of determining what and who is important in a corpus of text is by looking at the concepts of "centricity" and "betweenness". Counting the number of words in a document is a way to understand the content as well as the words that are occurring more than the average.

- The more the betweenness of a word, the more it appears connected with other words that represent different concepts.
- Centricity has more to do with the way that betweenness is represented in a network diagram. The idea of centricity has often been used with influencers' network mapping.

Predictive Text Analytics

Earlier we covered the differences between describing text (via word clouds) versus making predictions based on what is in the text. Describing relationships (a word map or word cloud) is useful, yet predicting which routes in a map will bring us to our destination more quickly is far more actionable. Text analytics uses the methods discussed: in this chapter such as linear regressions to determine probabilities. By using probabilities, decisions can be made on the probabilities calculated from the text being analyzed.

Simple Models and Linear Regressions

Everyone knows loan calculators that predict monthly payments over time and the impact of making changes to the amount owed minus interest; incidentally, this timeline can be charted linearly because the timeline is based on a model. Regression is used to forecast what is likely to happen and what can be applied to many domains of knowledge and industry with good results. However, regressions do not seem to work too well for many text analytics use cases, especially if you have too many variables involved.

Linear Regression

- In a linear regression, there is a variable that is forecast or predicted termed the "dependent variable" or "target variable"; the dependent variable is usually plotted on the Y axis.
- There is also an independent variable or predictor variable that is usually plotted on the X axis.

- A simple linear equation can summarize the relationship between the two variables such as y=3x+25.
- A constant shows the starting point of the line on the Y axis on the equation chart.
- Since regressions are all about straight lines we need a way to tell how close to a straight line the regression is, which is called the "R-squared" of the regression (which measures how well the regression performs).
- The value of "R" is a correlation coefficient; correlation is a summary measure that shows how closely two variable falls into a straight line relationship.

In a linear regression, a change in the value of the independent variable (or X axis), there is a corresponding shift in the dependent variable (or Y axis), which suggests a probabilistic relationship between the two variables.

Examples of Linear Regression

- Author age prediction from text using linear regression: Uses blogs, telephone conversations, and online forum posts a common model involving all three corpora together as well as separately and analyzes differences in predictive features across joint and corpus specific aspects of the model.[25]
- Movie reviews and revenues: an experiment in text regression: Uses linear regression with metadata around a movie; model attempts to predict a movie's opening weekend revenue.[26]
- Text analysis in incident duration prediction: Uses free flow text fields within incident reports of road blockages to predict clearance time, the period between incident reporting and a road's clearance.[27]

Logistic Regression in Text Analytics

Most of the things that dominate life are not linear – life is full of intangibles, even things we enjoy such as art, music, fashion, and sports are not linear in nature, and we should have some other way to make predictions on these. For complex tasks, such as classifying text into a known set of categories, logistic regression is a much better method than linear regression. Logistic regression relates a quantity x to the probability of it being a member of one of two groups and the likelihood of y having a value of 1. For example, logistic regression delivers, for any value of x, the frequency of the word "strange" and the log odds of the word refers to the Marvel Movie *Doctor Strange* (released on November 4, 2016). Logistic regression is often expressed as the odds of something happening or occurring or not and can consist of several variables that are interrelated to each other and impact the outcome.

Logistic Regression Examples

- **Multiple logistic regression analysis of cigarette users among high school students:** Binary logistic regression analysis was performed to predict high school students' cigarette smoking behavior from selected predictors based on a 2009 CDC Youth Risk Behavior Surveillance Survey.[28] The five predictor variables included in the model were 1) race, 2) frequency of cocaine use, 3) first cigarette smoking age, 4) feeling sad or hopeless, and 5) physically inactive behavior. The strongest predictors of youth smoking behavior were race, the frequency of cocaine use, and physically inactive behavior.

- **Lying words: Predicting deception from linguistic styles:** In an analysis of five independent samples, a computer-based text analysis program correctly classified liars and truth-tellers at a rate of 67% when the topic was constant and a rate of 61% overall. Compared to truth-tellers, liars showed lower cognitive complexity, used fewer self-references and other references, and used more negative emotion words.[29]
- **Fast logistic regression for text categorization with variable-length n-grams:** Instead of pre-processing text to clean it for text analytics, logistic regression was used to automatically tokenize text, even when it was unfamiliar.[30]

Classification Trees

Classification trees are a statistical grouping method that works better for text analytics than regression models. One of the most common classification trees used in text analytics is the CHAID method that splits the data into groups, then finds smaller groups within those groups that are significant, and keeps on doing that. The original intent of CHAID was to detect an interaction between variables. CHAID stands for "Chi-squared automatic interaction detector" and works s best with coded text generated through surveys and questionnaires.

Consider the Response CHAID Tree, in Figure 8.8. The overall response of 10% (from a population of size 1,000) can be predicted by marital status, gender, and pet ownership. Note: CHAID does not work well with small sample sizes as respondent groups can quickly become too small for reliable analysis.

Example

For a simple introduction to classification trees, see "5 Minutes with Ingo: Decision Trees".[31] Take, for example, a coin sorting system for sorting coins into different classes (perhaps pennies, nickels, dimes, quarters, much like the old coin dispensers

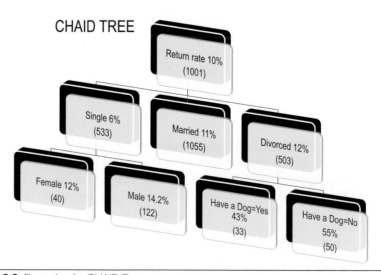

Figure 8.8 Example of a CHAID Tree
Source: Authors

that are rarely used these days). Coins usually differ in their diameter, and that can be used to devise a hierarchical tree system for sorting coins. Once we drop a coin into the coin sorter, based on its diameter, it is classified as a penny, nickel, dime, or quarter. The decision process used by the coin changer (or classification tree) provides an easy and common method for sorting a pile of coins, and it can be applied to a lot of different classification problems. Virtually all tree methods behave similarly.

Bayesian Networks

Bayesian network modeling is much more real world and realistic than results coming out of a regression network. One of the unique characteristics of the Bayesian networks is that they assemble themselves around the strongest patterns.

Applications

- Bayesian networks are used in a variety of situations such as aeronautics (guidance systems), public safety (nuclear power plants, police protection, etc.), medicine (cancer research, genetics research, etc.), national defense (persons of interest database, etc.). Originally, Bayesian networks were developed for scientists and researchers. Marketers are late in getting started using Bayesian (neural) networks – and they certainly lend themselves perfectly to text analytics.
- Bayesian networks have conditional probabilities and the change of any variable in a Bayesian equation impacts all the other variables in the equation. Bayesian networks can focus just on the variables that are strictly relevant to the "target" while getting rid of (ignoring) those that are not.

A "Markov Blanket" is a clustering of the most relevant variables that are the main elements of the analysis.[32] Bayesian models are difficult to run. Most software is expensive and hard to learn with a steep learning curve. Feature sets are very uneven across products, and some don't allow modifications of the network while others do, etc. Bayesian Models better model and predict the real world, which is why they are in many situations such as aeronautics, public safety, medicine, etc.

Example

There are known problems that would be very hard to solve without Bayesian math; take the yellow taxi/white taxi problem:

- In a city, there is an accident involving a white taxi cab.
- Someone witnessed the crash and reported the accident was caused by a white cab.
- In this city 85% of the cabs are yellow, and 15% are white.
- Police questioned the witness and determined they are 80% accurate in reporting the color of the cab.
- What are the odds the cab was white?
- The answer is 41.4%; in a Bayesian network, all the variables impact each other.

- To model the yellow taxi/white taxi problem with Bayesian math; build a network that links the actual color of the cab and the color that the witness saw with each being a network node.

It is beyond this book to cover Bayesian networks in-depth; we are simply alluding to them here because they are the best way to solve certain complex mathematical problems. For a simple introduction to naïve Bayesian networks see "5 Minutes With Ingo: Naïve Bayes".[33]

Clustering

Humans take different bits of information and group them in clusters (i.e., "foods we like", "people we like", "jobs we like", and so on). We cluster information when we look at landscapes and group the foreground, middle ground, and background; whereas, the landscape is much more complex, and our mechanism to cluster information is central to our ability to process the information and connect the dots in our mind and nervous system. Likewise, to derive meaning from textual data, we need to organize text data into groupings and then connect the dots. This paradigm of information retrieval and organization goes back to Marshall McLuhan's theory of media that the medium is the message, and the way we organize information profoundly impacts what we see and how we act on it. Some scientists believe that we do not see visual reality as it is. In fact, our brains simplify things to "hide the reality of what we are looking at", by not representing it literally. This is called "unconscious bias" – people tend to judge or process information based on preconceived information that will shape the outcome of newly processed information.[34]

Topic Analysis

There are any number of free text analytics tools that organize information, some of them surprisingly powerful, but in a narrow frame of data, limited to a small number of posts that are arranged to be processed by the tool. Topic analysis works best when the information is already cleaned and organized, but sometimes just running any text through topic analysis can reveal interesting patterns for further analysis, such as the cover page of *The New York Times*.[35]

The reader can try it by going to http://tweettopicexplorer.neoformix.com/#n=NYTimes and clicking on the various bubbles that are organized by the software into clusters. While the clustering is not based on the meanings of the sentences but rather the words used, it is an advance over simply looking at the text without structuring it.

Word Clusters and Similarity

The utility of word clusters is that they lump together words that reoccur more often than others. Clustering finds patterns of similarities in the sampled data (or the entire corpus being examples) between people or objects, creating groups in which every member of the cluster group is very like the other members, yet different enough from the members of other cluster groupings of words. Clustering of words is based on how closely the words are related (being the most similar). Text clusters are not particularly well suited to organize information in a useful way via similarity because we have first had to define what similarity means when we are seeking to organize the textual data for, and that is hard to do.

Ontologies

Ontologies show the relationships of words. Ontologies started becoming popular when object oriented programming (OOP) came into being in the late 1980s as the result of software programming platforms such as Unix and C/C++ that was prevalent at the time. Ontologies and OOP attempt to solve the same problem and provide self-contained data and the descriptors of the data so that it can be operated on as a unit, irrespective of where that operation takes place. Ontologies create a hierarchal order that applies context to words. Context is needed to derive meaning, so ontologies are relevant, especially having the right ones in place for the data being analyzed. Ontologies solve a problem we frequently see in text analytics, where a word or phrase has multiple meanings, and by using the best ontology, meaning is derived that is more accurate.

The following provides an example of the same words being interpreted differently based on their context in a sentence:

- **Low down payments** are desirable.
- She provided us with the **low down on which payments** to process.
- **Low down payments** are the least of his concerns.

Applying an ontology allows text analytics to determine the best meaning for specific words based on the other words they are surrounded by in a sentence.

Clustered Data Types

The information in ontologies on the web can fall within a few categories:

- **Nominal:** Values that are not numerically related and have no fixed scale – here's an example: Northeast =100, Midwest =200, Southwest =300, Northwest =400
- **Ordinal:** Numerical values that appear not to be related
- **Continuous:** Values that are numerical and have adhered to a fixed scale; can be an interval and/or ratio-based

OWL

OWL stands for the web ontology language, and it allows computers (software) to process content within information on the Internet before presenting it back to the reader. OWL is superior for this purpose to XML and other HTML mark-up languages that do not have the capability to process ontologies in the same way that OWL does.

Advice About the Clusters Used in Text Analytics

- K-means fails for useful text clustering
- Two-step clustering produces good cluster groupings
- A small number of cluster groups (3–5) works best

Hierarchical and K-Means Clustering Methods

Many of the high-powered text analytics tools use statistical engines to organize data. This type of software is not intended to be user-friendly. Statistical engines are useful (but not user-friendly) for a wide variety of enterprise data mining that can handle almost any type of data and run virtually any mathematical operation on it.

Iterative K-Means Clustering Algorithm

One of the most popular and useful way to organize information in the K-means algorithm.[36] K-means algorithm creates a specific number of groups (K) from a set of objects. It's a popular cluster analysis technique for exploring a set of data.[37]

K-means algorithm works in a similar manner to a simple coin changer that runs for as long as there are coins to sort. Algorithms are simply a set of instructions that are repeated over and over again on a set of data. The iterative part of the K-means algorithm uses the output of one state of the computation as the input of the next stage, continually re-running the K-means until the output and input no longer meaningfully change.

Many of the algorithms scientists use are based on simple operations; the challenge is to figure out the right algorithm(s) to use and how to organize the input and output. The main problem with using K-means clustering (See Figure 8.9) for marketing purposes is that the results often do not seem to be that useful; perhaps it is not the right approach to take (yet many vendors take that approach, which is why we are covering algorithms in this book).

So analysts and stakeholders run into a familiar problem with text analytics that is common with the other types of analytics we discuss in this book. Namely, while the algorithms and platforms are great, the amount of setup for the data to be usable (or useful) is often prohibitive. What we are saying is that K-means clustering works great if organizations are already organized and pre-digested the data, but if they haven't

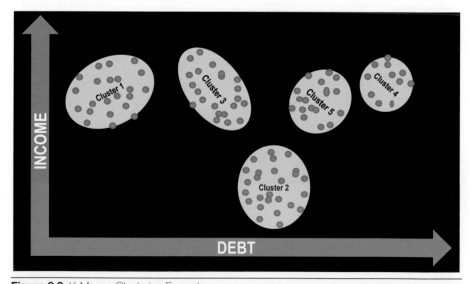

Figure 8.9 K-Means Clustering Example
Source: Authors

it may end up creating garbage clusters that aren't useful – and may be downright dangerous when used this way.

Choosing the right algorithm and running it effectively, is more of an art than a science at this point – K-means requires enough differences in the data that can be summarized to a few groupings, so it may be that K-means when used by marketers, is simply applied incorrectly by the marketing analysts (or whoever needs the output). Another point that has been made is that clustering data for marketing purposes is not the same as market segmentation: "Clustering is finding borders between groups; segmenting is using borders to form groups".[38]

Effective clustering requires analysts to have meaningful differences to form clusters with. But do they have meaningful differences? Are age, gender, and income meaningful differences to form cluster groups with? Not always. Increasingly, these clusters mean less and less – but that is the clustering most industry tools have settled on to build their platform reports; recipe for failure. K-means is a method to define market segments from a set of disparate data; whereas, marketers assume the data is grouped in the best way, even when that is not the case, and a better grouping exists, or should be created. The final point is with sampling the right frame – what if the data being clustered turns out not to be of significance for the marketing campaign? We could end up with segmentations (based on K-means) that aren't effective.

Cluster Analysis Representation

Once algorithms have been run, and we are satisfied with the results, then the fun part starts. Analysts must represent the data in a manner that makes visual sense to stakeholders; otherwise no one is going to understand the analysis!

Dendrograms

Clustering is not hierarchal or time sequenced – we live in a multidimensional world where there is hierarchy and sequence; what comes first, second, and third makes a difference, and some things are more important than others (just look at any organizational ORG chart). After clustering the data, we must organize it in a way that makes sense to stakeholders – enter dendrograms, tree clustering, and other visualizations.

- Dendrogram and tree clustering diagrams are produced by high-end statistical platforms, such as SAS Text Miner, IBM SPSS, Skytree, and even Google Analytics, etc.

Dendrograms may be an effective way of organizing text data but are not very popular with stakeholders and marketing executives.

Treemaps

Treemaps are produced by many kinds of software. Treemaps can also be broken down into subgroupings, which are also very useful. Statistical platforms produce word treemaps, but so do many web and audience analytics platforms such as Google Analytics.

Multidimensional Scaling

MDS is a statistical method that produces tables, such as the distances in miles between several cities.[39] High-end statistical platforms like IBM SPSS and SAS Text Miner and RapidMiner can produce MDS charts. While MDS works well for types of comparisons (such as distances in flight routes), it can also be used with text analytics (provided the data is manually reorganized by the analyst first).

Word Clouds

Word clouds are images composed of words, used in a text or subject, where the size of each word indicates its frequency or importance. Many text analytics platforms produce word clouds based on an analysis of the text examined.

- **Wordle and Neoformix:** Textual diagrams that shows how many times a word appears in a body of text
- **Clustering diagram:** Clumping words together in various ways using a statistical method called clustering
- **Tree diagram (dendrogram):** Analytical visual word map
- **Word clouds:** Text volume visual representation
- **Graph layouts of words:** Network of words showing interconnectivity
- **Heatmaps:** Show concentration of interest in the word map

Machine Learning: Supervised vs. Unsupervised Learning

There are two classes of machine learning techniques: supervised and unsupervised. In supervised learning, a model is created based on previous observations as a training set using a set of documents tagged by humans to be part of a category. Social media analytics tools like Crimson Hexagon work in this way. Once the classifier is trained, it can predict any given document's categories. Supervised learning classifiers are developed and used and score the input along predefined lines as shown in Table 8.2.

Supervised machine learning uses classifiers. When a classifier is fed new text (i.e., blog post, tweet, SMS message, call center record, etc.) to classify, it predicts whether the document belongs to a particular predefined category, and assigns a label for the document as well as a confidence score.[40]

SVM

SVM or support vector machine learning models are associated with machine learning algorithms that analyze data for text analytics. The SVM algorithm builds a model that assigns new examples into one category or the other, making it a non-probabilistic binary linear classifier.[41] Using SVM for text categorization comes down to an analyst or researcher's judgment call. For a simple video explanation of SVM, watch "5 Minutes with Ingo: Understanding Support Vector Machines".[42]

Table 8.2 Supervised Learning Example

Number	Color	Size	Shape	Fruit Name
1	RED	BIG	Oval shape with a depression on the top	APPLE
2	RED	SMALL	Globular, heart-shaped	CHERRY
3	GREEN	BIG	Cylinder that is long and curving	BANANA
4	GREEN	SMALL	Elongated oval shape appearing in a grouping that is usually cylindrical	GRAPE

Source: Authors

Unsupervised Machine Learning

Unsupervised learning is run when we are trying to discover patterns rather than trying to fit the data into the predefined structure. Clustering is an example of unsupervised learning. Unsupervised data assumes that nothing is initially known, and the software learns as it runs. Unsupervised machine learning differs because it is "not supervised by a human" and does not require a training dataset. Typically, the categories are not even known in advance. Unsupervised learning includes methods such as topic clustering and topic modeling (discussed earlier), and it is used automatically to find groups of similar documents within a collection of records. For example,

- **Analyze several corporate emails as part of a fraud discovery process**. At the beginning of the analysis, the analyst has no idea what the emails are about or topics they deal with, but we can use unsupervised machine learning to determine the most common topics present in the emails. Once the common topics are discovered in the email corpus, the analyst can then use K-means clustering algorithm to group the emails into a few distinct clustered categories.[43]

Classification Models Used in Supervised and Unsupervised Machine Learning

Classification models determine the way information is organized. The classification process involves organizing the text within a corpus of documents into categories for its most effective and efficient use.

- **Discriminant analysis** is used to classify text into clearly defined groups using statistical models.
- **Logistic regression** is like discriminant analysis but works better with data that doesn't clearly fitting into any category.

- **Classification trees** are a form of partitioning, organizing a space and are hierarchical (in some ways like ontologies we just covered in this section), and uses "if-then" rules.
- **Bayesian networks** represent the probabilistic relationships between a set of values and outcomes. For example, given certain conditions, the network can be used to compute the probabilities of the presence of various weather patterns.
- **Custom classifiers** are used when none of the common ways of classifying information are sufficient to classify the information for a task – in this case, creating a custom classification model makes the most sense.

Depending on what we are trying to accomplish, any one or a combination of the classification models mentioned in this chapter could be used.

Visual Text Analytics

Visual information is so much easier to absorb than text, and we are visual beings. Many of the same algorithms we have discussed in this chapter have been adapted and extended to deal with the visual realm (photos, videos, and live streaming).

Decoding Emotions in an Image

The software can decode basic emotions via text analytics (with differing accuracy) – now it's being done to images and video streams. Emotient is one of the companies at the forefront of visual emotion tracking and was acquired by Apple in 2015.[44] Apple likely planned to apply Emotient technology to Siri in later versions of the iOS operating system that runs on iPhones and iPads. Visual Analytics platforms that detect emotion are interesting to experiment with. However, the technologies need to improve and standardize before they can be deployed widely. Emotient had a demo anyone could use with their own computer cam, but once the company was acquired by Apple, the demo was removed. However, Emotient left a video on YouTube showing their emotion tracking demo.[45] There are several other vendors in the same space, such as imotions, which still offers a demo upon request.[46]

Visual Analytics Applications

This space is very dynamic, so there are always going to be new offerings – here are few we found interesting. For example, LaMem allows anyone to upload a photo, and the algorithm will determine how memorable it will be to a normal human viewer.[47]

Recommended Free Text Analytics Platforms

The following is a sampling of the free text analytics tools available at the time of publication for readers to experiment with:

- **MeaningCloud:** Install the free MeaningCloud Excel Plug-in[48]
- **Dandelion API** and a Google Spreadsheet Plug-in[49]

- **They Say API:** Paste some text below and then hit the button[50]
- **PINGAR Demos and API:** Explore the different features of the Pingar API for free[51]
- **Semantria for Excel:** Allows anyone to utilize sophisticated text analytics technology in free demo[52]

Recommended Paid Text Analytics Tools

- SAS Enterprise Miner/Text Miner[53]
- IBM SPSS[54]
- ODINText[55]
- Lexalytics[56]
- RevealedContext[57]

Common Text Analytics Terms

- **Natural Language Processing (NLP):** A field of computer science and artificial intelligence that focuses on interactions between computers and human language. Examples of NLP applications include Siri and Google Now.
- **Information extraction:** Extract structured information from: unstructured and/ or semi-structured data, such as text documents or webpages.
- **Named entity recognition:** Locate and classifying elements from text into predefined categories such as the names of people, organizations, places, etc.
- **Corpus:** Large collection of documents used to infer or validate grammatical rules, perform statistical analysis, and test hypothesis.
- **Sentiment analysis:** Use NLP to extract attitudinal information from a piece of text.
- **Disambiguation:** Identify the meaning of words in context using computational means (software). Example: use or develop an algorithm to determine whether when a reference to "Apple" in a verbatim (text) refers to the company Apple or to the fruit.
- **Bag of words:** Commonly used model for text classification; text (a sentence or a document) is represented as a bag of words with word order and word frequency used as a feature far training a classifier.
- **Explicit semantic analysis:** Understand the meaning of a text verbatim through a combination of the concepts found in that text.

Best Practices

- **Speed and scale iteration through software development:** NLP often requires a large set of data, much of it needs to be cleaned where multiple query steps feed one another.
- **A centralized location for both types of data and processing:** Most organizations have not figured out how to contain the data they collect so it can be worked on, even collecting it together so it can be processed is a challenge (since it is often collected and siloed for different reasons and needs).

- **Support for a wide variety of existing and emerging analytics tools:** This point directly addresses our textbook – there are so many new tools and methodologies that are developing, there is no possible way to stay entirely on top of all of them! Today, those toolsets include ETL, SQL, PL/Java, PL/Python, PL/R, Mahout, Graphlab, Open MPI, MADlib, Spring Data, Spring XD, MapReduce, Pig, Hive, web analytics, Tag Managers, and others. However, what will the toolset look like five years from now? It is hard to say as new platform tools are constantly being released.

Text Analytics Principles

1. Only work on a clear problem.
2. Be prepared to invest much more time preparing the data for analysis than initially planned.
3. Decide what is important and what is not.
4. Go for the simplest approach that explains what is important. Faulty analysis leads to faulty conclusions.

Text Analytics Issues

- Raw data needs to be cleared and organized before it will be useful for text analysis. For example, anything in social media might be considered data, but may or may not be useful.
- Regardless of the data out there to collect, unless there is a compelling reason to gather and study it, the data will usually not be collected or examined. That makes it easier to be good at finding and processing information that is valued and not so good at collecting and examining information that is less valued (or not valued).
- Text analytics requires a significant investment of time and resources. Software for text analytics ranges in price from free to enterprise level, with "enterprise level" being a secret code for "costing a lot of money". When there are great masses of text, usually there are also great masses of other types of data. One may need to invest in new storage, new hardware, and new software to handle this.
- There may be a need to hire additional people to deal with all the resources necessary to analyze text deeply.
- Even top text analytics researchers cannot program machines to correctly tag content in a document 100% of the time. The meanings of words in a document are contextual so that no matter how much the software is programmed, it cannot handle the variety of ways that people say things.
- There are some newer developments, such as adding emotion detection to text (i.e., Crimson Hexagon detects six emotions on Twitter data in its Buzz Monitors). However, such information, alone, will not be helpful until the data is filtered, cleaned, organized, and analyzed with very specific questions that connect to business goals. After all, programs will most likely take words literally unless there is some method to teach them to realize the entire context of the sentence. As analysts, authors, and professors, we have concluded that the biggest issue with text analytics isn't with the tools.

Sentiment Analysis Issues

Confusion Over Number of Emotions

Emotions are not standardized across different sentiment analysis software. Some vendors think people express six basic emotions (love, joy, surprise, anger, sadness, and fear, according to Parrott);[58] others suggest eight or 16 emotions will work better.

Opinions Cannot Be Accurately Extracted

Classifying a document or sentence as positive or negative in emotion does not add much value to analysis if we cannot tell what the opinion holder feels positively or negatively about.

Choosing a Text Analytics Solution

1. Determine if knowing more about a subject is going to make a difference in what actions an organization may take (if yes = proceed; if no = don't use text analytics in this context).
2. Determine budget: There are some free tools available, but they are not often that extensible or reliable, so a serious effort with text analytics should probably rule out free or low-cost software. Once consideration in platform tool choice is the form of the data that is going to be processed as not all platforms process all file/format types.
3. Determine how much data cleaning and reorganizing is going to be needed to make sense of the data.
4. Determine the right models and algorithms required to process the data – this is more of an art than a science since there are several ways analyze text (some are more effective for a given situation than others).

Why Many Organizations Are Not Using Text Analytics (Yet)[59]

1. Many organizations do not understand the value of the data in documents or how to extract it.
2. Researchers too often buy a technology solution when what they need is an insights solution.

Case Study: Tapping Into Online Customer Opinions

Founded in 1986, Frequent Flyer Services (Flyertalk.com) has created a unique niche for itself within the travel industry as a company that conceives, develops, and markets products and services exclusively for the frequent traveler. Its focus and distinctive competency lie in frequent traveler programs. Worldwide, these frequent traveler programs in the airline, hotel, car rental, and credit card industries have more than 75 million members who earn an excess of 650 billion miles per year. Flyertalk. com is one of the most highly trafficked travel domains. It features chat boards and discussions that cover the most up-to-date traveler information, as well as loyalty programs for both airlines and hotels. With millions of users generating millions of posts and comments, it wanted to tap into the explosion of customer opinions expressed online. Flyertalk.com knew that the feedback that current and potential customers provide on their website provided a rich source of feedback and was looking for ways to mine it. The answer to the problem faced by Flyertalk.com lies in text analytics.

The most innovative companies know they could be even more successful in meeting customer needs if they just understood them better. Text analytics is proving to be an invaluable tool in doing this. Flyertalk.com leveraged Anderson Analytics do the job. Anderson Analytics, a full-service market research consultancy, tackles this issue using cutting-edge text analytics and data mining software from SPSS that allows the application of scientific, statistical, and pattern recognition techniques to large text datasets. Note that the text analytics techniques applied, in this case, are not limited to discussion boards or blogs but can be applied to any text data source, including survey open ends, call center logs, customer complaint/suggestion databases, emails, and social media data, etc. A text analytics project is usually part of a much larger data mining project that would typically involve the identification of some core strategic questions, the allocation of resources and the eventual implementation of findings. However, the focus of this case study is to describe the tactical aspects of a text analytics project and to delineate the three basic steps involved in text analytics:

Step 1: Data collection and preparation
Step 2: Text coding and categorization
Step 3: Text mining and visualization

Step 1: Data Collection and Preparation

Having quality data in the proper format is usually more than half of the battle for most researchers. For those who can gain direct access to a well-maintained customer database, the data collection and preparation process is relatively painless. However, for researchers who want to study text information that exists in a public forum such as Flyertalk.com, data collection can be more complex and usually involves web scraping. Web scraping (or screen scraping) is a technique used to extract data from websites that display output generated by another program. Many commercially available applications can scrape a website and turn the blogs or forum messages into a data table. Here is how web scraping works.

The Web Scraping Process
- **Crawl:** Crawl the website and scrape for the topic, ID, and thread initiator.
- **Download:** Use topic ID from the first step as part of the URL query string to download messages.
- **Store:** The web crawls and stores message display pages.
- **Screen scrape:** Screen scraped web pages are extracted, and the data is stored in a structured format.
- **Link:** Link extracted posts with topics from the first step, along with other extracted fields to create the final dataset.

Even with the availability of powerful web scraping tools and techniques, text mining a popular blog or a message board like the one at Flyertalk.com presents unique data collection and processing challenges. The amount of free text available on such sites usually prohibits an indiscriminate approach to data scraping. A strategy with clear objectives and a clear data extraction method are needed to increase the reliability of data analysis in the latter stages of the research. In this case, researchers at Anderson Analytics narrowed the scope to just discussion topics within a 12-month period (from August 2005 to August 2006) on the five top forums intended for discussing the hotel loyalty programs of Starwood, Hilton, Marriott, InterContinental, and Hyatt hotels. Specific web scraping parameters differ depending on the structure of the target sites. In a discussion board format, the text data tend to follow a simple hierarchy. Typically, each forum contains a list of topics, and each topic consists of numerous posts, Therefore, the web scraping process of Flyertalk.com initially retrieves data, such as the discussion topics, topic ID, topic starter, and topic start date. Then, by using the topic ID, the web scraping application constructs and submits query strings to the Flyertalk.com site to retrieve messages associated with each specific topic. An excellent web scraping tool should allow the capture of information that exists in the source data of an HTML page, not just the displayed text. Therefore, hidden information such as the topic ID, date stamp, etc., also becomes available to the researcher. Besides making sure the fields in the final dataset are in the correct format, another problem unique to discussion board text needs to be addressed. It is very common for posters to quote others' text within their posts. These quotes should typically be extracted from the message field and placed in a separate field to prevent double counting and inadvertently adding weight to certain posts. In addition to the text messages posted on the forum, the web scraping process should also capture the poster's ID, and handle, as well as any other available poster information such as a forum, join date, and forum registration information (in this case: location, frequent traveler program affiliation, etc.).

Step 2: Text Coding and Categorization

Text coding and categorization is the process of assigning each text data record a numeric value that can be used later for statistical analysis. Text coding can apply either dichotomous code (flags and many variables) or certain codes (one variable for an entire dataset). Short answers to an open-ended survey question typically use certain codes. However, the amount of text included in most discussion board posts typically requires dichotomous codes. A typical text coding process has the following steps.

Text Coding and Categorization Process

- **Preliminary coding:** Use both computer and human coder to obtain the initial understanding of the data.
- **Initial classification:** Use SPSS Text Mining tool to perform initial categorization on a sample data set (1/100 of the entire dataset).
- **Computer classification:** Information and knowledge gained from the original concept extraction are used by the human coder to assist in computer categorization.
- **Coding and classification refinement:** Categorization and coding are an iterative process. Custom libraries are created to refine the process. Text extraction is performed multiple times until the number of and the details of categories are satisfactory.

- **Coding and extraction rules:** Once the coding result becomes satisfactory, the same coding and extraction rules are used on the entire dataset.
- **Categorization results:** Categorization results are exported for further analysis with tools such as SPSS Text Analysis.

Text coding is usually an iterative process, and this is particularly the case for coding messages on a site such as Flyertalk.com. Text information can be compared to survey answers. The text data on most discussion boards tend to be user-driven rather than provider-driven. Before creating categories, researchers at Anderson Analytics first randomly examine a sample of text messages to gain a basic understanding of the data. This step is required to understand the type of acronyms, shorthand, and terminologies commonly used ort the forum of interest.

SPSS Text Analysis for Surveys and Text Mining for Clementine are powerful tools. However, the text coding results can be significantly improved if the programs can be trained to better understand text information and topics of interest. With a list of industry-specific themes, concepts and words, the researchers at Anderson use tools such as SPSS Text Analysis for Surveys to create a custom dictionary. Then the SPSS text analytics applications can be utilized, in conjunction with an SPSS developed dictionary, to extract highly relevant concepts from the text data. In this case, examples of some of the basics in the messages that can be detected by the software include "rates", "stay", "breakfast", "points", and "free offers". The text extraction and categorization processes are repeated with minor modifications each time to fine-tune results.

Step 3: Text Mining, Visualization, and Interpretation

Depending on the needs of any given research project, the coded text data can be interpreted in many ways. In this case, the data is examined via the following methods:

Positive/Negative Comments and Overlapping Terms
The Flyertalk.com data indicates that negative discussions among the posters are centered on the payment process, condition/quality of the bathroom, furniture, and the check-in/out process. The praises seem to be centered on topics such as spa facility, complimentary breakfasts, points, and promotions.

Data Patterns within Different Hotel Brands
By comparing the coded text data of Starwood and Hilton forums, the researchers find that the posters seem to be relatively more pleased with beds on Starwood's board, but more satisfied with food and health club facilities on Hilton's board.

Longitudinal Data Patterns
As this study contains data from a one-year period, data can be analyzed to understand how topics are being discussed on a month-to-month basis. The data in this particular case revealed that the discussion about promotions on the Starwood board is especially frequent in February 2006. Cross-checking with Starwood management confirmed that special promotions were launched during that period. Text analytics is one way to measure the impact of various communication strategies, promotions, and even non-planned external events.

Analysis of Poster Groups

Web mining may clarify the aggregate motivation of some of the most active users of the products. Although it may be difficult to segment posters with only one post, frequent posters can provide a relatively comprehensive set of segmentation variables. In this case, some general motivational themes found were the need for "being in the know", "finding deals", and the desire to "give back".

Conclusion

Companies have discovered that they can compete far more efficiently if they gain a true 360-degree view of their customers. The feedback that current and potential customers provide in blogs, forums, and other online spaces provides a rich source of feedback. Using text analytics to monitor this information helps organizations gauge customer reaction to products and services and, when combined with analysis of structured transactional data, delivers predictive insights into customer behavior. This case described how text analytics was applied to information posted by users of travel and hospitality services, but the same techniques can be applied to other industries. A company might find, for example, that when it launches a special promotion, customers mention the offer frequently in their online posts. Text analytics can help identify this increase, as well as the ratio of positive/negative posts relating to the promotion. It can be a powerful validation tool to complement other primary and secondary customer research and feedback management initiatives. Companies that improve their ability to navigate and text mine the boards and blogs relevant to their industry are likely to gain a considerable information advantage over their competitors. Source: Anderson Analytics, LLC (www.andersonanalytics.com).

Review Questions

1. What is text analytics and why is it useful?
2. Differentiate between static and dynamic social media text.
3. Discuss different social media texts.
4. Explain the four main purposes of social media text analytics.
5. Explain the common social media text analysis steps.

Chapter 8 Citations

1. https://www.gartner.com/document/4346799?ref=solrAll&refval=366435729 – Quick Answer: How Should We Integrate the Use of ChatGPT into Our Automated Authoring Strategy? – Published 11 May 2023 – ID G00786759 – By Marko Sillanpaa, Stephen Emmott. Accessed June 2, 2023.
2. Redmore, S. "Text Analytics in 7 minutes." *Lexalytics*. April 27, 2016. www.lexalytics.com. Accessed May 30, 2023.
3. "5 minutes with Ingo: Making sense of Text Analytics." *YouTube*. March 18, 2015. www.youtube.com/watch?v=FsP3Z5ieos8. Accessed May 30, 2023.

4. "What is opinion mining (sentiment mining)?" *WhatIs.com*. http://searchbusinessanalytics.techtarget.com/definition/opinion-mining-sentimentmining. Accessed April 15, 2017.

5. "Identifying the political impact of US talk shows." www.qsrinternational.com/case-studies/impact-of-us-shows. Accessed April 15, 2017.

6. Hitlin, P. "Methodology: How Crimson Hexagon works." April 1, 2015. www.journalism.org/2015/04/01/methodology-crimson-hexagon. Accessed April 15, 2017.

7. Jurkowitz, M. and P. Hitlin. "Twitter users give Christie negative marks on bridge scandal." January 10, 2014. www.pewresearch.org/fact-tank/2014/01/10/twitter-users-give-christie-negative-marks-on-bridge-scandal. Accessed April 15, 2017.

8. "Demystifying #MachineLearning part 2." https://mymeediacom/stages/tech/post/24435859. Accessed April 15, 2017.

9. Bowden, G. "Bible and Quran, text analysis reveals 'violence' more common in Old and New Testament." *Huffington Post UK*. February 9, 2016. www.huffingtonpost.co.uk/2016/02/09/bible-and-quran-text-analysis_n_9192596.html. Accessed April 15, 2017.

10. Kalafatis, T. "Using data science on TripAdvisor reviews (Part 1)." July 19, 2013. www.smartdatacollective.com/themoskalafatis/135106/using-data-science-tripadvisor-reviews-part-1. Accessed April 15, 2017.

11. Huijnen, P. "From keyword searching to concept mining." December 4, 2015. https://pimhuijnen.com/2015/12/04/from-keyword-searchIng-to-concept-mining. Accessed April 15, 2017.

12. *Assessed from Google Books Ngram Viewer and* shortened via Bit.ly. http://bit.ly/compareDM-WA. Accessed April 15, 2017.

13. Woodie, A. "Predicting consumer behavior drives growth of Text Analytics." January 16, 2015. www.datanami.com/2015/01/16/predicting-consumer-behavior-drives-growth-text-analytics. Accessed April 15, 2017.

14. Press, G. "12 Big Data definitions: What's yours?" *Forbes*. September 3, 2014. www.forbes.com/sites/gilpress/2014/09/03/12-big-data-definitions-whats-yours. Accessed April 15, 2017.

15. Nguyen, C. "What 24000 Facebook confession posts tell us about college." June 23, 2015. http://motherboard.vice.com/read/what-24000-facebook-confession-posts-tell-us-about-college. Accessed April 15, 2017.

16. Watcher, B. "Natural language processing in health care: The breakthrough we've been waiting for." July 20, 2015.www.kevinmd.com/blog/2O15/07/natural-language-processing-in-health-care-the-breakthrough-weve-been-waiting-for.html. Accessed April 15, 2017.

17. Ellis, J. "The New York Times built a robot to help make article tagging easier." July 30, 2015. www.niemanlab.org/2015/07/the-new-york-times-built-a-robot-to-help-making-article-tagging-easier. Accessed April 15, 2017.

18. Elgammal, A. "Creating computer vision and machine learning algorithms that can analyze works of art." www.mathworks.com/company/newsletters/articles/creating-computer-vision-and-machine-learning-algorithms-that-can-analyze-works-of-art.html. Accessed April 15, 2017.

19. Brown, M.S. "Text & the city: Municipalities discover Text Analytics." January 16, 2014. www.allanalytics.com/author.asp?doc_id=271089. Accessed April 15, 2017.

20. Grimes, S. "Text Analytics 2014: Q&A with Fiona McNeill." *The Fluffington Post*. April 21, 2014. www.huffingtonpost.com/seth-grimes/text-analytics-2014-qa-wi_b_5146419.html. Accessed April 15, 2017.

21. Marshall, P. "NASA applies deep-diving Text Analytics to airline safety." *GCN*. October 26, 2012. https://gcn.com/articles/2012/10/26/nasa-applies-text-analytics-to-airline-safety.aspx. Accessed April 15, 2011.

22. Rose, S. "3 insurance business applications for Text Analytics." January 9, 2014. www.insurancetech.com/3-insurance-buslness-appllcations-for-text-analytics/a/d-id/1314975? Accessed April 15, 2017.

23. "Text, sentiment & Social Analytics in the year ahead." January 11, 2016. https://breakthroughanalysls.com/2016/01/11/10-text-sentiment-soclal-analytics-trends-for-2016. Accessed April 15, 2017.

24. Socher, R. "Parsing natural scenes and natural language with recursive neural networks." October 6, 2013. www.Socher.org/index.php/Main/ParsingNaturalScenesAndNaturalLanguageWlthRecursiveNeuralNetworks. Accessed April 15, 2017.

25. "Author age prediction from text using linear regression – Washington." http://homes.cs.washington.edu/~nasmith/papers/nguyen+smlth+rose.latech11.pdf. Accessed April 15, 2017.

26. Joshl, M., D. Das, K. Gimpel, and N.A. Smith. "Movie reviews and revenues: An experiment in text regression." www.cs.cnu.edu/~msheshj/pubs/joshi+das+glmpel+srrtlthjaacl.2010.pdf. Accessed April 15, 2017.

27. "Text analysis in incident duration prediction – MIT." http://ares.lids.mlt.edu/fm/documents/textanalysis.pdf. Accessed April 15, 2017.

28. Adwere-Boamah, J. "Multiple logistic regression analysis of cigarette use among high school students." www.aabn.com/manuscnpts/10617.pdf. Accessed April 15, 2017.

29. M.L. Newman, J.W. Pennebaker, D.S. Berry, and J.M. Richards. "Lying words: Predicting deception from linguistic styles." www.albany.edu/~zg929648/PDFs/Newman.pdf. Accessed April 15, 2017.

30. Ifrim, G., G. Bakir, and G. Weikum. "Fast logistic regression for text categorization with variable-length n-grams." August 24, 2008. http://dl.acm.org/citatlon.cfm?id=1401936. Accessed April 15, 2017.

31. "5 minutes with Ingo: Decision trees." *YouTube*. March 25, 2015. www.youtube.com/watch?v=xohJ1Vu-3xY. Accessed April 15, 2017.

32. "Startseite – Fachschaft Informatik." www.fachschaft.informatlk.tu-darmstadt.de. Accessed April 15, 2017.

33. "5 minutes with Ingo: Naive Bayes." *YouTube*. April 15, 2015. www.youtube.com/watch?v=llVlNQDk4o8. Accessed April 15, 2017.

34. Waugh, R. "Everything you see is illusion, scientist warns – and reality is MUCH weirder." *Metro*. http://metro.coi.uk/2016/04/25/everythlng-you-see-is-an-illusion-scientist-warns-and-reality-is-much-weirder-5838949. Accessed April 15, 2017.

35. "Tweet topic explorer – Neoformix." http://tweettopicexplorer.neoformix.com/ Accessed April 15, 2017.

36. "K-means algorithm demo." *YouTube*. May 2, 2013. www.youtube.com/ watch?v=zHbxbb2ye3E. Accessed April, 15, 2017.

37. "Top 10 data mining algorithms in plain English." May 2, 2015. http://rayli.net/ blog/data/top-10-data-mining-algorithms-in-plain-english. Accessed April 15, 2017.

38. "The difference between segmentation and clustering." *Mixotricha*. July 17, 2010. https://zyxo.wordpress.com/2010/07/17/the-difference-between-segmentation-and-clustering. Accessed April 15, 2017.

39. Young, F.W. "Multidimensional scaling." http://forrest.psych.unc.edu/teaching/ p208a/mds/mds.html. Accessed April 15, 2017.

40. "Text Analysis 101: A basic understanding for business users." January 20, 2015. http://blog.aylien.com/post/104768074963/text-analysis-101-a-basic-understanding-for. Accessed April 15, 2017.

41. "Support vector machine." *Wikipedia*. https://en.wikipedia.org/wiki/Support_ vector_machine. Accessed, April 15, 2017.

42. "5 Minutes with Ingo: Understanding support vector machine." *YouTube*. March 11, 2015. www.youtube.com/watch?v=YilWisFFruY. Accessed April 15, 2017.

43. "K-means clustering example (Python)." April 27, 2011. http://blog.mpacula. com/2011/04/27/k-means-clustering-example-python. Accessed April 15, 2017.

44. Winkler, R., D. Wakabayasií, and E. Dwosiln. "Apple buys artificial-Intelligence startup Emotient." *WSJ*. January 7, 2006. www.wsj.com/articles/apple-buys-artificial-intelligence-startup-emotient-1452188715. Accessed April 15, 2017.

45. "Emotient facial expression technology demo." *YouTube*. June 13, 2013. www. youtube.com/watch?v=7BiPZ1gHpEw. Accessed April 15, 2017.

46. "Request denlo." *iMotions*. January 6, 2017. https://imptlonsxqm/requestdeoq. Accessed April 15, 2017.

47. "LaMem.demo." http://memorability.csill.ilt.edu/demo.html. Accessed April 15, 2017.

48. "MeaningCloud text mining solutions." www.meaningcloud.com. Accessed April 15, 2017.

49. "Dandelion." https://dandelion.eu. Accessed April 15, 2017.

50. "API Demo." http://apldeoq,theysayio. Accessed April 15, 2017.

51. "Pingar API demos." http://apldemo.pingar.com/Default.aspx. Accessed April 15, 2017.

52. "Semantria sentiment analysis tools." www.lexalytics.com/semantria/excel. Accessed April 15, 2017.

53. "SAS Text Miner." http://suppqrt.sas.com/software/products/txtilner. Accessed April 15, 2017.

54. "IBM SPSS." www.ibm.com/analytics/us/en/technology/spss. Accessed April 15, 2017.

55. "OilnText." http://odintext.com. Accessed April 15, 2017.

56. "Lexalytics." www.lexalyilcs.com. Accessed April 15, 2017.

57. "Buyer beware: What Text Analytics providers won't tell you." *OdinText*. October 26, 2016. http://odintext.o0mbDlog/buyer-beware-what-text-analytlcs-providers-wont-tell-you. Accessed April 15, 2017.

58. "Emotions in social psychology." www.amazon.cam/Emotions-Soilal-Psychology-Key-Rea.is$/dp/0863776833. Accessed April 15, 2017.

59. "Buyer beware: What Text Analytics providers won't tell you." *OdinText*. October 26, 2016. http://oilntext.com/blog/buyer-beware-what-text-analytics-proilder-swont-tell-you. Accessed April 15, 2017.

Basic Web Analytics and Web Intelligence

CHAPTER OBJECTIVES

After reading this chapter, readers should understand the following:

- Web analytics versus big data
- Common tools used for analytics
- Intermediate metrics (Vanity Matrices) and web analytics
- Web analytics attribution models

Web Analytics

Web analytics, the practice of collecting and analyzing data from websites, continues to evolve with new technologies and techniques. Here are a few new and exciting aspects in the field of web analytics:

- **User journey analysis:** Web analytics now focuses on understanding the complete user journey across multiple touchpoints. It involves tracking and analyzing user interactions, behavior, and conversion paths across different devices and channels, such as websites, mobile apps, social media platforms, and offline interactions. This holistic view helps organizations optimize user experiences and identify areas for improvement.
- **Advanced analytics techniques:** Web analytics incorporates advanced machine learning and predictive modeling techniques. These techniques enable organizations to gain deeper insights, predict user behavior, personalize experiences, and optimize conversion rates. Organizations can make data-driven decisions to improve their digital strategies by leveraging large-scale data and advanced algorithms.
- **Customer segmentation and personalization:** Web analytics can segment website visitors into distinct groups based on their behavior, preferences, and demographics. This segmentation allows organizations to deliver personalized experiences, targeted marketing campaigns, and customized product recommendations. The goal is to provide tailored content that meets individual user needs, increasing engagement and conversions.

DOI: 10.4324/9781003025351-9

- **Real-time analytics:** Real-time analytics in web analytics is gaining importance. Organizations now have access to tools that can provide instant insights into website traffic, user behavior, and conversion rates. Real-time data allows for quick decision-making, timely optimizations, and immediate response to changing user patterns or trends.
- **Privacy and consent compliance:** With increasing concerns over data privacy, web analytics is adapting to new regulations and user expectations. Organizations are implementing privacy-friendly practices, obtaining user consent, and ensuring compliance with data protection laws, including anonymization of data, transparent data usage policies, and user-friendly consent management mechanisms.
- **Cross-channel attribution:** Attribution modeling has become more sophisticated, considering the impact of multiple marketing channels and touchpoints on conversions. Organizations strive to understand each channel's contribution to the user journey, both online and offline, to allocate resources effectively and optimize marketing strategies.
- **Voice and mobile analytics:** As voice assistants and mobile usage continue to rise, web analytics is expanding to include voice and mobile analytics. It involves tracking and analyzing user interactions, searches, and conversions on mobile devices and voice-enabled platforms, providing insights into user behavior in these emerging channels.

These new developments in web analytics reflect the need to adapt to changing user behaviors, technological advancements, and privacy considerations. They provide organizations with deeper insights, more accurate measurement, and enhanced personalization capabilities to improve their digital presence and drive business growth.

The Most Common Web Analytics Use Cases

- Optimize websites website performance against specific marketing goals and initiatives.
- Maximize the marketing placed on websites.
- Learn how site navigation, content, and aesthetics affect the bottom line, which should align with business goals.
- Learn from past marketing efforts on a website.
- Optimize future campaigns to increase conversion on a website.
- Recommend website or marketing changes based on an analysis of website behavior.
- Implement site changes or recommend changes to those in authority to do so.

Why Study Web Analytics?

Note: Since the first edition was published, the web analytics ecosystem continued to evolve and change with Google Analytics becoming the dominant web analytics platform, and it is accessible to most users in a free version for use and for learning purposes. As the current version of Google Analytics (Google Analytics 4.0) has a functioning e-commerce sandbox that connects to an actual website (The Google Merchandise Store), we will focus more heavily on Google Analytics when we discuss web analytics.

According to Avinash Kaushik, a prominent analytics evangelist for Google and co-founder of MarketMotive, a digital training consultancy, marketers use online data to address fundamental business problems by leveraging data relevant to their business.[1] Below is information about web analytics that marketers use to help them understand its foundation and capabilities:

- In the past, business owners and stakeholders depended on interpretative and proxy-driven success measurements. An example of a proxy success measure would be a click. It is often used as a measure that shows interest in a digital campaign. Using web analytics, business users can use data to measure success, instead of blind faith because the amount of capturable data has grown significantly.[1]
- The web provides access to an infinite amount of data at a low cost. By adding a tag to a website, anyone can collect an enormous amount of consumer behavioral data from a site, which provides a thorough understanding of successful and poor digital marketing strategies.
- Web and data analytics provide qualitative and quantitative data about monitored websites and customers, including customer intent for the organization and, at times, competition and desired outcomes for online and offline business goals. With these insights, there can be continuous improvement aligning websites with stated business goals.
- Web and digital analytics is a broad field that covers more than websites. It is no longer sufficient to group people into segments based on the web analytics supplied demographics or behaviors (via DoubleClick). Analysts are expanding their skill set to include R, Python, statistical programs such as IBM SPSS, and visualization platforms such as Tableau. It is more likely that in the foreseeable future AI chatbots will become more prevalent in web analytics platforms and reports. These chatbots are equipped with the ability to detect patterns and convey intricate information in a way that resembles human conversation and meaning. As a result, they are becoming more widely available. It's highly probable that this feature will be utilized more frequently in web analytics platforms in the coming years.
- Web and digital analytics are not part of big data.[2] Web analytics databases are structured by the platform vendors (via a consensus that evolved as the first web analytics appeared in the mid-1990s as illustrated in Figure 3.3 in Chapter 3 – it has been extended as the platforms take on more capabilities) to allow business owners and data analysts to understand a business better and to report their findings clearly and more efficiently to the right people. Conversely, big data must be cleaned, organized, and structured before it becomes useful for most applications.

When people speak about big data, it is usually unstructured or semi-structured data. Web analytics takes the raw data collected from a visitors' web browser and structures it into reporting suites (considered part of an organization's first-party data) for easy access and use for analysts and stakeholders, as illustrated in Figure 9.7 later in this chapter. Web analysts operate on structured data in reporting suites and produce detailed reports of website and marketing performance using segmentation against preset business and website goals. Web analysts do not need to be programmers, whereas with big data, it is a requirement.

In comparison, data scientists work with large sets of semi-structured and unstructured data (big data) to create interactive and predictive analytics intelligence against marketing goals, Data scientists must program in Python, R, or use IBM SPSS, SAS or another high-end statistical platform. In addition to the programming skills, data scientists need massive amounts of data to work with and run algorithms on. Web analysts work with the first-party data that is collected and structured for them and requires a different skill set, including business knowledge and business communications skills. However, web analysts and data scientists share a passion for data; it's just a different set of data.

Web analytics and big data are closely related. Both are solutions that deal with the complexity of data that is being generated and collected and provide stakeholders with information that leads to actionable results. Ideally, an analyst should be able to operate across the spectrum of analytics (see Figure 9.1).

Commonly Used Software Platforms Supporting Web Analytics

There are several free or inexpensive platform tools commonly used with web analytics. These tools are modular and easy to learn (for those who like to program). Below are commonly used platform tools for digital analytical projects:

- **R:** Statisticians and data miners use the R programming language for developing statistical software and data analysis. R's popularity has increased substantially in recent years. It has become one of the most commonly used languages for data analytics and big data projects.
- **Python:** Python is a high-level dynamic programming language that allows programmers to create software with a minimum of programming code.

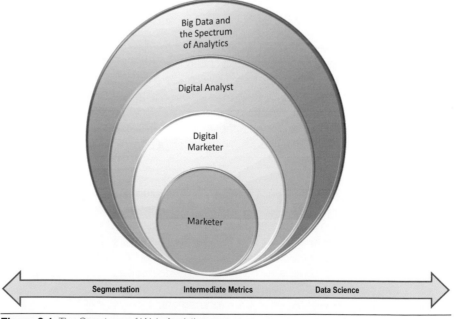

Figure 9.1 The Spectrum of Web Analytics
Source: Marshall Sponder

- **IBM SPSS:** SPSS (Statistical Package for Social Science) is a statistical package that can perform highly complex data manipulation and analysis with simple instructions.
- **Tableau:** Tableau is a standard data visualization platform for enterprise data.
- **Perl:** Perl is a high-level, general-purpose programming language that is used especially for developing web applications.

A Peek into the Future of Web Analytics, Circa 2026

Over the next few years, AI-based tools and chatbots are expected to become crucial components of web analytics platforms. These technological advancements have the potential to revolutionize these platforms, introducing various tools that are likely to become standard by 2026. AI can analyze vast quantities of data, predict customer behavior, and identify anomalies in web data. By analyzing past and current data, AI algorithms can forecast future trends, enabling businesses to plan their strategies effectively. AI chatbots can use natural language processing to interpret queries in a conversational way, making these platforms more accessible to non-technical users. AI can help create more complex and dynamic customer segments by learning from user behavior and demographics and adjusting these segments in real time. By 2026, new tools like explainable AI, voice-activated analytics, AR/VR technologies, and real-time AI coaching could be developed.

The Evolving Data Analytics Curriculum

Today, web analytics comprises of a mature set of web services and databases, continues to evolve, and that is particularly true about Google Analytics 4, which is the newest version of Google Analytics – and new features are added or changed on a very frequent basis. As a result, periodically we can expect that some of the information contained may look or behave differently when the reader uses Google Analytics 4 a year or two from now (or even a few months after this textbook is published).

The massive growth of online business has created the need for individuals that can measure the impact of digital marketing initiatives. Web analytics is expanding to cover more courses in the marketing curriculum at colleges and universities, including new courses that focus on big data and innovative uses of technology to improve business results. Many universities are adding digital analytics curriculum. Overall, in the workplace and at educational institutions, the consensus is that:

- Web analytics as a crucial skill for marketers in today's market and the value delivered by web analytics depends on how aligned an organization's business requirements are to the planning and initial setup of the web analytics platform installation. Most of the planning and setup information shared in this chapter can be used with any web analytics platform. However, this chapter focuses on Google Analytics 4. By extension, as Google owns the most popular web analytics platform and the most popular browser (Chrome), the best way to implement and test Google Analytics 4 is with the Chrome web browser; any of the examples that we examine in this chapter are best viewed in the Chrome browser.
- Digital marketing is a framework that needs to remain flexible enough to change and grow as digital and marketing technologies advance. That said, in order

to have a successful web analytics implementation, analysts and stakeholders need to confer and plan how the platform setup will proceed and what it must contain; this planning and documentation is a vital part of the implementation that must not be skipped; otherwise their value from that implementation will not be realized.

- With the right exposure, skills, and understandings, readers who are interested in perusing a career that includes web analytics activities have a better shot at finding great jobs and careers.

Requirements for Effective Web Analytics Deployments

To be effective with web analytics, it takes specific, organizational business context at a detailed level, combined with an understanding of how to use the analytics for high performance. Deep knowledge of business operations is required to harvest accurate analytics reporting that generates desired business results.

Guidelines to keep in mind when solving analytical problems include:

- Obtaining the right data to answer defined business questions. In fact, web analytics is a subject that can't be approached intuitively (yet). Like a highly tuned instrument, before you can get anything useful from any web analytics platform you need to understand how it functions and what inputs and outputs are required for optimal functionality in your environment; otherwise you will not be able to show value for the investment into these platforms to stakeholders of your organization (even if that stakeholder is reader!).
- Understanding a company's operation at a detailed enough level so that its data can be correlated with the business's digital activities. It starts with understanding the environment of the organization that is being examined are working, including how the organization functions and what they value the most.
- Based on the aforementioned, create a measurement plan (the measurement plan is often contained in an Excel table or a Word document with one or more tables included in it).
- Come up with a series of questions that need to be answered via web analytics – this can come from stakeholders/clients or analysts/clients, or even from the reader – you need specific questions to answer; otherwise there is no direction and not much use for the web analytics platform.
- In addition, should the web analytics platform be improperly configured to answer the majority of the questions that are going to be asked about website or app performance, then what good is it? That said, a good implementation plan may require several meetings with interested stakeholders until enough of the right kind of information is gathered where it makes sense to move forward with the analytics implementation.

Note: Third-party platforms such as Shopify that are focused on specific types of e-commerce activities may not require as much planning to set up because the analytics tracking is intergraded into the product databases. For example, if items (SKUs) are added to a web store all the needed tracking code is automatically put in place. It follows that features such as customer heatmaps and customer session recording can be easily integrated to a web store with other third-party software plugins such as HotJar, and so on. The point being made here is that web analytics can be a much more integrated experience when it is already built into the operations of certain types of websites that are built on top of e-commerce platforms.

What we are saying is that at the current moment, using a web analytics platform such as Google Analytics 4 or Adobe Analytics might be overkill if the business doesn't actually need that level of complexity. We are also putting forward the idea that general purpose web analytics platforms such as Google Analytics 4 can meet almost any use case organizations may require, especially if one uses the enterprise version and the full Google Marketing Cloud, but that doesn't mean that they are optimized for every use case. Just the reverse, to implement the level of tracking that Shopify provides an e-commerce website business would take much more work to replicate and maintain in enterprise web analytics platforms, such as Google, Adobe Analytics, or WebTrends.

- Delivering the reporting and insights to the right people, along with the right visualizations and language to garner the best responses.
- Before the web analytics implementation on a website(s) analysts and stakeholders must already know what is going to be tracked (and the analyst should already understand the nature of the questions that are going to be asked by stakeholders) and from the reporting data of the web analytics platform that will be monitored. Once a well-structured planning document is ready, the analyst should be able to answer the majority of the questions stakeholders in their organization will want answers to, providing part of the value that comes from a well-planned and implemented web analytics property.
- As many organizations are frequently putting into place ambitious development and web coding, implementing everything into the web analytics properly all at once is a mistake and it's better to prioritize what need to be tracked first and implement the tracking of those things, and then gradually introducing additional tracking on a manageable schedule.
- As always, all web analytics tracking code needs to be tested in order to verify that is working properly, and usually this is an iterative process, so allow enough time for that iterative process to properly play out.

Web Analytics: Path of Value

While web analytics provides great business value once it is set up well, there some things it is above to do very well and other things it cannot do, at all. It is important for that stakeholders' expectations are managed realistically when a web analytics platform is first implemented there is a list of functions it can do and others it cannot.

What digital web analytics is and what it can do

- Analyze data from a website or mobile app or something else in order to improve business outcomes
- Analytics can tell us what, when, where something interesting happened on a website or application, but not why it happened. For example, analysis of some, but not all questions a business has, such as what happened that resulted in a change of amplitude or frequency of data that is captured from a website or mobile application and where the source of the change came from. Unfortunately, most of the time digital or web analytics cannot determine why some event or change happened (which is usually a key piece of information the stakeholders want).

- Some third-party tools such as Microsoft Clarity can be combined with web analytics to better understand the "whys" and "where" of the root cause of changes happening on the website or application.

What digital web analytics is not, and what it cannot yet do

- Analyze data from the same sources only because we think it's interesting.
- Digital web analytics usually cannot tell us *why* an event or interesting thing that we are monitoring in the platform is happening (it cannot know the ultimate source and cause of the things being analyzed because it is beyond the scope of what analytics was designed to collect – this usually needs a human to connect the dots, when possible, back to the ultimate cause of an event or interesting change on the website or app).

The Goal as an analyst/vendor is **to create as clear a mental picture of how the organization operates as they can, as this contributes to the value the analyst or reader adds. If the analyst or reader can't get these answers, they will not be able to provide much value to the information and the organization that employs them will not be as happy with what they are getting. As if that wasn't enough, the analytics implementation probably won't work as well, either.**

A one-hour kick-off meeting is probably the best place to start, where a basic question can be brought to the table with the client/stakeholder/customer. The customer might not at this point have all the information required for web analytics implementation but we have to start somewhere.

What the analyst or reader could ask a client about, initially:

- **Ask about products and services the business offers as well as what makes this unique or better than** the average product or service of this kind, getting them to talk about why the offerings are better than what is already in place in the marketplace (this is something that the analyst or reader should take notes on).
- **Who does the customer/client believe their audiences are?** Whom are their audience comprised of now, and break it down by age, occupation, country, and region. See how this information can be fit in with the web analytics implementation because all of this information is necessary to create segmentation and target it properly, and even name it properly so it can be presented seamlessly into reporting later on.
- **Customer journey reporting:** Most organizations have done this research or paid for it by a third party, and it consists of a series of diagrams of how the organization gets its customers and what touch points does that place. Often, Customer Journeys are created though combining first and third-party data, such as web analytics, customer surveys, market research data, focus groups, and the people who put that together have studied how to do this, and they do this for multiple clients. Sometimes the organization does it internally, but it's usually better if it is done by an outside vendor who has expertise and does this for many, many organizations. Perhaps, the reader will want one of these customer journeys for each segment that was earlier identified in your questioning (or questionnaire, though this information is best done if it is orally facilitated by the outside vendor doing the customer journeying for the organization). The information gained will inform web analytics tracking put in place along with advertising that will be aligned

to the touch points that go with each customer journey – that's why analysts need this information before implementation of the analytics, if possible.

- **Marketing initiatives:** The analyst/reader needs to know any search advertising, including paid marketing, YouTube advertising, affiliate marketing, print advertising, offline (i.e., signboards, TV ads, flyers, etc.) that are running or will be run while the web analytics is being set up. They also want to know about organic search optimization and how that is going, and what's been done up to this point. While no special setup needs to be done for organic search, Google Analytics 4, for example, is able to provide statistics on visibility and CTR on search results in its own Google search engine, so it is good to know what SEO has been done or is planned during the implementation stage of the web analytics. Get the client to talk about what has worked for them with their advertising efforts and what didn't work.
- **How the organization currently uses their web analytics:** Ask the client organization how they use web analytics at the current time, as usually organizations have some sort of analytics in place even before you set your foot in the door! Ask what the client looks at the web analytics for (what information), and if they are happy with what they are getting out of their current analytics setup. Ask the client organization what they *want to get out of their web analytics* and what they expect you, the vendor/analyst to produce for them.
- **Ask if there are any customer** surveys the organization has done of their users (probably a customer email list is a good place to start). Let the organization share their findings as this may help in planning the web analytics implementation.
- **Is there already a web analytics team in place?** They have an analytics team or person in place (usually they do, in fact, that might be the person you are collecting the information from in your initial call with the client organization).
- **Ask about the web development** team and how it is structured.
- **Ask about anything else that comes to you** mind that you might want to know about the organization that could come into play with how the web analytics is implemented.

Once all the previously presented information is collected and put into some structured format where it is easy to update, any additional needed information can be covered on a follow-up call.

And in that next follow-up call, additional information could be collected such as

- History of the organization or company the analyst is doing this analytics enablement for and when and where it was established.
- Structure of the organization and the number of employees, offices, departments (this information can be important for campaign reporting, departmental reporting, setting up Zones in GTM, and many other things, so it is an important area to delve into).
- What is the role of the people who the analyst is conducting interview with – they are probably going to become the main stakeholders of the analytics enablement project, initially? Knowing the role and influence that the stakeholder has in the organizational hierarchy, org chart will help keep the analyst out of trouble with others in the organization that may feel threatened by the analytics project, etc.
  - **Note**: Often, there is a suspicion that other groups in an organization may have about people on the web analytics team, as they may fear that their previously well performing business unit results will be unfavorably portrayed by the web analytics team.

- At times, there can be open hostility towards the reports that web analysts share during organizational meetings as many stakeholders do not understand or trust the data, and often the reports are unfavorable or simply unhelpful.
- As if that wasn't bad enough, often other business units and stakeholders in an organization who both need the analytics for their own reports and decision-making, often submit their requests at the very last moment and don't allow enough time for web/business analysts to pull the data, arrange it properly, analyze it, and deliver a report that the stakeholder understands and can act on.
- For those reasons, knowing where the stakeholders or business sponsors of a web analytics enablement process are vital, as a project that doesn't have a strong executive sponsorship, it likely will not succeed. The co-author has heard this story many times even now and has lived it as well.

- You want to also know who is the one that makes the decisions about the implementation of the web analytics, that will be your most important stakeholder, initially, including what goals they are looking to reach with the web analytics implementation(s).
- Many organizations are created through mergers and acquisitions, and therefore, there are URLs that were previously used that might still be out there, and it is good to know about that, as sometimes there are still analytics connected to those old URLs, believe it or not!
- Just as with any project, analysts should collect the stakeholders and business sponsors' short- and long-term goals, including where they see this analytics implementation in six months, a year, and five years from now.
- Ask why the business website was created in the first place and if it has met its goals or not.
- Ask what the organization or business is best known for and if it is price, quality or service related.
- Ask what their KBRs are (Key Business Requirements) and their mission statement and vision statement.

As one reads these set of questions, it becomes clear and a serious implementation (i.e., enterprise levels) is complicated the time and costs associated with gathering the needed information are easy to underestimate. Typically, it could take as much as five to ten meetings before there is enough information to know what it makes sense to implement for the client, and of course, what the client is willing to foot the bill for.

Some have envisioned the field of web analytics as being functionally like a stack of dominos. One of the co-authors built his web analytics course on the Domino or Gartner model[3] as it seemed to be the most comprehensive of those examined.[4]

However, new maturity models appear with regularity, and there may be better ways to organize web analytics topics in the future. According to David Loshin, who writes at Data-Informed on issues related to evaluating and implementing big data analytics in business: "Executing this sequence in alignment with organizational needs requires people who can champion new technologies while also retaining a critical eye to differentiate between hype and reality".[5]

Defining the Five-Step Web Analytics Process

According to Avinash Kaushik, failure in digital marketing campaigns occurs when the real purpose of the campaign is not clear. Too often, business goals are unclear or are missing, so the success or failure of a campaign is undeterminable.[6]

How to Determine an Organizations Business Goals of An Organization for Analytics Enablement

- Find out (though meeting sessions) what the organizations business goals and look for those goals where web analytics can assist (not all business goals can be informed by web analytics, and we really need to determine which goals can be assisted by web analytics and those that cannot be).
- Once the business goals are defined and determined to be informed by the web analytics, its then time to ask the stakeholders how those goals will be met, going from the general to the more specific examples.

  - Business goals can be played out broadly and then made to become more specific (tactics).
  - Stakeholder and analytics project sponsors need to the source of the information used to configure the web analytics, it should never come from the analyst or their group.

- Once the business goals are defined and gathered by the analyst or analytics team, they should be written down in a document that is accessible to all stakeholders and be used to guide the initial implementation (or update, when there is already an existing web analytics implementation is in place which is being modified or added to).

Creating SMART Goals:

- SMART goals are an easy way to assemble goals that work.
- SMART goals are *specific* (i.e., set goals by X, Y, Z percent, or upset product Y to get more sales, offer a specific way to get more leads, etc.).
- SMART goals should be *measurable* (numbers, percentages).
- SMART goals should be *smart* goals should be *achievable* (a realistic target, such as growing revenue three times more than the normal rate may not be realistic based on the normal growth rate of the business revenue, and a more realistic revenue growth should be selected).
- SMART goals should be *relevant* in that it aligns with the business and its values, and relates to the market the business operates in. (i.e., if your client is a law firm, and they want to generate 100K new Twitter followers, will this actually increase their revenue? Perhaps, but in most cases this Twitter number is a vanity metric and not relevant to the main business goals of a law firm).
- SMART goals should be *time-bound*. There is a deadline and the goal needs to be reached before or by that deadline (for example, increasing revenue by X% needs to happen in specific defined period of time).

Below are the guidelines marketers need when creating a campaign:

- Identify the business objectives at the beginning of a project.
- Associate goals for each business objective.
- Define key performance indicators (KPIs) related to each business objective.
- Identify target values for each KPI.
- Determine the segments of people/behavior/outcomes to analyze why the project succeeded or failed.

Web analytics implementations in organizations that already have distinct business processes in place are usually more successful. The reason is obvious: when business processes are poorly defined, they are much harder to instrument and measure.

Focusing on Strategy – Deciding What Is Worth Counting (and How to Count)

As shown in Figure 9.2, a successful web analytics implementation moves down a path beginning with an overall strategy to lower level tactical business targets that can be measured. Later, the results are contemplated and communicated with midlevel managers, generating digital strategies and key performance indicators that impact stated business objectives. Finally, once the measurements are defined and campaigns implemented, analysts define behavior segments and business targets, as part of their day-to-day operations, to achieve the larger, stated goals.

Figure 9.2 is an example of a well-defined analytics and business strategy for a voter registration drive that an organization in that activity can operate with.

The Cycle of Improvement

The "Cycle of Improvement" (refer to Figure 9.3) is the continuous improvement cycle that businesses operate in, as market conditions, competition, and technology change. There are cycle charts for search engine optimization and search engine marketing that work in a similar way. The digital measurement process involved in the cycle of improvement includes mobile, social, campaign, survey, competitive, and offline data, such as closed sales from online leads (see Figure 9.4).

Key Business Requirements (KBR) vs. Key Performance Indicators (KPIs)

KPIs are a way to determine if an organizations business goals are being achieved or not (during a defined period of time), that's all they are, no need to mystify it. Once an organization defines their business goal(s), they need a method to determine if the

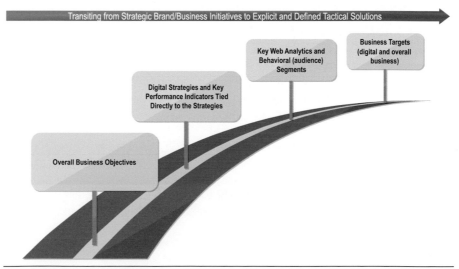

Figure 9.2 Moving From Objectives to Digital Strategies
Source: Marshall Sponder

Table 9.1 Measuring a Voter Marketing Initiative From Start to Finish

	Strategy A: Generate Awareness	Strategy B: Sign up Volunteers Who Are or Plan to Be Likely Voters	Strategy C: Generate Donations to Enact "Get out the Vote"
Overall business objective: Improve the relationship between voters and representative government in the United States.	*Objective A:* Launch a website dedicated to reaching active voters	*Objective B:* Use the website to recruit likely voters (get them on a consumer, customer list)	*Objective C:* Increase the collection of donations on the website
KPIs: Frequency, recency and time spent from web analytics	KPI: # of potential voters who signed up (via web analytics)	KPI: Revenue collected in USD (via shopping cart)	
KPIs: Social media metrics such as shares, followers, fans, pins, etc.	KPI: # of potential voters who respond (via webform/ email)	KPI: Donation size (goal is to increase it)	
KPI: Watch specific videos created to generate awareness and buzz	KPI: # of potential voters who have signed up by specific state voting districts	KPI: Respond to an email pledging to vote in the next election	

Source: Authors

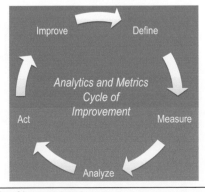

Figure 9.3 Analytics Cycle of Improvement
Source: Marshall Sponder

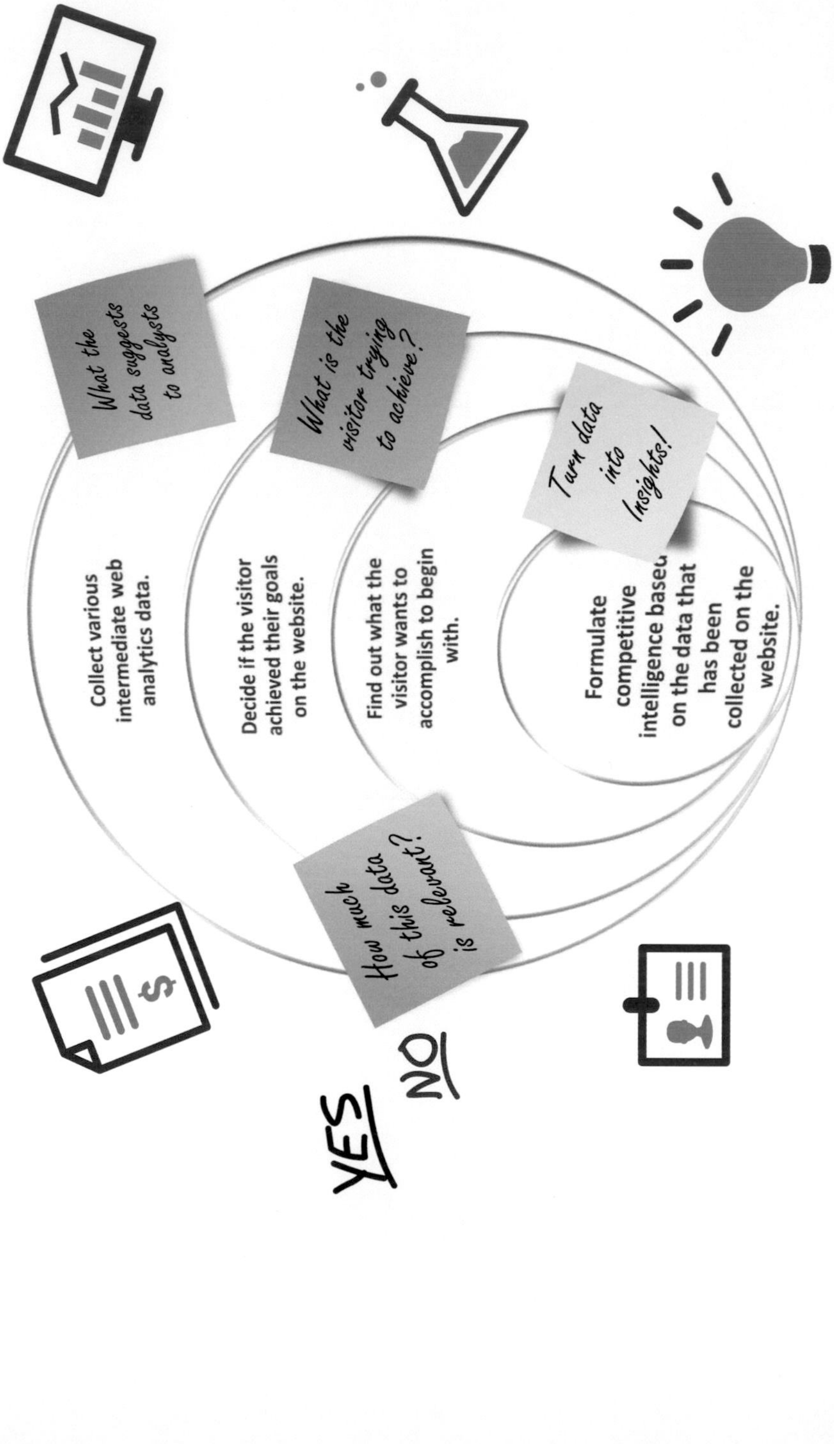

Figure 9.4 Moving From Web Analytics Data to Business Insights

Source: Marshall Sponder

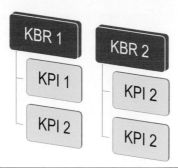

Figure 9.5 KBRs and KPIs
Source: Marshall Sponder

business(es) are meeting their business goals (performance based). The best way to know if an organization is meeting their business goals is to imagine the data that would be needed to ascertain if the organization is meeting its defined business goals. Each KPI chosen must be measurable (something that can be captured in a web analytics report, ideally) and directly tied to one or more specific business goals (for example as shown in Table 9.1). Metrics in and of themselves can be or could not be useful, it all depends if the metric can meaningfully be part of KPI that is tied to a business goal or not. Web analytics metrics, for example, would not be of much use for digital analytics if they are not tied to a specific business goal.

People working in any specialty tend to get involved with the terminology and lexicon commonly used in that community. For marketers, individuals involved in analytics planning and implementation tend to communicate using certain terms such as KBRs and KPIs. Key performance indicators (KPIs) are the digital measurements marketers use to track progress, whereas key business requirements (KBRs) reflect the business requirement or goal that the processes are meant to realize. For instance, referring to the schema shown in Figure 9.5, if KBR 1 is a business requirement to encourage types of member content to be shared more often, then the implementation of the share button and the number of times it is clicked on becomes one of the KPIs that informs KBR 1.

KPI EXAMPLE:

- Are page views per session that can be supplied by any web analytics platform a good KPI or not? (It depends.)
- If the business goal is to acquire more business leads that lead to more product sales, then page views per session would not be a particularly useful KPI. In this case, there is not a clear correlation between pages viewed per session of a business lead and sales that resulted from viewing those pages.
- But if the business is a type like a news website, where a major source of revenue is page views where there are ads displayed on those pages, then page views per session might be a great KPI (metric) in this case.
- Different businesses tend to have KPIs that are more typically use for that kind of business and vice versa.

People have strong opinions about these lexicons. Gary Angel, author of *Measuring the Digital World: Using Digital Analytics to Drive Better Digital Experiences*, expresses his opinion about traditional KPIs many marketers use: "The challenge with KPIs is *most of the standard digital metrics are almost useless* to make marketing decisions because they were designed to measure the wrong things and do it in the wrong way".[7]

Angel stated his belief that "our reality is constrained by the tools we experience it with", and addresses his concerns about the accuracy of web analytics platforms. He is brazen about his opinion because web analytics platforms do not represent the activities or outcomes most marketers care about. Instead, they provide diagnostic readouts. Marketers should be skeptical of various marketing platform analytics because most do not reflect the true needs of most marketers or customers.

Below are reasons why web analytics fall short of marketers' standards:

- The first digital analytics tools were built to read weblogs, not to measure the digital world. Though the capabilities of the tools have improved the basic views they provide, they have not changed much, according to Angel.[7]
- Humans build the websites for specific purposes. Web analytics tools are not able to determine the purpose of a website. If they could, analytics reports would be more useful.

Mapping KBRs to KPIs (as shown in Figure 9.5) is an essential part of getting the value from web analytics deployments. Using web analytics effectively requires that stakeholders and analysts exercise a degree of introspection" – to understand what the real needs are and a useful way to measure the process of getting those needs met (refer to Table 9.2).

Table 9.2 illustrates how to formulate the goals or KBRs shown on the left, for the website (which should include mobile apps), along with the specific conversion events

Table 9.2 Mapping Key Business Requirements to Key Performance Indicators in Web Analytics

Key Business Requirement	Conversion Event	Key Performance Indicators
Increase revenues (online)	Finish checkout process	Purchase, checkout initiation rate, buyer conversion rate, order conversion rate
Increase revenues (online)	Add products or services to shopping cart	Product browse to cart add ratio, category browse to cart ratio, shopping cart addition
Decrease customer support costs	Decrease traffic to "contact us" pages	Percent of visitors viewing "contact us" pages, percent of visitors searching for "contact related" content
Decrease customer support costs	Drive traffic to "self-service" pages	FAQ/service document take rate, percent of visitors using site search, site search yield rate, CSAT scores

Source: Authors

Note: In Adobe Analytics, conversion events are set up by administrators. Google Analytics does the same by limiting goal setup to users with administrative access.

(that happen on the website or app) smack in the center of the chart. The final part is how the activities on the website or app will be measured (on the right). However, the specific KPIs used to measure conversions will depend on the capabilities and implementation of the analytics platform (which an analyst or strategist ought to know well – this is the level we will focus on in this section).

Web metrics (i.e., pageviews, visitors, time spent on page, etc.) are, too often, called KPIs and used to measure marketing, the designation is misleading for the following reasons:

- Most of these so-called KPIs are intermediate metrics that are produced by the platforms at their convenience, and they have almost nothing to do with any real business marketing outcome. They are indicators, much like the dashboard of a car indicates diagnostics about the speed and health of the vehicle.
- KPIs presented out of context have little meaning for marketers. By connecting KPIs with circumstances and business goals, they become actionable.
- Most of the metrics/KPIs commonly used by digital marketers are outdated, particularly those commonly related to top SEO rankings.[8]

The best metrics for an organization will almost always be customized to an organization's most valuable business requirements and goals.

Table 9.3 KBRs and KPIs by Industry

	Media/ Advertising	Technology	Retail	Personal
KBR	Draw repeat visitors deeper into site content	Generate leads	Draw more visits to product pages	Lose 20 lbs.
Conversion Events	How content is consumed	Complete a form	Product view, cart addition, checkout	Weight on scale (being 20 lbs. less)
KPI 1	Pageviews	Leads generated	Revenue	Weight (lbs.)
KPI 2	Monthly uniques	Lead conversion rate	Average revenue per visit	Weight (lbs.) trend
KPI 3	Pageviews per visit	Cost per lead	Orders/order conversion rate	HDL
KPI 4	Visits per visitor	Web inquiries	Average order value	LDL
KPI 5	# of subscriptions	Inquiry failure rate		

Source: Authors

Figuring out what to implement first and the ordering of implementation

- We can't implement everything at the same time, we just don't have the bandwidth or budget to do it all at once or the process could be influenced by what we already collected, and so it is impossible for foresee everything in advance.
- The best practice for implementing web analytics it to determine which goals and events are the most important and implement them first. For this purpose, analysts should create a spreadsheet to plan what to implement first; this spreadsheet will be updated as new features are added to the implementation.

We created an example of the KBRs and KPIs that well-known brand Starbucks might have used. For KBRs and KPIs by Industry, see Table 9.3.

Example: Starbucks.com

The first Starbucks store opened in 1971 in Seattle. Upon creation, its self-proclaimed goals were to "share great coffee with our friends and help make the world a little better". The goal surpassed being a company of passionate purveyors of coffee but also achieving a replicable franchise with a full and rewarding coffeehouse experience, regardless of its location. If Starbucks were interested in creating a strategy that included KBRs and KPIs for their digital marketing efforts, it might look like the one in Table 9.4.

Table 9.5 shows important KPIs that could be used by Starbucks across different industries and channels.

Table 9.4 KBRs and KPIs by Digital Marketing Initiative

KBRs	Increase Brand Awareness	Increase Use of Rewards Cards	Grow Mailing List	Increase Online Product Sales
KPI 1	Unique visitors	Click path	Click path	Unique visitors
KPI 2	Click path	Sign-up rate	Mailing list joins rate	Purchase rate
KPI 3	Pageview count	Login rate		
KPI 4	Page depth	Card member page view count		
KPI 5	Organic search keywords			
KPI 6	Click-through rate on online ads			

Source: Authors

Table 9.5 Common KPIs by Industry and Channel

Industry	E-Comm	Social Media	B2B	Content Marketing	SEO	Facebook	Twitter	Instagram	Pinterest	YouTube
KPI 1	Conversion rate	Follower growth	Total cost savings	Unique visits	Return on investment	Likes	Followers	Followers	Pins	Subscribers
KPI 2	AOV	Link click-through	Quality of service	Geography	Keyword ranking	Reach	Follower	Total media	Pinners	Views
KPI 3	Days to purchase	Shares	On-time delivery	Mobile readership	SERPs	Impressions	Impressions	Likes	Repins	Likes/dislike
KPI 4	Visitor loyalty	Referrals	Inventory availability	Bounce rate	CTR	Engaged users (page)	Engagement rate	Total reach	Impressions	Playback source
KPI 5	Visitor recency	Publishing volume	Contact compliance	Clickstream	Goal conversion rate	Engaged Users (post)	retweet	Impressions	Clicks	Comments
KPI 6	Task completion rate			Pageviews	Backlinks	PTAT	favorite	Engagement rate	Engagement rate	Sharing
KPI 7	Share or search					Edgerank				Estimated time watching

Source: Authors

Table 9.6 Comparing Traffic and Conversion-Based Metrics and KPIs

	Site-Wide Metrics	Report-Specific Metrics
Traffic Metrics (out of the box)	Pageviews, visits (sessions), visitors	Reloads (page specific), time spent on page, and others
Conversion Metrics (requires deliberate setup)	Revenue, orders, units, shopping cart events (e-commerce events in Google analytics), custom events	Product views, any configured campaign reporting, and conversions (goals and events in Google Analytics)

Source: Authors

Calculated Metrics

Most web analytics platforms provide out of the box metrics by default. They have variables/dimensions that can be customized: Users configure the platform to collect the data they want, and they can create a calculated metric to include in dashboard visualizations and custom reports. Table 9.6 shows general types of metrics.

Traffic metrics, such as those shown in Table 9.6, usually do not need any setup by users or platform administrators – they are out of the box reporting that the platform vendor sets up, but they are also intermediate metrics that don't provide much business value, when they are taken literally (out of context). The conversion metrics shown in Table 9.7 must be configured manually, by an administrator of the web analytics platform, and are intended to represent events that have tangible business value, such as the view of a brand's product page (perhaps, by a prospective purchaser).

- Adobe Analytics supports calculated metrics that are numeric, percentages, currency-based, and time-based. For example, a "time to complete" calculated metric can be created that counts the elapsed time in hours and minutes between the beginning of an event and the end of it.
- Creating a calculated metrics called average order value (AOV) is quickly set up by driving revenue/orders (both conversion events are configured by administrators).

In Adobe Analytics, conversion rates and calculated metrics are automatically updated in the funnel reports. Users can configure several calculated metrics in Adobe while the free version of Google Analytics allows five calculated metrics per profile (GA Premium probably allows far more).

Google Analytics 4 Events, Dimensions and Metrics:

Events, Dimensions and Metrics are different elements of Google Analytics 4 and they are also similar to other web analytics platforms although they may be called by other names in those other platforms.

Event	Metric
1. ID of some element in the monitored website that was clicked	1. Count of transactions (number of items sold, etc.)
2. Transaction ID (usually e-commerce related)	2. Product quantity (how many items were purchased)
3. User's registration country (country where the event was initiated)	3. Conversion rate (the average rate of conversion compared with everyone else on the website)
4. User's pricing plan (usually a membership level, etc.)	4. Sessions, users (usually page and site related metrics)
5. Product category, etc. (usually an item or SKU number)	5. Time on page (how much time did the user spend on a page).

- A dimension is an analytics construct; it's an attribute that describes an event, context, user, etc. I think the best way to compare a dimension a language construct is to think of it as a noun, a person, place, or thing.
- A metric is a quantitative measurement such as the number of transactions or conversation rate; basically it is count of something specific.

  - So if a dimension is a thing, then the metric would be a count of the number or quantity of that thing, etc.

Different Web Analytics Platforms

While Gartner expects that much of what we have been calling web analytics will converge around 2027 to a broader digital analytics category that covers web, product, and digital experience analytics.[9]

What this potentially means to us is that you having a web analytics platform might not be enough to provide all the insights needed for organization about their digital activities and that many of the functions that used to be handled by different platforms and different teams within an organization are converging.

Is 2027 the date for that convergence or not? We don't know, but our best is that Gartner uses a hype cycle methodology in order to plan out future expected changes in the markets it is analyzing and strategizing about, and 2027 comes in the hype cycle that focuses on web analytics tools. In fact, looking at the Gartner Hype Cycle, Table 1, titled "Priority Matrix for Analytics and Business Intelligence, 2022" seems to confirm that may be a single use case around 2027, but for now the web analytics platforms don't offer every type of insight that one might want, and the different vendors that still remain such as Google, Adobe, and WebTrends are all offering their own marketing and analytics stack solutions that may or may not be the best fit for any particular organization.[10]

In this chapter we are mainly focused on Google Analytics 4, and Adobe Analytics (although, Adobe is no longer as directly involved with working with universities to offer a sandbox, that program called the "Adobe Education Academic Initiative", sadly ended in May 2020).

Installing and Using Google Analytics 4.0

We are going to remain very high level in this outline, but for our readers who want learn web analytics with the current version of Google Analytics 4, here's a high-level series of steps that readers can take to install GA4 and gather insights from it.

Our readers can also gain insights on how to work with the Google Analytics 4 demo property, that is a fully functional e-commerce website called the Google Merchandise Store (https://shop.googlemerchandisestore.com/).

Lately, searches in Google Search often bring up local listing for Google's own merchandise stores in certain locations such as New York or Mountain View, but we're not talking about the local stores, but the online store.

Useful Information Before Installing Google Analytics 4

Here's some useful links to use when opening up a new account or adding a property to an existing GA account.

- https://marketingplatform.google.com/about/analytics/ (page about GA4)
- https://analytics.google.com/analytics/web/ (log into to GA4)
- https://support.google.com/analytics/answer/6367342#zippy=%2Cin-this-article

1. **Set up your own account and GA4 (Google Analytics 4) property, if possible**, that way you have admin access to all features of the analytics platform; this is true even if you don't yet have a real website or app to connect to GA4, yet. Also, for studying web applications that run on mobile devices, they can look at the Flood-It account that is also available with access to the Google demo properties (note that the Flood-It property is distinct from the Google Merchandise Store property, though there are implementations [GA4 properties] that can merge website and app data, the demo does not offer this at this time).
2. Once GA4 is installed (or you can look at the current settings in the Google demo, but you will not be able to change or play with them due to permissions levels) focus on the account and property settings in the admin menu.

    a. **Reporting identity** – allows the Admin to tell GA4 how to collect the data on a user who visits the website or application monitored by the Google Analytics 4 property. Depending on how the admin specifies it, the reporting identity, data being collected with be organized differently, which can have interesting ramifications to what the data is going in your reports and how it corresponds with the users being tracked by GA4. Note that any changes you make in reporting identify can be changed later as the underlying data is not altered (https://support.google.com/analytics/answer/10976610?hl=en&utm_id=ad&visit_id=638029151138041248–2531683157&rd=1) The default is "Blended", but there are two other options, "Observed" and "Device-Based". As GA4 is integrated with machine learning and artificial intelligence, the "Blended" identity allows for blending in AI derived information from computer modeling when there is enough confidence in the data to add it into the mix.

    b. **Reporting attribution model** – There are a number of attribution models that come with GA4, which determines how much weight each step is given when a conversion takes place.

c. **Look back window** is the amount of time GA4 looks back at the user data to associate that data with a particular user for attribution purposes. Look back windows are usually sent to 30 days or 90 days, and it depends on how your business functions what makes the most sense.

d. **Property change history** (or Account Change History) Shows changes made to the account or property, and is similar to an "audit log" of the activity on a property of the analytics users on it.

e. **Data deletion requests** – When data is collected that perhaps should not have due to privacy issues, and data was sent to Google Analytics that should not have been sent, then the admin of a property can request that Google Analytics delete that data – the deletion request usually takes about week before the data is removed on the Google Analytics servers.

f. **Set up default currency, industry, reporting time zone, and so on.** Depending on what type of business is being operated the time zone will be set up differently. For example, if the site is for a set of local restaurants then the time zone should reflect where those restaurants are located, but if the property reflects restaurants all over the country, then the time zone may better be set to where the corporate offices are located in that country.

g. **Setup of user access to GA4 – Property Access Management:** User access permissions and metrics settings are also covered in this area of admin module of GA4.

h. **Setup of user access to GA4 – Property Access Management:** User access permissions and metrics settings are also covered in this area of admin module of GA4.

i. **Data collection settings**: DataStreams allow data from monitored websites and apps (iOS or Android) are covered in the admin module as well, and you can specify them there. **Data collection** is where you can enable Google Signals which enables first and third-party cookies that sends data from double click remarking from advertisers, which enables inter agrarian with Google Ads and remarking data integration with your Google Analytics property.

ii. Enabling Google Signals is necessary in order to receive cross-device data, including user interests, age, gender of those users who enabled personalization features in their Google accounts. Therefore, whatever demographics data one gets here will be incomplete, and possibly, sparse, but it may still be valuable to some businesses.

iii. However, the problem with enabling Google Signals is that the data collected may run afoul of certain local regulations in the areas your business operates or where your users may be located. Caveat, while such data could be collected, it is often against the law to do so, fully – so maybe a legal consult is needed here.

i. **Data retention** – Impacts how long Google Analytics Explorer reports are maintained in memory – the default is two months, but it can be set to 14 months. That said, the retention settings only impact Google Analytics 4 Explorations (custom reports) while data in standard reports remain available for up to four years.

j. Data from outside Google Analytics such as advertising cost data can be imported to Google Analytics via a.csv file in a particular format.

k. **DataStream creation**: GA4 requires a datastream be created for to capture the data from a website (or app), and a property can have more than one datastream.

l. **Enhanced measurement**: GA4 allows the admin to set up tracking for data that used to require additional analytics configuration and tagging such as pageviews, page scrolls, outbound clicks, site search, video engagement and file downloads. Recently, form interactions were added but are not yet particularly useful for form tracking.

m. **Web code tagging**: Currently, Google Analytics supports two choices, Global Site Tage (GTag) and Google Tag Manager (GTM).

    i. Gtag (Global Site Tag) – usually used by developers when they are adding the same Gtag code to all pages of a website. If a website is already using Gtag.js, then you could connect the existing website to a new GA4 property, but this is not recommended because GA4 is different enough from GA3 (UA) that the analytics setup and tagging may need to be rethought out (*as is discussed in the course*). **GTM (Google Tag Manager) is the preferred method because it provides analysts much more flexibility**. With that said, we will not cover GTM in any depth in this chapter, other than refer to it as the preferred method for installing and maintaining Google Analytics properties.

    ii. **GTM is a middleman** or better put, a layer of software that manages the configurations and interactions between one or more websites or apps and third-party software and applications such as Google Ads, Google Analytics and pretty much everything else in the marketing technology stack. *It's not the only tag manager,* as there are several, but it is the most common and accessible tag manager, and the one we will discuss in this chapter.

    iii. **Create a GTM account by going to** https://marketingplatform. google.com/about/tag-manager/ and create a tag manager account. [NOTE: GTM is constantly being updated]

    iv. NOTE: Best practice is to have one GTM account per business (not per website), as one business can have several websites, and all of these could be managed by one GTM account, with each website having one container, as usually the tracking codes are different for each website.

    v. If you already have a Google account, you can just log in (two-step verification). If you did not have a Google account until now, then you will be promoted to register a new tag manager account.

    vi. Choose a WEB container and press "create", and "HEAD" and "BODY" JavaScript code is generated that needs to be pasted onto the code of every page of the website (being administered by GTM). Note: there are other container types including iOS, Android, AMP, etc.

n. **Additional settings:**

    i. There are at the current time at least three additional advanced settings that can be added in to the GA4 configuration, though they are not always used.

    ii. Connected site tags

    iii. Measurement protocol API secrets

        1. This is an advanced feature used by developers to connect data between servers – it requires coding development is out of the scope of this course (chapter).

2. More Tagging Settings

    a. Modify events

    b. Create events

    c. Collect Universal Analytics events

3. Tag Configuration

    a. Configure your domains

    b. Define internal traffic

    c. List unwanted referrals

    d. Adjust session timeout

o. There is a lot more to installing Google Analytics than we will cover in this chapter, but one advantage that Google Analytics 4 offered admins and developers is the ability to debug their installations of Google Analytics with a feature called "DebugView" that is currently located in the admin interface of Google Analytics 4. However, in order to take advantage of DebugView, the data being sent to Google Analytics must contain certain a debug parameter; the best way to do that is with the Adswerve DataLayer Inspector Chrome plug-in, and all Google Analytics debugging is done from the Google Chrome browser. Readers can also make use of a **Google Analytics Debugger** such as https://chrome.google.com/webstore/detail/google-analytics-debugger/jnkmfdileelhofjcijamephohjechhna?hl=en To test that GA4 is installed properly and functioning. Use the GA Debugger in the browser to inspect the website and see if the necessary information is detected in the debugger than GA4 is installed properly.

p. **Opting out of being tracked by Google Analytics** – Some browser extensions can block Google Analytics data from being sent to a Google Analytics 4 property, one of the Chrome extensions that is good for this is **Google Analytics Opt-Out** and, if someone does not want to be tracked by Google Analytics, install this Chrome extension.

q. **Setting up cross-domain tracking** – Analysts can have multiple domains that are part of the same user journey, and ultimately, the same GA4 property, for example, someone may go to a website, view something at that website and then go to another website (domain) and make a purchase there. As long as the other websites are considered part of the user's journey to ultimately purchasing a specific purpose or product and under the control of the same GA4 admins, the user journey won't be captured fully in web analytics without setting up cross-domain tracking. And, the reason why web analytics doesn't normally track users across different domains is that a randomly generated client id is generated for a user in each domain and stored as a cookie in that domain (via browser cookie), and when the user goes to the next domain in their user journey and new client id is generated and saved to a cookie in the other domain. Normally, each website (domain) only has access to its own cookies, so it will have no awareness of the user and their actions and another domain other than its own.

    i. Websites must be tracked by the same DataStream (and be under the same GA4 Property).

r. The setup for multiple domains is now located in **the Configure Tag settings** in the Datastream submenu of the admin settings. ***NOTE: Subdomains of the same domain are handled automatically by GA4 and do not need cross-domain tracking***.

s. **Filtering internal traffic out of your reports in GA4 –** While testing tagging implementation, it is useful to isolate other internal traffic in your domain (say, coworkers) from your own traffic by defining what is considered to be internal traffic. Go to Admin settings/Datastream/Modify Tag Settings/More settings/Define Internal Traffic. Once the internal domain IP address or range of addresses that information is inputted (remember to test it with GTM and DebugView) traffic from those specified IP addresses should be marked as "traffic type = internal".

t. **Getting rid of unwanted referrals such as payment gateways in your GA4 reports** (see https://support.google.com/analytics/answer/10327750) Goto Admin/Data Settings/Data Stream/More Tag Settings/List Unwanted Domains and put the domains you want to exclude such as PayPal.com there.

u. **Testing a website with GA4 (maintaining a testing environment).** Most organizations do not deploy new code on the production website, they test it first on a QA or testing/staging website first – hopefully that staging website is set up to mimic the online production website as closely as possible (but we know from the real world, that is not always possible to do fully). Both websites must be separate GA4 properties with identical settings – that is very important! GTM container information needs lookup table code that can distinguish between the urls of the production (live) website and the development/test/QA stating website, and inject the test code into on the staging website and not the live website.

Web Metrics Breakdowns

Breaking down web analytics data to very accurate reporting is done in a few different ways. Each platform has a slightly different name and procedure. The more specific the question, the better the report can be (when the data and context are available to inform it).

Adobe Analytics Breakdowns

Table 9.7 illustrates how certain web analytics platforms, such as Adobe Analytics, allows analysts and stakeholders to get report readouts that are specific to what they are interested in knowing about (i.e., a certain page, device, location, etc.).

Types of Web Metrics

There are two kinds of web metrics, activity-based traffic versus conversion event-based metrics. Depending on which web analytics platform used, the reports may have different names, but the same functionality exists on almost every web analytics platform.[11] Readers are encouraged to compare Table 9.8 and Table 9.7 – they are very similar. Both tables indicate that a base set of web metrics are provided with every web analytics profile or reporting suite (left column), but the real business value comes from defining and configuring custom metrics (right column). Consequently, setting up useful calculated metrics requires introspection and experimentation

Table 9.7 How Adobe Analytics Classifies Behavioral Data Collected on a Website by the Platform

	Correlations (traffic)	Sub-Relations (conversions)
Definition	Breaks down traffic reports by other traffic reports to show pageview distribution	Break down conversion reports by other conversion reports to show success events
Reports	Pages, site sections, custom traffic	Products, campaigns and custom conversion events

Source: Authors, derived from Adobe Education

Table 9.8 Activity (out of the box) Metrics vs. Milestone Metrics (configured)

Activity/Traffic Metrics	Events/Milestones/Conversion Metrics
Pageviews	Purchase metrics (revenue, orders, units, etc.)
Visits	Cart metrics (opens, adds, checkouts, etc.)
Unique visitors (daily, weekly, monthly, etc.)	Custom events (registrations, form completion, etc.)
Path related metrics (entries & exits, single access, reloads, time spent on page, average page depth)	Report-specific metrics (product views, campaign click-throughs, instances, etc.)

Source: Authors, inspired by Adobe Education

to determine what should be measured, and multiple iterations for a successful implementation.

Traffic Metrics vs. Conversion Metrics

All web analytics platforms make a distinction between activity metrics, such as entries and exits, time spent, pageviews, and visits that focus on the presence of activity by a visitor (during a visit or session) versus actual destination metrics, such as a purchase, registration, form completion, and so on. Traffic or activity metrics are out of the box data, unconfigured web analytics platforms. Conversion/milestone metrics must be set up deliberately and customized (by someone who has the necessary admin permissions in the web analytics platform) and depend on the use of custom variables and program memory to run. Web analytics platforms, such as Adobe Analytics, do not allow administrators to combine traffic breakdowns with event breakdowns due to their different nature and purposes.

Correlation Filters

Adobe Analytics and Google Analytics offer report filtering, but they are evoked in various ways. Adobe Analytics has secondary dimensions but calls them correlations. Analysts select several correlations at one time, if desired. For example, a correlation filter can be configured that shows how many confirmed registrations took place from 25–29-year old visitors to a fashion retail website during a given period. If the data is collected in the web analytics platform, there is probably a breakdown or correlation filter report that will be able to inform a specific business question.

Metrics Configuration

In Adobe Analytics, the following metrics are set up by administrators:

- **Props:** Used to track page-by-page site traffic activity in Adobe Analytics (they do not persist between pages of the website) – props capture the value of pageviews, visits, new and repeat visitors connected to a specific page. Using props is a way to save memory usage in Adobe Analytics as well as speed up processing.
- **eVars:** Used to track conversion events and traffic activity in Adobe Analytics. Most implementations come with a standard set of eVars that can be configured and more can be added (for additional cost), and these variables are enduring (they track events across visits).
- **Events (conversions):** Custom events set up by administrators in Adobe Analytics to track conversions – the event tracking is at the core of web analytics (together with the integration with the Adobe Marketing Cloud), as without a custom set of events that are measured stakeholders might as well run Google Analytics for free.
- **Products:** Track products that are viewed, sold, added to a shopping cart, or removed from a shopping cart. Adobe Analytics assumes that retailers will want to sell products and track them, thereby creating a variable class and reports to support it built around just that function (no doubt it made the platform more popular with publishers, retailers and financial organizations that are bottom line sales focused).

Both Adobe Analytics and Google Analytics allow users to create custom dimensions and custom metrics. Adobe Analytics' custom reporting requires the specialized setup of props, eVars, events (conversions) and products to deliver business value to stakeholders. One fundamental difference between both platforms: Google Analytics is free to use (so using resources does not generate a charge), but there are limits to how many custom dimensions and metrices reporting are allowed.

What is the Best KPI for a Website?

Start by determining the questions that web analytics is put in place by a business to answer – this line of inquiry will drive organizations to find data and metrics that will best inform their question(s).

- The KPIs are going to differ from organization to organization, although industries generally focus on similar sets of metrics.
- KPIs and KBRs demand a very well-defined set of business processes that have key entry points where web analytics systems can be deployed.

Choosing Relevant Web Metrics

Metrics are the currency of web analytics, which is an excellent bean counter containing much built-in intelligence about web traffic and conversions taking place on a monitored website. Some of the more common metrics are visits, unique visitors, pageviews, revenue, and time spent.

- Each business is unique, and KPIs should be tailored to the company's needs.
- Knowing how an industry or organization operates makes it easier to determine what to look for and benchmark.

Intermediate Web and Social Media Metrics

Intermediate metrics are marketing data that falls within the range from impression to purchase, such as bookmarks, views, recall, the number of followers, shares, clicks, retweets, likes, pins or downloads (note: the authors refer to Intermediate metrics as action metrics in several other chapters of this book). Google convinced the world to believe in the click. Facebook has done the same with the "like", Twitter with the "follower", and Pinterest has with the "pin". Web analytics did the same thing with "visits", "visitors", "pageviews", "hits", and "bounce rate", to name a few of the better-known metrics. From the authors' perspective, Figure 9.6 and Figure 9.2 in this chapter are two sides of the same coin; web analytics, and social media analytics have created their own currencies, but they are not interchangeable, and they should

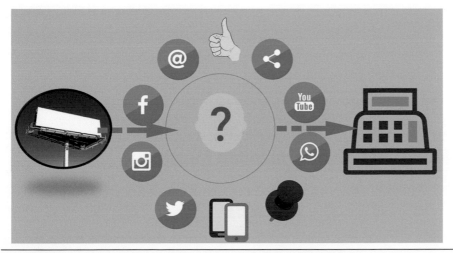

Figure 9.6 Intermediate Metrics and Their Impact on Return on Investment
Source: Authors

not be combined in a single metric with integrity (because they measure different behaviors from different audiences). Consequently, they are not very useful as a proxy for business analytics metrics. Unfortunately, intermediate metrics are too often used by stakeholders as a proxy for business activity metrics (likely by uninformed stakeholders or their analysts.)

Consequently, while intermediate metrics are useful as a measure of audience engagement, they should not be considered the end point of a return on investment calculation. Perhaps, the only use case we can think of offhand where intermediate metrics work as ROI is a publisher or advertiser who is paying for clicks on their ads or content, outright, as part of a campaign, with designated landing pages and e-commerce transactions. As marketers learn to deliberately instrument their goals, strategies, tactics, and KPIs, they are more likely to be successful aligning their KPIs as intermediate metrics, to their stated business goals.

This much we can say about most intermediate metrics:

- They are *not* the end goal of most businesses, and they rarely correlate to established business outcomes *in and of themselves*.
- Analytics platforms are incapable of doing attribution from intermediate metrics alone.
- Example: Domino's Pizza – how many of those people who "liked" Domino's Pizza have placed an order online or been to the store? Intermediate metrics such as a Facebook "like" provide much useful information but are not a proxy for actual sales data, and while advertising efforts are effective, they do not always inform fundamental business questions.

One of the issues with social media is that brands are incorrectly basing their successes on increasing metrics such as page likes and account followers, which are too simplistic to inform their actual business initiatives or tell enough of the story to be that useful. Often, there are many subsequent actions connected to intermediate metrics that can't currently be tracked (or at least, cannot easily be tracked).

Where Intermediate Metrics Could Be Useful

- Start-ups
- Any organization building brand awareness
- Individuals who are building their personal brand (i.e., blogger, publisher, celebrity, politician, etc.)
- Advertisers and publishers
- Situations where measuring sales and revenue is almost impossible to determine

Viewpoints on Intermediate Metrics

- Intermediate metrics act more as barometers for interested parties on commonly intangible attitudes of a potential or *de facto* online audience, while they are not perfect, just like the weather forecast, they show the trend. Intermediate metrics should be treated as characteristic data points that measure aspects of web performance but aren't comprehensive.
- Intermediate metrics produced by social media platforms such as Twitter and Facebook are publicly available and often free to collect, and perhaps that is why

Table 9.9 Custom Variables in Google vs. Adobe vs. Webtrends Analytics

	Preconfigured Variables	Semi-Free Custom Variables	Free Custom Variables
Definition:	No influence on how variables are filled or called and are provided out of the box by the platform provider (Google, WebTrends, Adobe, etc.)	Reporting context is limited in scope, often come out of the box but need to be configured	Totally configurable, can be used in any context and are open to all admins
Examples:	Technology, URL/page, geography, referring sites, search keywords	Adobe "pageName", GA on-site search terms, ecom variables, custom events, props, success events	GA and WT Custom dimensions and metrics, Adobe eVars

Source: Authors

they are so popular. The intermediate metrics are *tangentially indicative* of how a website/web presence performed in the past and how it is currently performing.
- Connect Intermediate Metrics with a campaign – it is a mistake to apply them more broadly.

Custom Variables

The value of analytics implementation comes from precisely setting up conversion metrics using custom variables, which is a step many business owners fail to do well, or at all (also refer to Tables 9.7, 9.8, and 9.9 in this chapter).

Designing KPIs That Work

There is an art to developing a useful KPI, and here is one approach:[12]

- Define the business problem (what are the main issues the organization faces?)
- Choose a single issue (per KPI), at least one designated stakeholder, and a designed KPI indicator that would be useful to that stakeholder.
- Define three or four processes associated with the KPI (but don't get too specific, yet).
- Define a statistical measure that will be linked to each of the: processes related to time KPI. By instrumenting an indicator and setting thresholds with a high/low action for each process, it becomes possible to place the KPI in a dashboard and act on it. In a nutshell, connect each business process with a data source that will inform it.
- Define the measurement algorithm for the KPI as a formula when possible.
- Define the procedure to conduct/measure the KPI.

Please note that many businesses create KPIs that are not based on web analytics. For example, many universities create KPIs that are meant to measure the effectiveness of the instructors and course quality. The metrics used in KPIs are diverse; most have nothing to do with web analytics. This chapter focuses only on the metrics that are used to formulate web analytics KPIs.

The Promise and Failure of Web Analytics for Stakeholders

The KPI approach appears to be both mechanical and logical, and akin to decision support systems that are common in many industries, such as automotive, aerospace, construction, etc.[13] Web analytics works best in organizations that have very defined business processes – the same kind of processes that facilitate KPI development. Incidentally, web analytics was created to satisfy tactical measures that business owners defined (before proceeding to instrument web analytics in their businesses – if they have not done that, the analytics reporting will not be very helpful). That is because web analytics was created (or at least initially sold to users/ subscribers) based on the idea that it would help mature business organizations solve their problems, activities or issues with more actionable data. As it turned out, many organizations – that have not done the necessary set up work, in this sense, they are immature – are not ready or able to spend the time or resources to set up analytics well enough to benefit from it.

Common Use Cases for Web/Data Analytics

Use cases are examples of where an organization uses web analytics to perform a business function.[14]

Below are the most common for web analytics:

- Collect visitor data to owned media websites (to better understand customers or potential customers)
- Performance measurement (against KPIs)
- Marketing optimization (measure and understand, through analysis, how campaigns are performing and improve the performance by making changes based on the data obtained)
- Content optimization (understanding why the website exists and whether the content on the monitored site contributes to that purpose, making changes based on the collected data to improve the content)

How Web Analytics Track User Web Data

Internet data is primarily gathered from web server log files or JavaScript tags (third-party APIs to external data sources are an additional method, they are discussed in more depth in later chapters). Most platforms use the JavaScript method because it requires less overhead and is considered superior for most situations (but not all). The web analytics tracking process is shown in Figure 9.8.

- **Server log file analysis:** Web server log files contain information on file downloads and search engine crawlers not tracked by web beacons.
- **Web beacons:** Every page tracked by web analytics has a small snippet of JavaScript code that executes when the page is loaded by a web browser. The JavaScript code on the webpage is customized by the marketer to capture the exact information marketers need for their web analytic and financial business reports.

Web Beacon Tracking (Most Common Method)

When a visitor visits a site, the web server sends page information while the page displays in the browser. As the page loads in the web browser and the web analytics JavaScript Beacon code on the page executes, it sends a request to the analytics server as a transparent 1-pixel-sized image along with various raw data that is captured from the visitor's session (visit).

By installing web analytics tracking code on a website, the visitor's browser activity on the site is tracked by an analytics server in parallel with the website's web server. When a page loads in a browser, the JavaScript code on the page is executed as the page renders. All following activity on the page in question is tracked by the web analytics collection server as raw data where it is processed into reports. Once the data is fully processed, the raw data is dumped (to save on system resources and data storage). We believe that many organizations are

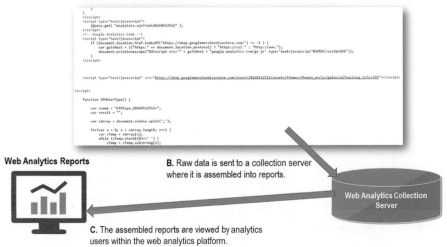

A. Web Analytics JavaScript Collection Script (executed by a web browser upon rendering web pages that are monitored by a web analytics platform such as Google Analytics, Adobe Analytics or WebTrends)

Web Analytics Reports

B. Raw data is sent to a collection server where it is assembled into reports.

Web Analytics Collection Server

C. The assembled reports are viewed by analytics users within the web analytics platform.

Figure 9.7 Web Analytics Tracking Pixel and Data Collection Mechanism
Source: Authors

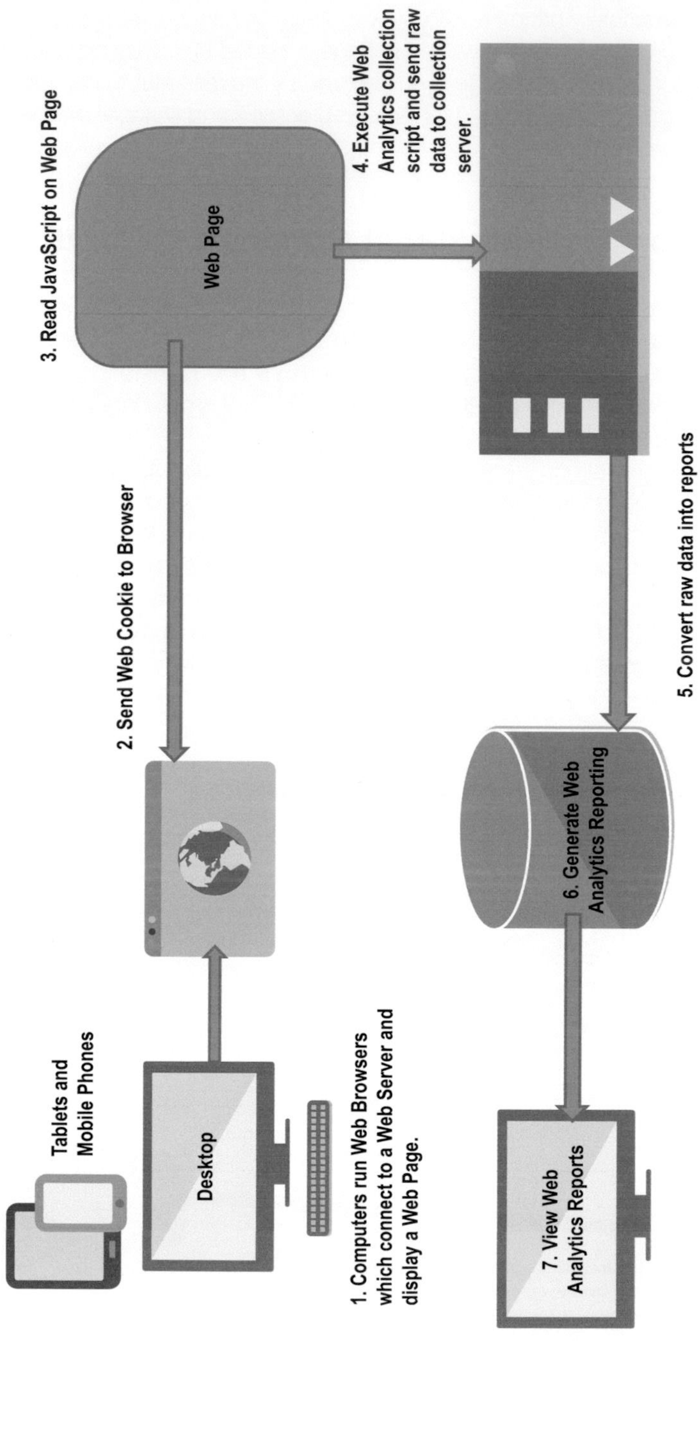

Figure 9.8 Web Analytics Tracking Process

Source: Authors

not entirely informed of the drawbacks of web beacon (JavaScript) tracking, that is why we are highlighting many of the disadvantages first. Drawbacks to JavaScript tracking include

- Analytics tracking that is improperly implemented is not recoverable once the analytics server creates the reporting from the raw data that is collected from visitors' browsers. Consequently, potential data loss should be a concern that organizations must address because of using JavaScript tracking.
- Some visitor behavioral activities (such as file downloads, video views, Flash and Shockwave files, mouse hovering movements, Ajax web code, pageviews, podcasts, vidcasts, and streaming media, in general, etc.) on the website that are being measured using web analytics are not normally trackable using the default configurations of all web analytics platforms. However, web analytics can track virtually all visitor activity on the website – but it takes a significant cost in time, effort and business expense (ultimately).

The advantages of using JavaScript tracking are evident:

- Reduced infrastructure costs – most of the raw data is processed and stored in the cloud and can be scaled on demand (Google Analytics has successfully done this) and offered to users at a reduced price (for many, such as those who use the free version of Google Analytics, the platform is free).
- Superior tracking of many (but not all) visitor activities that can be merged with third-party data (such as DoubleClick).
- Extensibility of the analytics implementations. There is literally no limit to the number of websites that can be tracked with this method.
- The analytics providers (particularly Google) have an enormous swath of humanity they are tracking via their websites – the collected data can be used for industry and site benchmarking, behavioral targeting, and market intelligence (second- and third-party data) for analytics users, advertisers, and publishers.

To deploy web analytics effectively, it should be part of a company's strategic initiative and team (occasionally dubbed the "Center of Excellence") to receive requests and funnel the insights to the rest of the organization. Well-defined business processes and business strategies are a prerequisite to getting substantial value out of web analytics platforms.

For example, if a company wants to increase visitation to a page on their site by 25% next month, they should take steps beforehand to be sure they can collect all the data necessary to measure their progress, before beginning the advertising campaign. While it is possible to implement processes in analytics as one goes, it is better to set up the analytics before launching a new program or campaign.

The Digital Analytics Maturity Model

When deploying web analytics, consider the model outlined in Table 9.10 (i.e., organizations must choose a solution, set it up and train users in Phase 1 to be able to do basic and advanced reporting in Phases 2 and 3).

Table 9.10 Defining the Digital Analytics Maturity Model

Phase	Functional Definitions of the Digital Analytics Maturity Model
1.	Strategic consulting to establish the right framework for an organization
2.	Basic training on how to use the analytics platform to run and refine is reporting
3.	Advanced consulting to customize analytics measurement to the very specific needs of each client
4.	Visitor intelligence to connect the dots and make sense of the collected data to further business goals
5.	Integrating and converging data collection and reporting, which is very hard to do, expensive, and time-consuming

Source: Authors

No one is perfect. No organization (or individual) *always* acts sequentially – we are all inconsistent frequently; in real life, we learn from our mistakes, improvising, integrating, and improving our actions and insights as we go along.

Iteration and Learning from Mistakes

The Digital Analytics Maturity Model presented in this chapter is not mutually exclusive with learning how to deploy web analytics by making several iterations and mistakes to discover what works (in real life both processes can take place simultaneously) – our takeaways depend on the context of the learning. Since no one is perfect (even a machine or a program as both are fashioned by humans), no one is going to have a perfect implementation of web analytics, ever. Nothing is a mistake if we learn something valuable from it – the biggest mistake we make in life (and web analytics) is not learning anything from our mistakes, and by extension, over time, not recognizing what our mistake was.

If we do not make mistakes and continue to iterate off those errors, there is no progress. Nothing we put forward in this book should be taken as the only acceptable way to accomplish the subjects we cover in this book.

The Role of Iteration Within the Digital Analytics Maturity Model

Perhaps, a better way of conceptualizing Table 9.10 is to add in a more iterative component – most organizations will move back and forth between the maturity model phases.

- **Phase 1/Phase 2:** Many organizations will move to Phase 1 and Phase 2 (perhaps forever) until they reach a fulcrum point of a well-informed stakeholder and management consensus, thereby allowing the organization to move on to Phase 3 (where useful standalone applications are developed for stakeholders).

- **Phase 3:** At Phase 3, standalone analytics insights are successfully developed for departments and lines of business (LOBs), but the data produced by the applications cannot be used extensible or easily combined. Analytics data and insights are usually effective because they are localized and contextual. At this stage, the data cannot be combined with other information within the organization. Eventually, organizations find that stalling at Phase 3 in the analytics implementation creates too many reporting silos and analytics vendors (duplicating the same functions) that cannot be combined.

- **Phase 4/5**: Phases 4 and 5 require a significant commitment to business alignment, along with the necessary resources to instrument and implement the business technology alignment. Consequently, few organizations are receiving the full benefit of their analytics investment because they are unable to progress to Phase 4 or mature into Phase 5.

There is no universal and extensible list of companies that are functioning at Phase 4 or 5 in the Digital Analytics Maturity Model, as far as we can tell (although we can guess that organizations such as Amazon and Google are probably right up there at Phase 5). What is more troubling is that many organizations are skipping the necessary first two phases, which guarantees an epic analytics implementation failure (for example, if we suddenly find ourselves behind the wheel of a moving car, but we do not know how to drive).

To sum up, the sequence of the Digital Analytics Maturity Model phases that an organization goes through is far less important than skipping the early phases, or beginning of Phase 3 (i.e., skipping Phases 1 and 2 and suddenly purchasing an off-the-shelf third-party application to solve a critical, yet under-defined business problem).

Two Case Studies About Web/Data Analytics Implementation

1. Caesars Entertainment invested in an Adobe Analytics implementation (Adobe's Digital Marketing Suite) to manage their numerous online properties of more than 60 websites for various properties and services. Caesars also had 40 Facebook pages by 2013 to be more data-driven as an organization and collect data in a usable, actionable form.[15]

   a. Two main customer segments were identified consisting of Frequent Independent Travelers (FITs) and Total Rewards Members (TRMs) that were driven by different needs and behaviors. Using A/B testing, content was tested and optimized for both segments, which increased conversion rate by up to 70%.

   b. Caesars used web analytics to measure the impact of social media across FIT and TRM segments.

2. Motor Insurers Bureau created as a microsite to generate awareness of motor insurance in specific geographical locations across the UK (House of Kaizen) and used Google Analytics to provide an integrated view of a multichannel marketing campaign with site interaction metrics.

   a. A custom implementation of Google Analytics provided an in-depth understanding of their location data with custom dashboards reflecting KPIs showing what content was most effective.

Most web analytics platforms have several different ways to customize data collection and reporting.

Defining What to Measure and How to Measure It

The best way to deploy web analytics is to begin with an introspection process that business leaders and stakeholders within the organization go through (see Table 9.10, Phase 1) to determine what the company cares about or wants to accomplish (this is typically conducted by strategic business consultants such as McKinsey & Co, or a web analytics vendor such as Adobe). At the start of Phase 1, business leaders and stakeholders provide input about everything they want to know more about, defined and matched up with analytics capabilities and the costs that are involved in obtaining the information. After this process is concluded, an initial web analytics implementation can be mapped and approved with a few clear deliverables that make sense to instrument.

Helpful Questions for Phase 1 (Discovery Process)

- **What is the business paying for?** For simple businesses, it is easy to figure out where the time, energy, and money are being spent. A simple implementation of Google Analytics (free) is more than enough for small businesses. For more complex organizations, a highly customized web analytics implementation is necessary.
- **Where does the business spend most of its time?** There is an old saying that "time is money"; to find out what is important, determine how organizations or businesses focus their time. Web analytics requires that business value (of a process or activity) to be defined in a way that the analytics can measure.
- **What is driving the focus on money, resources, or time?** For example, consider the. key business requirement of losing weight could be remaining fit and attractive. One of the KPIs is the weight of the person on a scale from day to day, as measured in pounds, kilograms, or stones (in the UK).

When an organization, business, or individual defines what drives their main metrics of value, web analytics can provide most of them. Having said that, as shown in Figure 9.9, the most important business goal of B2B marketers appears to be an intermediate metric that web analytics can provide: web traffic. Web traffic is an activity metric and should never be the end point of a business goal (although it can be considered a campaign goal), suggesting that marketers need more clarity regarding what they really want to accomplish before they define their goals. Once the business goals are defined, they can be instrumented using a DSS (Decision Support Services) approach.[16]

As an instrumentation example: "If we knew that [KPIs] were consistently rising/falling over the last week/month, we would [ACTION]".

Once we can define the driver of change in a business metric, we can begin to instrument the key performance indicator – so the change can be measured. The next step is finding out what actions are needed and who takes them.

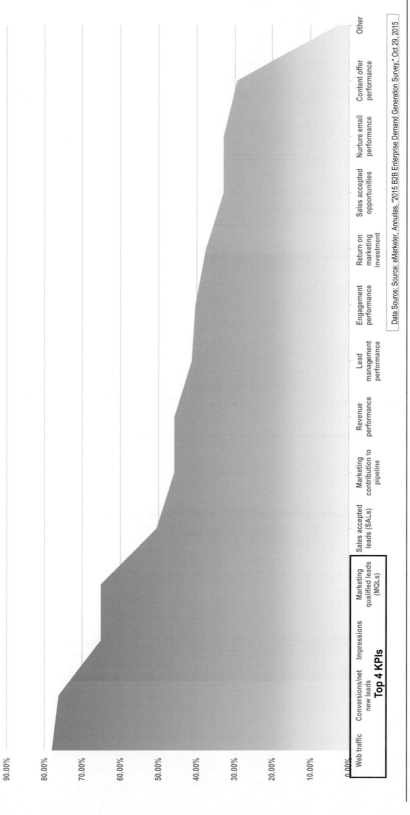

Marketing Performance KPIs Tracked by US B2B Enterprise Marketers, Aug 2015 (% of respondents)

Figure 9.9 Marketing KPIs Used by US B2B Marketers

Source: Marshall Sponder with data sourced from eMarketer.com

- A weather alert flashes on the iPhone of an umbrella street vendor that there is a 95% chance of heavy rain in the next 15 minutes nearby.
- If the umbrella street vendor is well-positioned for a lot of foot traffic and well-prepared, they could act based on this signal and quickly sell their entire stock of umbrellas. The retailer would arrive at a busy intersection in their city with several umbrellas to sell to pedestrians whose goal is staying dry.
- Both the umbrella vendor and the pedestrians passing by (who don't have an umbrella and do not want to get wet) achieve their goals.
- Acting on the weather alert while it is raining creates measurable value for the umbrella retailer and the pedestrian. We used this example to highlight that DSS systems using web and data analytics should lead to outcomes that are mutually beneficial to all parties Involved. Conversely, we should, on principle, examine that our business goals and initiatives provide measurable value to both sides of the equation (the seller and the buyer).

Data Can Be Applied in Different Contexts

If we strayed inadvertently into the realm of economics with the umbrella vendor example, forgive us. In our view, all subjects we study in universities are interrelated – the more we can create interrelationships on the various topics studied, the better. It's also more likely students will retain the information they read about and study if they can apply it in different contexts. The best way to start on that path (interrelationships of the curriculum in the context of digital marketing) is to think of applications where web analytics and text analytics can illuminate market strategy, consumer behavior, economics, public affairs, environmental policies, and vice versa.

For too long, in our view, universities have focused on their own program curricula, or businesses their own business context. It is a common saying that if we are going to catch more fish, we need to cast a wider net, and to begin to think more broadly.

Types of Data Marketers Value the Most

Figure 9.10 illustrates a well-known desire of many digital marketers to harness the power of the Internet to gather first-party data from their digital properties, perhaps combining it with third-party data from data brokers or other third-party applications, business partners, or affiliates.

Web Analytics Attribution Methods and Algorithms

The path the customer takes to find out about a product or service and purchase it is commonly referred to as the customer journey. Due to the fragmentation of media the customer or consumer can discover and engage with digital content via many touchpoints, perhaps in a circular or zig-zag process that is rarely linear (except with direct marketing campaigns such as PPC ad appearing on Google Search).

Because of the rise of social media, mobile devices, and media fragmentation (not to mention audience fragmentation), the customer journey is much more complex

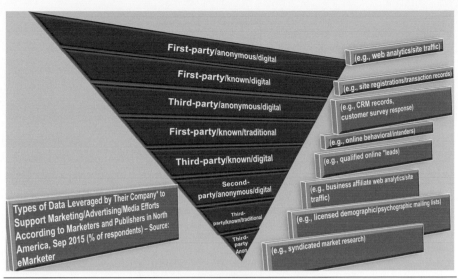

Figure 9.10 Top Eight Data Sources of US Digital Marketers in 2015
Source: Marshall Sponder from data provided by eMarketer.com

than the digital activities web analytics platforms can track out of the box.[17] It is much harder to get a complete picture of the customer journey using web analytics even with newer additions such as Adobe Social, various CRM additions coming from Google, Adobe, and IBM. The Third-Party Marketing Clouds from Salesforce, Oracle, IBM, and Adobe have evolved to capture and harness customer data, but they are expensive to deploy and manage. There are methods that web analytics platforms use to determine the attribution of web visitation and to evaluate or weight it, from an ROI (return on investment) perspective. Most of these methods take additional configuration, although some are in place by default, such as last-click attribution modeling.

Attribution Models

Attribution models are a method that web analytics platforms decide which sources of traffic are making a bigger contribution to a conversion event (such as a web purchase, file download, etc.). For example, Figure 9.11 is sourced from a standard Google Analytics report showing how web analytics determines the origins of web traffic that leads to a conversion event. The top referral patterns of online visitors to an e-commerce website are presented in Figure 9.11.

Site Pathing Analysis

Up to this point, we have examined how a business acquires a visitor – now will we talk about how to track the visitors' behavior once they arrive on the website. Web analytics tracks visitors' movements as they transverse a website visitor arrives on a site – this is called site pathing analysis. Figure 9.12 shows two pathing methods that web analytics uses to track visitors on a website (based on the first page browsed during a session/visit).

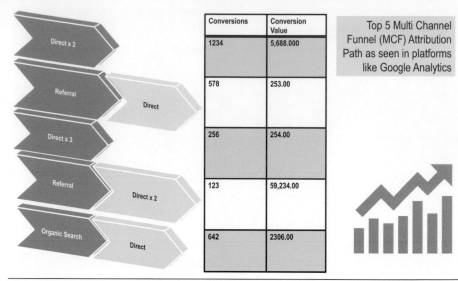

Conversions	Conversion Value
1234	5,688.000
578	253.00
256	254.00
123	59,234.00
642	2306.00

Top 5 Multi Channel Funnel (MCF) Attribution Path as seen in platforms like Google Analytics

Figure 9.11 Visualization of Google Analytics Multichannel Funnel Attribution and ROI
Source: Marshall Sponder from Anonymized Google Analytics Data

- **Point to point:** Used when businesses are more interested in knowing if the customer reaches the end point (i.e., that a user purchases an item is all that matters).
- **Direct path:** Used to optimize the visitor flow on the website (i.e., visitors are dropping out and leaving the site before purchasing anything, and we can track the pages where this occurs more frequently).

Depending on what the goal of the web analytics analysis is, point-based analysis might be all that is needed; whereas, if site performance is going to considered, then direct path analysis might make more sense, providing it is set up in a fair and equitable way.

Providing Actionable Web Analytics Reporting for Stakeholders

Web analytics collects a lot of website data (some believe web analytics collects too much data), but it is diagnostic in nature. Figure 9.13 illustrates four types of interested parties that require different analytics reporting. One reason data lakes, data marts, and data warehouses exist is to allow the information produced by analytics platforms to be more atomic, so it can be broken apart, reassembled, and messaged into different types of reporting that are stored in the cloud or private data repositories. In the schema shown in Figure 9.13, it is extremely unlikely that stakeholders who are marketers are going to benefit from a website data performance report provided to the enterprise team, or vice versa. Making the data more atomic seems to make sense if the necessary business context can be created or added in when reporting is created and/or delivered.

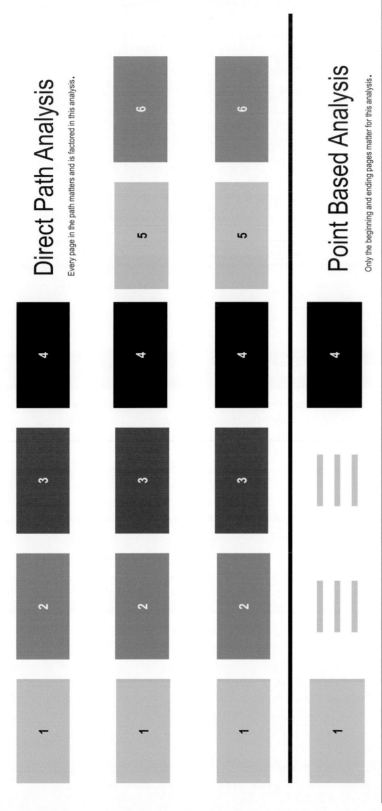

Figure 9.12 Comparing Direct Path and Point-Based Path Analysis

Source: Marshall Sponder from concepts taught by Adobe Education

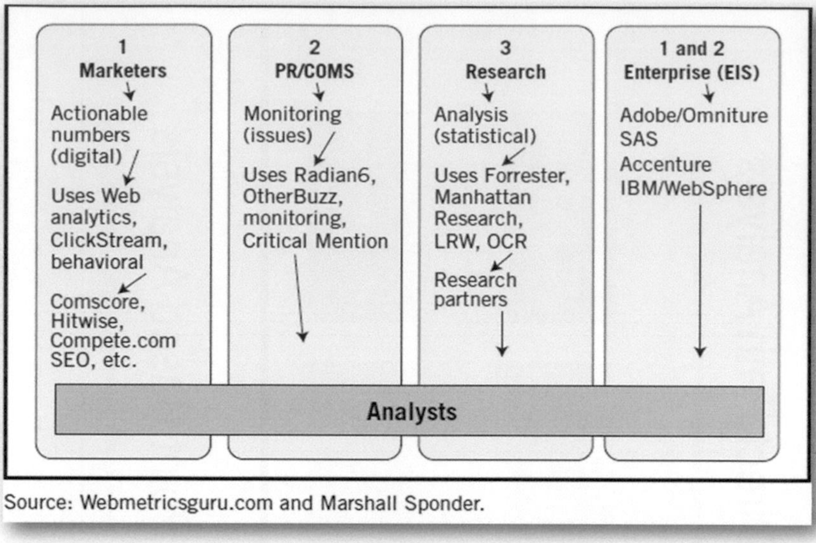

Source: Webmetricsguru.com and Marshall Sponder.

Figure 9.13 Customizing Reports for Different Types of Stakeholders
Source: Marshall Sponder

Review Questions

1. Define what web analytics is typically used for? What are some non-typical applications of web analytics? (Try to think of a few.)
2. Define the five-step web analytics process. Do you think there could be more steps to add to this process?
3. What do the terms KBR and KPI stand for? Who defines them?
4. What is a calculated metric? Does Google Analytics allow calculated metrics? What about Adobe Analytics – do they enable users to create calculated metrics?
5. Define the difference between point-based analysis and path-based analysis (for pathing/attribution).

Chapter 9 Citations

1. "Simplilearn." August 26, 2015. www.youtube.com/watch?v=BuEYkl2_b5l. Accessed June 2, 2023.
2. Nerney, C. "Soon, everybody will be a data scientist." August 29, 2014. www.cio.com/article/2600624/big-data-analytics/soon-everybody-will-be-a-data-scientist.html. Accessed April 15, 2017.
3. Dykes, B. "Analytics: 5 key steps to generate value." October 3, 2012. www.analytlcshero.com/2012/10/03/analytics-5-key-steps-to-generate-value. Accessed April 15, 2017.
4. Hamel, S. "Review of maturity models." September 1, 2009. http://blog.immeria.net/2009/09/review-of-maturity-models.html. Accessed April 15, 2017.

5. Loshin, D. "Achieving organizational alignment for Big Data analytics." July 17, 2013. http://data-informed.com/achieving-organizational-alignment-for-big-data-analytics. Accessed April 15, 2017.

6. Kaushik, A. "Multi-channel attribution modeling: The good, bad and ugly models." November 8, 2013. www.kaushik.net/avinash/multi-channel-attribution-modeling.good-bad-ugly-models. Accessed April 15, 2017.

7. Angel, G. (2016) *Measuring the Digital World: Using Digital Analytics to Drive Better Digital Experiences*. Upper Saddle River, NJ: Pearson Education, Inc. Emphasis added.

8. Accessed June 2, 2023. https://www.gartner.com/document/4014089?ref=solrAll&refval=366662942

9. Accessed June 2, 2023. https://www.gartner.com/document/4016569?ref=solrAll&refval=366666341&toggle=1

10. Accessed June 2, 2023. https://www.gartner.com/document/4014089?ref=solrAll&refval=366662942

11. Spiegel, B. "Ditch your digital top 10 metrics now!" August 1, 2013. http://marketingland.com/ditch-your-top-10-metrics-now-53525. Accessed April 15, 2017.

12. Sandhu, A. "Web Analytics comparison." March 11, 2013. www.slideshare.net/maverickaman/ga-wt-omtr. Accessed April 15, 2017.

13. Savkin Follow, A. "Design KPI." June 20, 2010. www.slideshare.net/asavkin/design-kpi. Accessed April 15, 2017.

14. "Pulse." www.amazon.com/Pulse-Science-Harnessing-Internet-Opportunities/dp/0470932368. Accessed April 15, 2017.

15. Smith, S. "How do companies use Web Analytics?" http://smallbushess.chron.com/companies-use-analytics-54630.html. Accessed April 15, 2017; "At Caesars, digital marketing is no crap shoot." February 1, 2013. www.dmnews.com/marketing-strategy/at-caesars-digital-marketing-is-no-crap-shoot/article/277685. Accessed April 15, 2017.

16. "Pulse." www.amazon.com/Pulse-Science-Harnessing-Internet-Opportunities/dp/0470932368. Accessed April 15, 2017.

17. "Marketers struggle to map multichannel customers' journeys." April 24, 2015. www.emarketer.com/Article/Marketers-Struggle-Map-Multichannel-Customers-Journeys/1012398. Accessed April 15, 2017.

Advanced Web Analytics and Web Intelligence

CHAPTER OBJECTIVES

After reading this chapter, readers should understand the following:

- Web analytics stakeholders
- Basic and advanced segmentation in web analytics
- Goal-setting and conversions

Google Analytics 4

Google Analytics 4 (GA4) is the latest version of the web analytics platform offered by Google. It was introduced in October 2020 as the successor to the previous version known as Universal Analytics. Google Analytics 4 introduces several advanced implementation issues that can be interesting and challenging for marketers. GA4 provides businesses and website owners with valuable insights into their online activities, user behavior, and marketing effectiveness. Here are a few noteworthy aspects:

- **Event tracking and enhanced measuremen**t: GA4 places a stronger emphasis on event tracking compared to the traditional pageview-centric approach of the now sunsetted Universal Analytics. Implementing event tracking for business insights requires careful consideration of the events to track, event parameters, and mapping them to specific user interactions and goals on your website or app.
- **Enhanced e-commerce tracking: GA4** introduces enhanced e-commerce tracking features that provide more detailed insights into user behavior throughout the customer journey, from product views to purchases. Enhanced e-commerce tracking requires additional data layer implementation and configuring parameters for tracking product details, add_to_cart, transactions, and more.
- **User identity and user properties: GA4** focuses on user-centric measurement rather than session-based tracking (but it offers both methods of tracking). Marketers should implement user identity tracking if they want to recognize and track users across devices and platforms. Utilizing user properties allows for more granular segmentation and personalization. Implementing user identity and

DOI: 10.4324/9781003025351-10

user properties requires careful integration with user authentication systems or implementing unique user identifiers.

- **Data streams and data import: GA4** supports multiple data streams, allowing marketers to collect and analyze data from various sources such as websites, apps, or other platforms. Implementing data streams and integrating data from different sources may involve additional configuration, data import, or integration with third-party platforms. Each data streams points to a different source of data (i.e., a website or collection of websites, vs. a mobile app, where the website(s) and app(s) have separate data streams).

- **Cross-domain and subdomain tracking**: User interactions across multiple domains or subdomains can be more complex in GA4 than in Universal Analytics. Marketers must ensure proper cross-domain tracking configuration, implement linker parameters, and define referral exclusions to track user behavior across domains accurately.

- **Custom dimensions and metrics**: GA4 introduces custom dimensions and metrics that provide flexibility in defining and tracking custom data points specific to your business needs. Implementing custom dimensions and metrics requires planning and proper configuration to ensure accurate data capture and reporting.

- **Privacy and consent management**: With increasing privacy regulations, GA4 includes features to manage user consent and data privacy. Implementing these features requires compliance with relevant privacy regulations, integrating consent management platforms, and configuring settings to honor user preferences.

These advanced implementation issues in GA4 require a solid understanding and technical expertise, along with a familiarity with the platform's main features. Google Analytics implementation should be carefully planned, and it is recommended that analysts consult Google's documentation and best practices and seek assistance from developers or analytics professionals to ensure accurate and effective implementation.

Once web analytics platforms are deployed, they should be configured to capture all the information needed to make business decisions concerning the website that is being measured. The information web analytics platforms collect also need to be communicated to stakeholders and decision-makers within the organization/enterprise.

Stakeholders

The Stakeholder Ecosystem

The business stakeholder has become an interesting brew, so to speak, in many organizations. Everyone seems to want the data that web analytics produces, but hardly anyone knows what to do with it. The reaction of most business owners is that the data readouts are too technical, and were created for analysts (which is true). But, web analytics contains a wealth of information that could inform any business function, once the data is taken out of the platform and put into the context the extended stakeholder needs it to be in. In this regard, it's worth spending a few paragraphs discussing whom the extended stakeholder might be, as illustrated in Figure 10.1. Some of the more advanced thinking about stakeholders comes from companies like IBM. Per IBM, Big Data & Analytics Hub[1] presents a newer way to

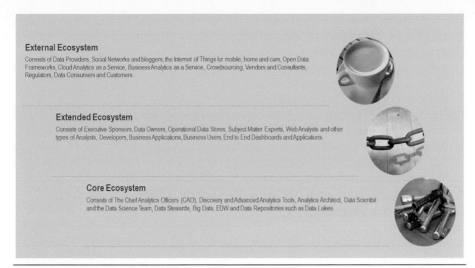

Figure 10.1 Web Data Analytics Ecosystem
Source: Marshall Sponder

group stakeholders that it terms a "data hub". The data hub encourages enterprise data collaboration, something that a siloed stakeholder-based organization inhibits.

Three interacting spheres define the *data hub* analytics ecosystem:

- **Core ecosystem:** Individuals and technologies assemble the data that is required, analyze the data to generate insights, and determine actions based on these ideas to achieve business outcomes. In this grouping, web analytics and the centers of excellence should be placed because analytics has become a critical business function.
- **Extended ecosystem:** Individuals, groups, and systems direct the analytics projects, collaborate with the core team, provide raw data, consume the outputs, and act on the insights. In this grouping, LOBs (lines of business) and various departments within an organization should be placed who need critical business data but do not have the means to gather it directly.
- **External ecosystem:** Customers, business partners, vendors, data providers, and consumers interact with the organization to help deliver the full potential of big data goals. Many organizations have business partners – even competitors can be business partners in some arrangements, and certain data can be shared between parties, which should be considered the external ecosystem.

The old way of dividing stakeholders into separate constituencies created mediocre results because the needs of different stakeholders were too often not aligned. Unless web analytics data can be put in the proper context, it is unlikely to be useful to anyone – usually requiring an analyst to interpret the data readouts.

Stakeholders' Roles Are Key

The most important characteristic a stakeholder has is what kind of actions they can take in an organization – their very specific roles will determine the kind of web analytics reporting they need. We covered a lot of the interview/questions that should be asked at the beginning of a analytics engagement in the previous chapter, and in this chapter, we view stakeholders more strategically.

Questions to ask stakeholders before delivering web analytics reports:

1. What is your role in the organization?
2. In the interest of providing you with actionable information to inform your decision-making, what types of actions do you take in your role(s)?
3. What information do you need from the web analytics team?

Advice: Let Stakeholders Believe That They Are Driving the Reporting

Typically, stakeholders have a very limited, stereotypical view of what web analytics data contains and how it can be used; they need to be educated. The best way to generate actionable web analytics reporting is to present a series of options of the data they can have in their readouts and reports (i.e., do you want A, B, or C?). Caveat, when presented with the specific reporting deliverables that were chosen, the stakeholder(s) may push back, and respond that the report they received was not what they asked for. That is due to the nature of reporting, in general, which is iterative in nature.

Avoiding Becoming a Report Monkey

When stakeholders receive the reporting that they asked for, it is often different than what they claim they requested. This disconnect could arise from the analyst or the stakeholder, or an imprecise way of defining what is to be delivered. In this case, analysts are invited to redo the report, tying up web analytics in an endless stream of report revisions and late working hours. Analysts can streamline their workload by delaying reporting until the stakeholder requirements are nailed down; when that is not possible, just produce an ad hoc, one-time report. We also want to put forward a point of view that repeating analytics reporting due to constant revisions and omissions may sap any time or energy left to discover new and exciting insights into the organization. Becoming a report monkey is the fastest way to burn out of the analytics industry. We all need some to time to play with these platforms and discover something new, especially if industry believes in the mantra of data being the "new oil". Consequently, all analysts should spend time discovering new patterns in the data (whatever data they are asked to examine), and not exclusively focus on daily, weekly, and monthly deliverables, support tickets, and ad hoc requests. In other words, there needs to be some room for discovery and play in the analytics process or else we burn out quickly.

The Type of Information Stakeholders Want

We examined the extended stakeholder ecosystem in Figure 10.1; let's examine what kind of data the recipients in the ecosystem want to know (that web analytics platforms can illuminate). Organizations purchase and deploy digital analytics platforms to fulfill several business priorities such as targeting, content optimization, and social engagement. However, web analytics usually does not contain information on real-time marketing, social media analytics, programmatic optimization, mobile optimization, content optimization, and social media engagement in a ready-to-use format for stakeholders.

Examples of marketing operations web analytics can/can't inform:

- **Multichannel campaign management:** Omnichannel analytics requires proper JavaScript tagging of all digital assets. Web analytics reporting supports this schema, but it must be set up beforehand and be regularly maintained.
- **Marketing automation:** Usually handled by third-party platform services rather than web analytics platforms. However, web analytics reporting informs customer targeting, digital advertising, and email marketing, when configured to track those activities.
- **Customer scoring:** Customer scoring is not usually in web analytics platforms (although content scoring is).
- **Mobile optimization:** Web analytics platforms possesses a wealth of data originating from the mobile devices of visitors to the tracked website.

Top Growing Digital Priorities Are (as per eMarketer, 2022)

1. Adjust marketing strategy to prepare for the economic uncertainty and the impacts of inflation.
2. Improve the ROI/effectiveness of marketing.
3. Reduce unnecessary marketing spend.
4. Consolidate marketing e-orts to our most impactful channels.
5. Bring certain outsourced technologies or services back in-house.

Enriching Web Analytics Reporting With External Data Sources

Web analytics captures the actions of visitors that take place on tracked websites, but not the marketing activity happening in other locations, outside of the site or offline (although there are other ways to extend the data and reporting contained in web analytics platforms via analytics APIs, custom variables, and database writes – aspects of external data capture are examined briefly in previous chapters).

We have established so far that to get a fuller, more actionable picture of consumer activity, web analytics alone is not sufficient – we must add other data, such as weather information and road traffic data (listed in Table 10.2) and merge it with tracked website behavior (which informs user/customer behaviors).

In the example of the umbrella street vendor in Chapter 9, it was easy enough to get climate data pulled from the Weather Channel/IBM Watson, which informed a direct action, capitalizing on an impending rainstorm in a nearby outdoor pedestrian area. If the vendors were working for a single company who controlled all such operations around the city, they would need to be alerted and supplied with enough umbrellas before it rains to make it worthwhile to stand out in the rain and sell them to interested pedestrians. Such an application needs website data via web analytics, combined with geo-data and climate data. While this example may seem somewhat far-fetched and whimsical, it's a very tactical example of what combining first-, second-, and third-party data can accomplish.

The Web Analytics Ecosystem

The world of digital analytics may seem complicated, but it is not so complex – Google Analytics evangelist Avinash Kaushik[2] did a splendid job of simplifying it, as shown in Table 10.2.

We think Table 10.2 covers Phases 1, 2 and 3 of the Digital Analytics Maturity Model shown in Table 9.11, in Chapter 9. Avinash deals with a simple web analytics implementation that deploys structured data to several departmental and enterprise business requests – that is as far as web analytics can illuminate, by itself. To reach Phases 4 and 5 of the digital analytics maturity, we must go past web analytics aid explore all the kinds of data that exist or would be useful and put them in a data lake or data warehouse. But if we just confine ourselves to web analytics implementation, Tables 10.2 and 10.3 serves us well.

Kaushik breaks down the implementation of web analytics into three phases as described in Table 6.4, which will take up to three years from start to finish to complete. However, we do not have independent research to support this view, and it is presented as bespoke findings from Avinash Kaushik, based on his writings. Perhaps companies will jump through Phases 1–3 of Table 6.4 faster or maybe they get stuck in Phase 2 (the most frequent outcome).

Notwithstanding the aforementioned, the duration of the stages of web/data analytics implementation will probably take closer to three years, per Kaushik.[3] Implementing the technology is part of the reason; the way the organization communicates internally with its stakeholders and customers is the other part.

Organizations who are not committed to analytics improvement will also have a hard time progressing beyond the first three steps of analytics projects as shown in Figure 10.2. Incidentally, Kaushik's Implementation Phases 1–3 in Table 10.3 line up very nicely with the first three stages of big data adoption presented in Figure 10.2– that's because they are common measures in any data implementation, regardless of the data or tools we are discussing.

Table 10.1 Comparing Unstructured, Structured, and Internal House Data Types

Unstructured External Data	Structured External Data	Internal Data
Utility Usage	Census Data	Sales Transactions
Search Terms	Partner Data	Web Analytics
Financial Market Data	Some Geo-Data	Product Shipments and Returns
Travel Traffic Data	Social Profiles	Inventory Data
Climate Data		Call/Contact Center Data
Geo-Data		Invoices
Blog Comments		CRM Data
Social Media Data		Employee Data
News		Marketing Campaigns

Source: Authors

Table 10.2 Parts of the Web Analytics Ecosystem, Detailed

Step	Element of Web Analytics	Analytics Ecosystem Definition
1.	Choose the web analytics platform/tool vendor	Google Analytics 4, Adobe Analytics (latest version) or other web analytics platforms designed to perform similar functions, etc.
2.	Choose the metrics to track (this may take some introspection/trial and error and experimentation to settle on the right set of metrics)	Metrics are simply numbers.
3.	Define business goals	Increase revenue by 20% in the current quarter from the last quarter
4.	Develop/choose key performance indicators (KPIs)	A KPI is a metric that helps you understand how you are doing against your objectives (such as bounce rate).
5.	Set dimensions for measurement	A dimension is an attribute of visitors to the website such as traffic sources, search keywords, referring sites, campaigns, countries, etc.
6.	Pure data pukes (customize reporting)	Find analysts that enjoy looking at the data
7.	Analysts/big brains	Hire the right people to live with the data and interpret it for stakeholders
8.	Custom reporting	Reporting is further developed, and new reports (and metrics) are created as needed.
9.	Custom data pukes	Develop analysts that know how to find the relevant data needed
10.	Set up advanced segmentation	Advanced segmentation, looking at the entire universe of website data to focusing on micro-clusters for actionable insights
11.	Develop Insights	From the data form a concept of what is happening on the website and why
12.	Take action(s)	Implement changes to improve performance and measure the results
13.	Competitive realities	Perform a SWOT analysis using your web analytics (and third-party data)
14.	Business impacts	Quantifying what will happen once the actions are taken
15.	New opportunities	Opportunities that are developed by using the collected data

Source: Authors based on data from Avinash Kaushik

Table 10.3 Phases of Implementation of a Web Analytics Ecosystem, Detailed

Phase	Characteristic	Description	Time Frame
1.	Data Capture	Putting tools in place and identifying the first set of metrics; this will quickly be followed by an effort to understand business priorities.	First six months
2.	Data Reporting	Many reports generated but not much business value from them (yet).	Months 7–12
3.	Data Insights	Generate actionable reporting that moves organizations forward.	1–3 years

Source: Authors, based on Avinash Kaushik

Developing and Managing Big Data Analytics Projects

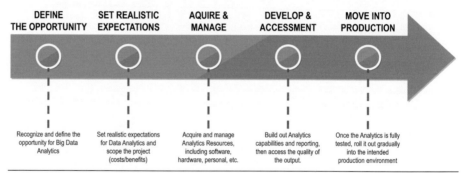

Figure 10.2 Managing the Process for Big Data Analytics Adoption
Source: Marshall Sponder

Evaluating Websites

Web analytics platforms are designed to measure the behavior of visitors on a website, and website design (UX) on visitors. Once website KBRs are defined and matched to appropriate KBRs, it is possible to determine whether the site is fulfilling its intended purpose or not. In fact, evaluating the impact of website design and functionality on visitors is one of the main use cases for web analytics as shown in Figure 10.3.

Pragmatic Web Analytics

A conversion action refers to a specific activity or set of activities that you want website visitors or app users to complete (see Table 10.4 for Google Analytics 4's example). The following questions can serve as a rough guide when looking at any website's web analytics for the first time, and every web analytics platform should be able to shed light on the following:

- Which pages are working well for the purposes they are intended?
- Which pages get low or no traffic?

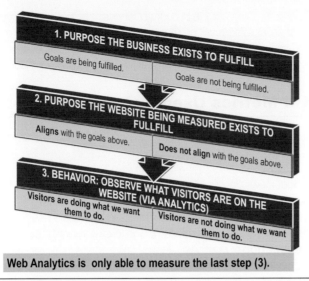

Figure 10.3 Questions to Ask When Understanding if a Website Implementation Is Successful
Source: WebMetricsGuru Inc.

Table 10.4 How Google Analytics 4 Defines Conversion Actions

Type	Description	Example
Destination	A specific page location loads	A thank you page, webpage or application screen
Duration	Sessions that last a specific amount of time, or longer	Ten or more minutes spent on a support website
Pages/ pageviews per session	A user views a specific number of pages or pageviews	Five or more pages or pageviews have been loaded
Event	An action defined as an event is triggered	Social share, video play, ad click, etc.

Source: Authors from information provided by Google Analytics Developers Portal

- Which areas in a website do visitors drop off/leave?
- Which pages are high exit pages?
- Which campaigns are driving success on a site, and which ones are just costing us money but not providing business value?
- Which products or services are selling and which are not?

This series of questions helps to deliver practical, diagnostic mini-insights that can help an organization optimize their websites, especially if they have first defined what each page is intended to do and how they would like visitors to interact and move around the site.

Goals and Conversion Events

Goals can be KPIs, often these are defined ahead of knowing what would be best to track. Fortunately, most analytics platforms allow stakeholders to define several goals, so it is usually possible to add new targets and/or refine the goals that are already in place.

There is always something unique in every business. It is likely that custom metrics and key performance indicators will be more useful than the standard, out of the box intermediate metrics that analytics platforms provide. Business value arises from how the data is customized, that seems to be a universal for every subject we deal with in this book.

Typical KPI Metrics Used by Industry

This is just a sample; there is lots of variety, customization, and creativity that can be applied here.

- **Retail:** product view, checkout, purchase
- **Media:** subscription, contest sign-up, page view, video view
- **Finance:** application, submission, login, self-service tools usage
- **Travel:** booking (purchase), internal campaign (click-through), search (pricing itinerary)
- **Telecommunications:** purchase, leads, self-service tools usage
- **High-tech:** whitepaper download, RFP, form completion, support requests
- **Automotive:** lead, submission, request a quote, brochure download

Definition of Good KPI

The perfect metric is the one the stakeholder or business user can understand and act on (see Figure 10.4). A key performance indicator is chosen because it informs business strategy and measures business growth.

Data Segmentation

Web analytics platforms provide customized segmentation (slices of data) that can inform business decisions – and in this respect, they excel over other types of analytics platforms.

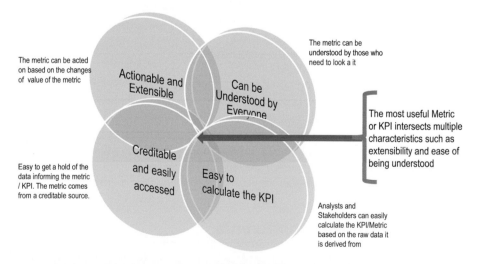

Figure 10.4 Defining the "Perfect Metric"
Source: Marshall Sponder

Example of Behavioral Segmentation of an eCommerce Business Website

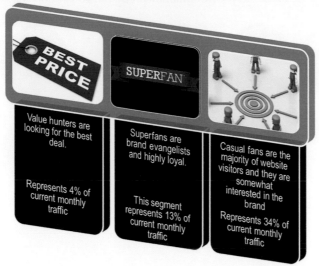

Figure 10.5 Example of Behavioral Segmentation on an E-Commerce Website
Source: Marshall Sponder

The behavioral segmentation shown in Figure 10.5 illustrates three custom customer segments to an e-commerce website. Custom segments are available for most reports and provide analysts and stakeholders with unique insights. Even free platforms such as Google Analytics provide amazing segmentations based on such visitor demographics, ZIP code, or neighborhood, and the sky is the limit for what web analytics can track provided extra coding and enablement are in place. Web analytics collects custom traffic metrics administrators define and configure such as newspaper signups, spend velocity, or anything else stakeholders and analysts define, once the data is captured in the analytics platform, and assigned to the metric. However, in the clear majority of websites, almost no instrumentation is done. Analysts should educate stakeholders about what insights it is possible to get with these systems.

Custom Segmentation

Web analytics platforms can divide visitors into different groupings, called segments.

What Can Go Into a Custom Segment

Web analytics tracks visitor location (usually at the city level) including where visitors are coming from, what device they used, the browser, connection, time of day, day of the week, and so on. No doubt, server web logs also contain similar information about location, date, time, etc.

Segments are comprised of many kinds of data (as per Figure 10.6) or a combination of them (provided the data be available/captured by the platform). It is best to focus on the characteristics and needs of the organization being analyzed and specific stakeholders when creating a custom segment. While web analytics allow analysts and

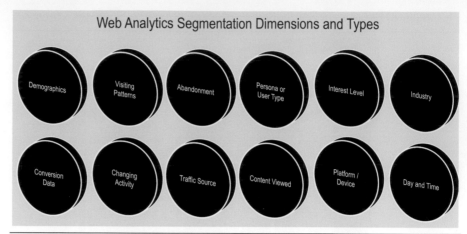

Figure 10.6 Segmentation Types in Web Analytics
Source: Marshall Sponder

administrators to create custom segmentations they should be validated against any stated or implied marketing task/goal by analysts and stakeholders. Segments exist for a specific marketing purpose; segments should be tested and validated against the intended goal for that segment, before using it for reporting. If the segment is not capturing the intended data, it should be improved until it does or discarded.

Adobe Analytics Custom Segments

Adobe analytics has enhanced segmentation shared across multiple groups in the same organization, and similar segmentations capabilities exist in most web analytics platforms.

Adobe Analytics Segmentation Types

There are three basic types of segmentation, along with a new enhanced programmable segmentation type that were released in the spring of 2015. You can create programmable segments when certain defined Boolean logic conditions occur. Boolean segmentation (programmable segments) are a hybrid grouping type we have not seen in the other web analytics platforms we have used. More likely, if they don't exist in Google Analytics today, they probably will be added, eventually.

Analysts can define and reuse segments when needed and even build segments from other segments along with preset segment templates (Adobe Analytics). Also, multiple segments can be applied at the same time and compared with other segments. In Google Analytics, custom segments are even easier to create and apply than Adobe Analytics (the user interface is easier to manipulate and more intuitive). However, it is far more challenging to define the best segment to build (and then test it). According to Gary Angel:

> Segmentations divide people into interestingly differentiated groups. Every business has segments, and for every business, they are potentially infinite and unique. There's no single right segmentation, but segmentation is always useful. I have never studied a digital property that can't or shouldn't be segmented.[4]

Usually, there is a business need to examine the behavior of a heterogeneous group of visitors or visits, and that reason drives the creation and iteration of the segment.

Custom Segment Examples

By now readers should have an idea that segments are created to examine situations where stakeholders and analysts want to know more about certain visitors. Web Analytics platforms support various kinds of segmentations (these could be set up with Google Analytics free version as well – anyone could create segments, even without administrative access, when needed).

How Google Analytics 4 Works With Segmentation

We have to discuss segmentation types in Google Analytics 4 before we can discuss segmentation in any detail in Google Analytics 4. Segments allow us to pick certain users of our website or app (property) and analyze how they are behaving. Segments are a very complex subject that is difficult to explain all at once and take a while to get used to. Table 10.5 shows the Adobe Analytics segmentation types while Table 10.6 shows Adobe Analytics segmentation examples.

Table 10.5 Adobe Analytics Segmentation Types

Segmentation Type	Definition	Example
Hit Based	Actions happening on a specific page or a specific resource such as a link to a page	Clicks on links on a specific page – a conversion event that exists only on a specific page (i.e., shopping cart checkout might be one example).
Visit Based	Visits occurring due to a campaign or anything that happens during a specific visit	Paid search campaigns, tracking if a visitor is logged in or not during their visit (when authentication is present) and viewing specific content during a visit are some examples.
Visitor Based	Information about the state of visitors to the website (over a series of visits)	New vs. repeat visitors, registered vs. non-registered visitors, new customers vs. loyal customers and any geo-demographics such as age, gender, location
Programmable (Logic Group)	Boolean logic triggered, exists if certain conditions are met (using "if-then" statements).	Visitor contribution goes beyond a certain value trigger, creates a segment and stores information about the visitor.

Source: Authors, based on material from Adobe Education

Table 10.6 Adobe Analytics Segmentation Examples

Segment Example	Segment Type
Anyone who spent more than $600 on the retail website	VISITOR (set Revenue 600 US)
A specific visit where $600 or more was spent	VISITOR (set Revenue = 600 US)
Visitors that hand spent more than $600 over the lifetime of their visits to the website	VISITOR (set Revenue = 600 US)
Males in the United States who purchased an item during a visit	VISITOR (set Gender = Male AND Country = the United States)
All visitors to specific sections of the website	VISITOR (set Site Section = Men AND Site Section = Woman)
Collect all the visits to the Men's Apparel page AND viewed two specific Men's Wallet pages (leather AND snakeskin) within 16 pages of each other (uses a logic group)	VISIT (set Page = Men's Apparel) THEN (within 16 pages of each other) (Page = Men's leather wallet AND Page = Men's snakeskin wallet)
Collect visitors that have more than ten visits to the website OR visitors from a specific campaign and spent at least $110 during that visit	VISIT (Visit number = 10) OR ((Campaign = Snakeskin Wallets paid ads AND Campaign Click-throughs = True) AND Revenue >= 110 USD))

Source: Authors, based on material from Adobe Education

Types of segments: (example: ***add_to_cart*** *event*, this is often used as an event in e-commerce websites as part of conversion tracking):

- **User:** Includes actions a user took in totally, across sessions. For example, if ever a user added a product to a shopping cart on the website, even if it were a month ago in a previous segment, they will show up in the segment if the "add_to_cart" event was added, and we looked at active users, etc., as metrics.
- **Session:** only the sessions where a user added a product to the cart are counted.
- **Event:** Only includes sessions where "add_to_cart" occurred (irrespective on the user or other events).

  - Event Scope:

    Look for a sequence of events that happen and include them into the segment.

  - Event Exclude (exclude certain events that happen on a website or app that are not added to a segment).
  - You can also specify of users not to include based on events they did or didn't do.

Segmentation examples in Google Analytics 4:

- People who visit several pages, more than four pages, for example (a marker of being more engaged with the website's content).
- Segments/Session Segment/page_view/Condition = <event count> >4/Apply.
- Sessions (or users) include "view_search_results" and apply it to an exploration and compare it to "all users" and looked at average revenue per user. The insight here is that people who use site search tend to spend more money on the website, and the action to take would be to encourage users to use the site search more often.
- New Users vs. Returning Users: Create user segment/"session_number =1" – this matches user that had their first session during a certain time period.

General considerations about segments:

- At the current time, segments are available in explorations (custom reporting), only.
- Certain explorations allow only one segment (such as path exploration).
- At the current time segments created in one exploration cannot be used in another exploration and need to be recreated. There is currently no way to save a segment that can be used across segments, which is seen as an annoying feature and a limitation of the platform.
- There are "Suggested segments" that can be used and adapted (modified) that serve as "templates".

  - Among the segments you can use are the **predictive segments** that use machine learning to learn which users are transacting and those who are not transacting and then predicting new users who are likely to transact on your website property.

    - Unfortunately, the predictive segments need a lot of traffic and transactions to benefit from the predictive segments due to the machine learning requirements (machine learning usually requires a lot of data to operate on, and most smaller sites don't have enough data to satisfy the algorithm's requirements).
    - Google Analytics has some predictive segments that most properties can use if they have enough website or app traffic. To trigger the conditions necessary for the 7 day likely purchasers your website property would need in the last 28 days to have a 7-day period where the website property received at least 1000 return visitors who made a purchase (predicting condition) and at least 1000 returning visitors *did not* make a purchase (see Google Developers website documentation https://developers.google.com/search/docs). Not every business or organization can have these levels of numbers.

      - Caveat is that you can play with these segments using the Google demo as it has decent website traffic (although, honestly, the number of transactions, purchases, may not be enough to fully benefit from these segments).

Segments can be imported and modified within the exploration easily (i.e., country=US for US based traffic and country does not equal US for non-US traffic). You can also distinguish between the type of segment (user vs. session), depending on what you wish to measure.

As Google Analytics 4 is being regularly updated, there are still some features that are missing or not optimally available at the time of the writing of the second edition.

Segments vs Comparisons vs Audiences: There Are Differences in How Each Can Be Used

- **Comparisons** can be used in any standard report in GA4.
- **Segments** can be used just in the Explore: Explorations part of GA4.
- **Audiences** can be found in the "Admin" section of GA4, to Audiences, and there you can add new audiences if you have sufficient permission (we do not have permissions to do so in the GA Demo property, but we would on our own properties).

  - **Audiences are not retroactive and collect data from the point they are created.**

Locations	Segments	Audiences	Comparisons
Standard Reports	**No** (unless you first convert the segment into an audience)	**Yes**	Yes
Explorations	**Yes**	**No** (unless the first convert audience into a segment)	**No** (must be converted into a segment in the Explorer and are not retroactive)
Comparisons	**No**	**Yes**	
Google Ads	**No**	**Yes**	**No**
Retroactive	Yes	No	• Yes, under certain conditions in certain detail reports, when exported into the Explorer, you can then make segment out of it. • However, audiences uses in comparisons are not retroactive, and only represent data from the date they were created.

This table shows that for whatever an analyst or stakeholder may want to visualize, the current Google Analytics 4 platform has only certain options available which may or may not impact how crucial business data is reported to stakeholders and decision-makers.

Workarounds to Google Analytics reporting limitations.

Replacing or workarounds for a UA construct (views) in GA4: Universal Analytics allowed a subset of a property such a blog to be viewed as a report. In GA4, we no longer have views, so here are some workarounds. (see – https://support.google.com/analytics/answer/11526072)

- While Google Analytics 4 does not support views, it does support "sub-properties", but at the current time this feature is only available for paid GA4 customers.
- If you have a need to see the specific information from a part of your business such as just the blog or just the website or just the test/qa website, or just the support website, etc., then you have to use the same GA4 property for all of these.

  - Example: *If you wanted to only view the blog data of your property but nothing else, there is nothing convenient at this time, but there are workarounds.*

Workarounds for views using other features of GA4:

Workaround	Drawback 1	Drawback 2
Comparisons	Not persistent, must recreate on every visit to GA4.	Does not apply to Explorations.
Explorations	Must be manually set up.	Applies only to the specific exploration it was created in *(but tabs in a single exploration can share the same setup)*. *However, another way to get the segment to apply other explorations is to duplicate and then modify the exploration to what is needed.*
Filters (in Explorations)	Must be manually set up.	Applies only to the specific exploration it was created in *(but tabs in a single exploration can share the same setup)*.

(Continued)

(Continued)

Workaround	Drawback 1	Drawback 2
Filters (in Standard Reports)	Must be manually set up but any filtering applied is persistent and is a superior solution to using comparisons. However, to have the same filter apply to other standard reports you just go through the same steps with each report, copying it, modify it with the filter, saving it, then adding it in the library to the lifecycle reporting, etc.	Must be admin or have edit permissions to the property.
Segments (in Explorations)	Only Event segments will yield reliable data.	User and Session segments cannot be relied upon for totally accurate data.
Looker Studio (Data Studio)	You can use Looker to create reports to share with your stakeholders, but it requires the analyst to learn another tool.	Looker Studio has a deep learning curve, so we can make simple charts easily, but more complicated charts require additional learnings.

- **STANDARD REPORT BASED**: Example: a website (single GA4 property) that operates websites in multiple countries (i.e., US, UK, FR, DE). NOTE: ***This workaround does not apply to Explorations.***

  - Where the data from all four websites are showing up in the same GA4 property, but where you want to look at each separately.

    - Use a standard report and add a comparison with a dimension such as "site_name" and removing "all users". (this will depend on how the subdomains are set up). "page_path" is another alternative depending on the way the subdomains are configured.
    - The same comparison remains in all the additional standard reports viewed, though once you leave Google Analytics and come back to it (on another day, for example) the comparison is gone and needs to be recreated (ouch!).

- **STANDARD REPORT BASED**: Your business has an app in the same property as a website, but you just want to view the app data by itself (the equivalent of a view in UA).

  - Create a comparison in a standard report that filters on "Stream_ID" and get rid of any other comparison such as "all users". You can see what this looks like by using the Flood-IT property in the GA4 Demo. ***This workaround does not apply to Explorations.***

- The same drawback is present in that the comparison is not persistent, and when you come back to GA4 later (next day), the comparison is gone and you need to recreate it, which could be an inconvenient process.

- **EXPLORER BASED:** You just want to see a part of your business (subdomain) as a segment in an Exploration.

  - This can be done easily in the Explorations, say by creating a segment, where you include traffic from the "hostname" (which will be the subdomain).

- **EXPLORER BASED:** You just want to see a part of your business (subdomain) as a segment in an Exploration using **a filter**.

  - Use a filter such as "site_location" (when the dimension is added first); however, this solution isn't always reliable from what we have heard.

Another limitation is that using events in user or session segments doesn't always yield the expected results such as, engaged users where "page_views">5 and "learn.analyticsmania.com" does not yield only engaged users in a certain subdomain, but also other data, and so it's not possible to get really clean cuts of the data as one would expect at the current time.

Unfortunately, filtering doesn't yield a good solution either because it still includes data from the segment which includes other data we wanted to filter out, meaning that we can't really filter it all out, as much as we try.

Google Looker Studio (formally Google Data Studio)

Looker Studio solves some problems yet creates others that we didn't have before such as quota limits (however, these quotas have been increased so they allow most reports to be displayed).

Looker is a data visualization tool that allows the user to look at data from different sources (including outside GA4) and visualize it various dashboards.

See: https://lookerstudio.google.com/u/0/navigation/reporting.

Creating a Simple Dashboard Using Looker Studio

- Create tables, charts, maps, and adapt the design for the organization the analyst is reporting for (or for themselves).
- Start with a blank report and connect the data from various sources using the connectors that are available. At the time of this writing there are 23 Google connectors and 752 partner connectors.
- For the purposes of this short introduction to Looker, choose the Google Analytics connector. Based on your account permissions, you will be shown a list of properties you can connect to, pick the Google demo (GA4). You will now be able to add data from the Google demo to the Looker Studio dashboards you are building. A sample table is added, but we will delete it and start afresh.
- You can add a table or chart, click on those from the top navigation (graphics) and you will be shown several options. Let's create a table of the most popular pages. Modifying the table will be very similar to working with an exploration.
- Create a simple table with a couple of metrics such as views, sessions, and total users.
- Copy the table (Control+C), then paste. Change the style of the copied chart to time series or any other type you wish.
- Add a dashboard (sessions is default), copy the dashboard and change the metric to total users. Add previous reporting period to both dashboards to show

the percent change from the previous period.

- Copy both dashboards and change them into spark charts and get rid of the previous period comparison.
- Change the style using Theme and Layout in the top menu.
- Add additional pages (you can add several pages if needed), change the name to page 1 and page 2, etc., or you can give them names.
- Preview the report (eye icon in upper right).
- You can export the data as a PDF file once you're happy with it.
- You can share the report with someone else in your organization or outside of it, and give them viewer or edit permissions. You can set up the delivery time of reports that you share and even make it a weekly report (to your manager or team) on a certain day/time, as a recurring task. There is even a new "Present" mode when you're showing the report as part of a in person or remote meeting.

Workarounds with Google Looker Studio

1. **Use a filter for each element of a Looker Studio report to include only the hostname or subdomain of the GA4 property you want to report on.** The filters in Looker Studio many be more powerful than those in GA4 Explorer of Comparison. You can even name the filter and apply it to more than the element you selected (say to all elements, the filter you created for one element could then be applied to all elements if desired).
2. Additionally, along with the filtering, a "drop-down filter" can be added by adding a control (top menu). You can change the dimension to something that gives you what you want (i.e., hostname).

- Add an additional control (say, for date)

There's a lot more to learn about Looker Studio than we can cover here, but the information provided allows readers to start to use Google Analytics 4 and other data sources with Looker Studio to create customizable dashboards that inform chosen stakeholders within an organization.

Tagging Marketing URLs (anything that needs to track in Google Analytics except for organic search traffic)

- **Medium source, campaign, content, term**

  - See https://support.google.com/analytics/answer/9756891?hl=en

Understanding marketing channels and the source of traffic has driven web analytics to create a vocabulary and structure (grammar) for this, and it's still popular to use and organize reports based on this way of looking at acquisition traffic in terms of dimensions.

Now, as the marketer is setting up their marketing campaigns, they need to tag them appropriately, using UTM parameters in Google Analytics (this part is the same for UA and GA4); in fact, this type of tagging with parameters is needed in all analytics, as otherwise the platforms are not intelligent enough (yet) to understand these things (who knows, someday, with enough AI, they may be, but that is still not the case, today).

- **Medium** is a dimension that describes where the visitor comes from.

  - CPC, Organic

- **Source** is the name of the traffic source where visitors come from.

    - Google, Facebook, LinkedIn, email, etc.
    - For example: CPC, Google = the source of the traffic is paid advertising

- **Campaign** is a category of paid advertising.

    - Summer campaign, graduate campaign, undergraduate campaign

- **Term** is usually a keyword associated with a campaign.
- **Content** is the specific ad (or slogan) associated with the term (keyword) of a campaign.

GA4 automatically sets the medium/source of some traffic (i.e., traffic from Google, itself). When the user clicks on an add (which has the "gclid" parameter in the URL of the ad) then the source/medium will be cpc/google, etc.

Note that each UTM parameter maps to a dimension in Google Analytics.

The implication of that is if a marketer comes up with a completely novel UTM, they will probably need to first create a custom dimension for it – I have seen this myself with mapping Lat/Long parameters in earlier versions of Google Analytics. The marketer is free to create novel parameters, but they must create the inherit structure with the analytics to understand, process, and store these parameters so they can be displayed in reports.

UTM Parameters Classic Parameters

- utm_medium (dimension: medium)
- utm_source (dimension: source)
- utm_campaign (dimension: campaign)
- utm_term (dimension: term or keyword?)
- utm_content (dimension: content?)

Newer Parameters

- utm_id (dimension: campaign id)
- utm_source_platform (dimension: source platform)
- utm_creative_format (dimension: creative format?)
- utm_marketing_tactic (dimension: marketing tactic?)

Naming Marketing URLS with UTM Parameters

- Remember to keep everything in lower case as UTMs are case sensitive.
- Spaces are represented in UTM parameters with "+".
- Use the Campaign URL Builder – see https://ga-dev-tools.google/campaign-url-builder/.

Channel Groupings in Google Analytics 4
By Default, Google Analytics 4 has a default channel grouping (see https://support.google.com/analytics/answer/9756891?hl=en)

Channel groupings are the way to group your incoming traffic to more useful groupings. There are rules that are built into GA4 that determine how incoming traffic is classified into various groupings – see https://support.google.com/analytics/answer/9756891?hl=en.

Note:

- If you see a lot of unassigned traffic in your channel grouping reports, it means that the company is using a lot of custom values for utm_source and utm_medium that are not recognized. Before coming up with new values, always refer to the official GA4 documentation.
- The default channel grouping is case insensitive. It means that if you have utm_medium=email and utm_medium=Email, they will both be included in the "Email" default channel grouping. This is mentioned in the documentation.

Traffic and User Acquisition Standard Reporting

Standard reporting is the top level of reports that are visible as soon as a user logs into Google Analytics and play a similar role to the reports that were present with the now sunset Universal Analytics (also called GA3). However, Universal Analytics had many prebuilt reports that came with the platform and marketers did not need to know very much to get some useful information from them. On the other hand, Google Analytic 4 has very few standard reports compared to earlier versions and most reporting is customized using the Explorer section. There are several Explorations that we will cover later in this chapter.

Traffic and user acquisition reports are part of the e-commerce reporting that is enabled once Google Analytics 4 is set up with conversion events, traffic channel. With that said, most customer journeys to purchasing an item or a service aren't so linear and, in the journey, and several visits/sessions to a website (and other websites or apps) to conversion, how should the credit be assigned?

Attribution modeling is the process web analytics uses to assign credit to a conversion; it helps us decide with touch points get the credit for a conversion, and every step in the customer journey is called a touch point, attribution settings, attribution models, and data-driven attribution are covered in more detail at the Google Developer website.[5]

In Google Analytics 4, it has decided that first click, linear, position and time-decay attribution count for less (are depreciated, in other words) and are used less in conversion tracking, overall, and the reason is related to how much website data that used to be tracked automatically no longer is because it requires a user's consent. Attribution data can be said using the admin menu, with sufficient permissions, that is, to any of the number of models, and that setting is retroactive.

The attribution model is a calculation on the underlying data, but fortunately, Google analytics separates the data that it collects with the attribution model. The **default attribution model is cross-channel data-driven attribution**. The attribution model decides which channels and which sources get credit for the attribution. That said, there are certain areas in GA4, where choosing the attribution model has no impact, and those include the acquisition reports for users and traffic, and the advertising menu (left Nav), where analysts with sufficient permissions can change the attribution model on the fly and see the changes in attribution model applied immediately to all relevant data.

Look Back Window

Lookback window is a setting in Google Analytics 4 that sets the period of time that Google Analytics 4 can track the touchpoints of a customer journey, with the default being 30 days and the maximum being 90 days; any change in the settings applies only to future data and is not retroactive.

Data-Driven Attribution

Data-driven attribution is the default attribution set up in GA4. With DDA (data-driven attribution) machine learning algorithms decide which channels get the most credit for a conversion in certain situations by examining each touchpoint in the customers journey and then calculating the "conversion probability". The algorithm is actually not that hard to understand at a high level, as it looks at each touchpoint in a journey by excluding it, then calculating the overall probability of the rest of the journey touch points, and so on, and assigned weight to each touchpoint as a result of its calculations. On the plus side, certain underestimated marketing channels might be given more credit for a conversion than other models might ordinarily assign. On the minus side, it's a black box, and we don't know how the algorithm made the actual decision.

There is no perfect attribution model for an organization – they need to be compared to see what makes the most sense on a case-by-case basis. One of the things that is most confusing about the cross channel data-driven attribution is that it ascribes credit for the attribution to the last known traffic source what was not *direct*. As much of the data that lands in the direct traffic source contains traffic that was either not property tagged or comes from a source such as a PDF or Word file that does not generate a referrer URL. By lessoning the importance of the direct channel of traffic and using algorithms and user data from the Chrome browser that are logged in their Google Accounts.

Attribution Models in Google Analytics 4

Before you can get anything meaningful from attribution reports, there must be e-commerce tracking (conversions) set up in the website or app Google Analytics property.

- **Traffic Attribution standard report uses the "last-click" attribution model by default**.
- **User Acquisition standard report uses the "first click" attribution model by default;** that's because any report based on first user is based on the "first click" the user takes that arrives on the website (being measured in the GA4 property).

The issue with traffic and user attribution reports (and models) is that they assign all the credit for a conversion to either the first or last click and ignore all the other touch points of the user journey. It is more realistic to find a way to attribute some credit to every touch point in a customer journey, but the standard user or traffic acquisition reports fail to do that, resulting in overvalued or undervalued traffic sources in the standard reporting in GA4, or in most any web analytics platform.

The value of a touch point as a conversion will vary based on the conversion model that is being used, to compare the changes by model, go to Advertising/Attribution/Model Comparison, where the different models we currently have available to us can be compared in how they impact the attribution reporting.

When we are given "cross channel last-click" attribution and "cross channel data-driven" attribution models to compare (in the advertising reports of Google Analytics 4), but that's it at the current time. Analysts can compare different channel groupings and see how they compare across the two different attribution models just to get an idea of how the attribution model employed can impact how the attribution reporting is impacted by the attribution model used. Frankly, the two attribution models produce almost identical attribution results, though there are slight differences in the numbers, but they are fractional.

You can also change the two models that are compared by the drop-down next to each model to select a different model from those available (there are several available models).

The best way to compare attribution models is by looking at a single conversion event; by default, all conversion events are selected when comparing models. This can be done by clicking on the filter at the top of the report. Certain touch points will change in the conversion value based on what attribution model and how it counts the conversion-based touch points and the value attributed to the touch point. That said, there is no perfect attribution model for a business, it depends on what the business is doing and how they value their own marketing efforts, etc. With that said, data-driven cross channel attribution uses AI to fill in the gaps and tries to figure out the probable contribution of each touchpoint. Sometimes the attribution modeling can be used to justify or encourage more spending in one or more channels when reporting the results to stakeholders.

With Attribution modeling, it's best to have stakeholder's questions in mind before looking at the model comparison reporting, otherwise just comparing the different attribution models won't be very illumination or productive. Also, it's best to analyze campaigns several weeks after they end as some attribution results will not have taken place or attributed yet, and in this type of reporting, it's best to have patience and wait a few weeks before analyzing the conversion results of a campaign. Also, in some models what give credit to multiple touch points will have fractional values.

Accuracy of Attribution Reporting in Google Analytics 4

- Always take GA4's attribution data with a grain of salt for the following reasons:

  - Privacy regulations and user content affect attribution accuracy
  - Apple's Intelligent Tracking Prevention may a come into play on Apple devices and browsers
  - Browser restrictions
  - Ad blockers
  - Different devices
  - First-party cookies that expire or are delegated

Workarounds to Improve Attribution Reporting in Google Analytics 4

- **Server-Side Tagging** is a separate solution for some organizations as it places an internal tag management server inside the organization's firewalls that can clean data that is being sent back to analytics and advertising server outside the organization.
- **Server-side tagging can address cookie deletion and expiration issues.** Yet, it's not a total solution due to the complexity and overhead, but also because most acquisition is working with new users who are not authenticating (logging in, and don't have an account with your website/business yet). Therefore, there is no complete solution to the incomplete attribution data inherit in all web analytics systems at this time.

Custom Reporting (Explorations in Google Analytics 4)

Funnel Analysis

- **Funnel analysis** is an analytics technique used to map linear user journeys to see user drop-offs; though we may not know why users are dropping of, but at least we can pinpoint where they are dropping off (losing interest/leaving the website, etc.).

- Caveat, the customer journey is not linear, though funnel analysis a linear analysis technique and non-linear paths customer journeys won't be possible to visualize or analyze with this technique. So in order for this type of analysis there is the need to simplify the user's desired path into something linear, so we can analyze it.
- Another issue with funnel analysis is that impulse buyers can distort the results of the analysis.
- Yet another issue with funnel analysis is that they may be too simplistic to realistically represent a customer's journey through your website or app experience to the desired outcome or destination. User journeys are a mess, in general, and they are almost never linear.
- Funnel analysis requires an analyst know how their website or app is structured as well as the desired outcome for a user transferring the website (measure as a GA4 property).
- The best way to plan out a funnel is to connect it to some event you want to see take place on your website or app (say a purchase) – that is the goal, and then consider the steps needed to take place getting to the goal. Those are the steps of the funnel analysis you will likely set up. Best to map the steps you want the user (Customer) to take in the way you are hoping they will perform.

Funnel Analysis Best Practices

- Prepare for a fair amount of debugging that's needed to get the most benefit out of a funnel analysis.
- Don't try to figure out if users are navigating your website when you're planning your first few funnels analysis.
- Focus your funnels (at least) initially, on "quick wins", things that generally happen quickly; this also helps your stakeholders and management see your value as an analyst.
- List an event on social media and get new users (visitors) to sign up (pay up, etc.).
- Show ads on Facebook and get new users who are purchasing the product.
- Viewers who watch a video on YouTube you placed (paid or organic) and decided to come to your website, sign up for a program or purchase a book, etc.
- Find the events that already are bringing in revenue successfully and build your initial funnels from that – rationale is that a successful process that is driving results may be even more successful if it were better optimized. Funnel analysis is good for that type of use case.
- When working with websites that have less traffic, pick a longer period to analyze data such as three months or six months so you have enough data to analyze.
- Add device category as a breakdown to see if there are bigger drop-offs in one type of device than another.
- If possible, have developers set up error tracking on the website or app, then it will be possible to use funnel analysis with error codes when users are running into certain tracked error conditions.

Analyzing What Funnel Analysis

Here are some additional ideas of the most common reasons why people are dropping off at specific stages of funnels.

Potential Leaks at the Top of the Funnel

- Targeting wrong people
- Irrelevant messaging
- Slow page loading speed
- The content of the ad does not match the content of the page (the expectation of a visitor is not met)

Potential Leaks at the Middle of the Funnel

- Too many distractions (the page should always have a single goal, e.g., purchase, acquiring a lead). Having too many options or distractions can hurt the end result
- Unqualified leads progress through the funnel
- The sales pitch starts too soon without properly educating the potential customer about a problem that you solve or providing enough free value first, if this applies to a business model

Potential Leaks at the Bottom of the Funnel

- Sales pages/checkout technical issues
- Not enough payment methods
- Cost of shipping, taxes
- Confusing checkout process

Find where the drop off is happening the most and analyze that. Usually the closer to the purchase, the more serious the drop off is, as a decrease there really impacts the bottom line of a business's income.

Google Analytics 4 Explorations That Are the Most Useful

The Google Analytics product team has provided several types of explorations (custom reports) but just a few of them handle most analytics questions.

- **Freeform** – you can build your own custom report from scratch.
- **Funnel** – analyze a predetermined pattern of traffic on a website, app, webpage or webform.
- **Pathing/reverse pathing** – analyze how users navigate through a website or app.

Note: Several standard reports can also be made to generate explorations when a comparison is added, and they are usually designated by the "Explore" button in the bottom left pane of a screen.

Standard Reports that Generate an Exploration

The following standard reports usually can generate an exploration (Custom Report).
    One great feature of Google Analytics 4 is that many of the standard reports allow for the generation of a custom report from the standard report (exploration);

the exploration that is generated from the standard report allows analytics users to customize their reporting and use the standard reporting as a starting point for a deeper analysis of the website patterns, behaviors, and traffic. To access the exploration, start with a comparison and then look at the lower right corner of the screen where there is an "Explore" button. When clicked on, an exploration based on the standard report is created, and this can be modified by the analyst to dig deeper and perhaps, create their own custom report.

- **Traffic acquisition**
- **User acquisition**
- **Event/event name**
- **Conversions**
- **Pages and screens**
- **Landing page**
- **E-commerce purchases**
- **In-app purchases**
- **Publishers ads**
- **User purchase journey**

User Privacy and User Consent in Google Analytics 4

Recent developments in European privacy laws consider Google Analytics to be illegal to use due to the GDPR legislation that has been in place for the last five years.[6]

Options and Features of Google Analytics That Have Arisen to Remedy User Privacy and User Consent Gaps

- IP anonymization
- The control of Google Signals + regional settings
- Disable Google Signals and ads personalization programmatically
- Mark events and user-scoped custom dimensions as NPA
- Data retention
- Data deletion requests (or delete users in user explorer)
- Consent mode

In early 2022, Austrian regulators stated that an Austrian website was using Google Analytics and according to GDPR it is illegal (because GA sends the data and IP address to servers in the United States; as a result, several other countries followed the same path).

- A similar argument is being used to propose banning TikTok in the United States as it has been found to be sending its data to servers in China (and TikTok is said to be controlled by the Communist Party).
- Another case involves recent elections in Arizona where some data vendors were sending election data to servers in China.

And as a prominent and popular analytics evangelist as mentioned recently,[7] "This is much bigger than just GA. If you are using any provider/tool/CRM/etc. that stores data in the US, they are part of this. But at the same time, there are still some unknowns in this situation". And later on, Julius Fedorovicius stated that "This affects A LOT of SaaS providers. So, my guess would be that more businesses will implement solutions for this".

Finally, Julius affirms that he thinks we should let the dust settle a bit and let's see what happens next. So, for now, don't panic. In the meantime, configure your setups and ask for valid consent before tracking anyone.

- Interim Solution: Google announced that GA4 will not be sending IP addresses to the US. Instead, all requests from the EU will be sent to EU GA4 servers, IP addresses will be removed there, and then data without anonymized IP addresses will be sent to US. This will not affect IP-based internal traffic filters because filtering happens before that. See – https://support.google.com/analytics/answer/12017362

Essentially, internet walled gardens are being set up to conform with recent legislation, and I think this solution will become more widespread over time, but whether it solves anything long-term remains to be seen. However, advertising data (re: Google Signals) was modified to allow it to turn on and off data collection on a regional basis, but the implementation of data collection and sharing will increasingly be subject to whatever legislation is in place in wherever the business operates to collect data, even if the business or organization is run from somewhere else.

See Privacy Settings in GA4:

- GA4 has more privacy controls than UA had because the entire web analytics industry, and online industry itself, is moving to a privacy first approach.
- Consent mode data is now used not only in conversion modeling but also in behavioral modeling. Meaning that now more gaps can be filled in, and you will see higher numbers in users, events, conversions, etc. This is not enabled by default; you have to configure Consent Mode + Use Blended reporting identity.

Table 10.7 Privacy Control Table

Feature	GA4	UA (GA3)
IP ANOMIZATION reduces PII	123.123.223.123 is changed to 123.123.123.0 and is the default. However, the full IP address is still sent to other countries, though it is not stored before IP ANOMIZATION is put into place. Caveat: to achieve full IP ANOMIZATION, Server-Side Tagging must be used.	123.123.123.123 must be manually configured to 123.123.123.0.

Feature	GA4	UA (GA3)

Google Signals (used to collect more information about your users)	By default, Google Signals is not enabled.
	• Should consult legal team to decide if it's OK to enable Google Signals and collect more (demographics type) data on users.
	  o Caveat: if Google Signals is enabled, it will collect user data regardless of users opting out of having their data collected.
	  o One solution is to use GTM to programmatically enable or disable Google Signals by user opt-in (REGEX)
	Using GA4 with GTM, Google Signals can be activated or deactivated per user opt-in.
		Not implemented?

Ads Personalization	Can be enabled or disable based on the country (region).	Not implemented?
Google Consent Mode (this is a gray area)	1. If enabled, certain consent settings are loaded onto a page, and by default they are denied. Nonetheless, some advertising data is still sent to ad servers, though it is anonymized. 2. Next, a pop-up is served to the user to ask them for their consent to collect the users' data.	Not implemented?

(Continued)

Table 10.7 *(Continued)*

Feature	GA4	UA (GA3)
	a. If the user gives their consent for tracking the normal, data is sent to GA4, or to floodlight servers, etc., with cookies. b. If the user doesn't give their consent to be tracked, then the rest of the data is sent but does not use cookies.	
Audiences	Allows NPA (Non-Personalized Ads) • Any event that is collected can be marked as "NPA" by the admin, • When an audience that has been defined uses an event that has been marked "NPA", it will be ineligible for Google Personalized Ads.	Not implemented?
Custom Definitions	User-Scoped Dimensions can be marked as NPA.	Not implemented?
Data Retention – Reset user data on new activity	Depending on what the legal team says about retaining data older than 2 months, data retention can be set to 14 months or left at the default 2 months. • However, with "Reset user data on new activity", a user's data can be stored for longer periods than 14 months if they periodically and often return to the website.	Same

Feature	GA4	UA (GA3)
Data Deletion Requests	Admin can delete certain data from their reports. • When PII user information is collected via a parameter the admin can ask GA to delete the data (by date). • Filtering can be used to further focus on specific collected PII data to be deleted. • The deletion request takes about a week before is acted on by Google Analytics, so if you change your mind in the meantime, you can cancel the deletion request. • Specific user data can also be deleted by going to the Explorer/User Explorer, find the user you want do delete, and click the delete icon in the Explorer, which will delete all the data on that user. o However, if the website has a lot of users, it might be very hard to locate a specific user and then delete them. And the same is true of a specific user exposed to specific advertising, and this process will be improved in the future but is hard to use at this point.	Not sure this is implemented

Google Analytics 4 can be set up to programmatically opt in users who give their consent to be tracked; otherwise, everyone is by default opted out of tracking, and this is best done with Google Tag Manager. However, the ins and outs of how to set this up using GTM is somewhat beyond the scope of this chapter but is doable if one is using GTM at an intermediate level of familiarity. However, allowing users to opt out of data collection means significant data loss as a recurrent issue and roughly 50% of user visitors will *not* consent to be tracked, so we have to use the other 50% and model the data, which is what GA4 does.

What to do about the data loss:

- Look for patterns and trends in your data (and make assumptions based on that data).
- Even though we are losing about 50% of the data (due to GDPR+), the patterns and trends of the data are enough to work with to improve the website and conversion experience.

As readers can see, setting up and using web analytics involves complexities and limitations well beyond the platforms themselves, and call into play issues with existing and new legislation currently in place that puts significant constraints on what analytics platforms can legally track.

Where are we today with user privacy laws and how does it impact web analytics data capture?

As web analytics is used quite a bit for the advertising and marketing use cases, it has been several years since GDPR and other privacy legislation have been adapted in Europe and often used all over the world. Here's where we are with GDRP currently.

- The increasing importance of first-party data, as brands and advertisers shift their focus towards building direct relationships with consumers and obtaining their consent. Third-party data providers are being challenged by the user privacy restrictions that have been caused by recent legislation; they are coming up with alternative strategies such as contextual targeting and influencer marketing. Overall, the US ad industry is adapting to the privacy landscape and exploring new approaches to maintain effective advertising while respecting consumer privacy rights.[8]
- Online publishers are prioritizing the development and utilization of first-party data. The article discusses how publishers are actively investing in data infrastructure, such as data management platforms (DMPs) and customer relationship management (CRM) systems, to collect and analyze valuable first-party data to comply with privacy regulations, reduce reliance on third-party data, and enhance audience targeting and personalization. There are now many challenges for publishers who are managing and monetizing their first-party data, as they are evolving strategies to overcome these obstacles. Overall, publishers are recognizing the value of first-party data as a key asset in driving revenue, engaging audiences, and building sustainable business models in the changing digital landscape.[9]

  - For example, the NHL is leveraging social media and QR codes to enhance fan engagement and reach diverse audiences. Rather than duplicating content across all social media channels, the NHL aims to provide unique posts for each platform.

- The league has increased its spending on digital advertising, with a significant portion allocated to Meta platforms like Facebook and Instagram. The NHL has introduced a bingo game within its Fan Access app, which generates player and team-related stats in real time. QR codes are being used to drive fans to the app during the Stanley Cup Finals, with the potential to win prizes like merchandise and gift cards.
- The NHL is also investing in YouTube Shorts to attract Gen Z hockey fans and adapting its content strategy based on fan feedback to ensure continuous improvement.[10]

Goal-Setting

The most important reason to implement web analytics is to gather the data regarding a website's chosen KPIs to provide the standard from which to compare changes in values over time. When starting with KPI measurement, take a baseline measurement of the metrics that comprise the KPIs – this will usually be an amount or percentage to gauge progress. Note that KPI ideation and formation should come first, but more often it happens the other way around because it is hard to know what to measure until you know what web analytics is capable of measuring. In other words, we do not know what we do not know, until we learn about it first-hand or hear about it second-hand and go ahead and experiment (try something new). When looking at deploying web analytics as a constantly evolving process, there is no perfect way to implement it in the complex business environment that most organizations operate in, and there will always be something done that should be better. As mentioned earlier, when beginning a new web analytics implementation, it is likely some of it may be changed later, as more information surfaces. The web analytics iteration process supports our belief that web analytics is a process, rather than a deliverable product.

Measuring Customer Acquisition

When a visitor visits a website, they generate data. Marketers can measure the impact of visitor activities as they happen on the site.

As we covered earlier in this section, while the customer journey is not truly a funnel, the visualization of a funnel is closer to how marketers envision the traffic traversing through their websites.

Traffic Sources

Except for the origin of the traffic, the reports for each traffic source are similar.

- **Organic search:** All the web analytics platforms report on a search engine, search keyword, and website referrals (links) by domain and pages. Search engine reports show the exact keywords that visitors type into their browsers (in search engines) that lead to a visit to the website.

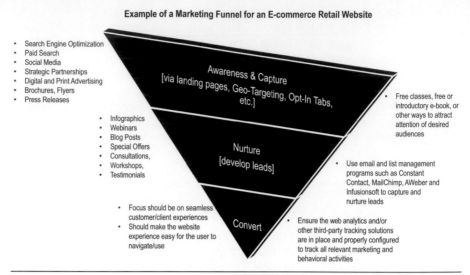

Figure 10.7 Marketing Funnel for a Health Club E-Commerce Site
Source: Marshall Sponder

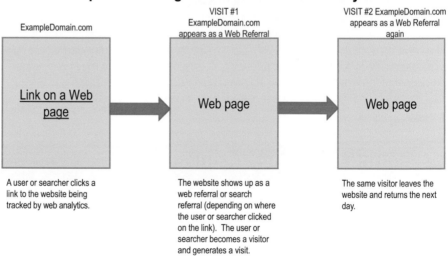

Figure 10.8 How Web Analytics Records Web Referrals
Source: Marshall Sponder

- **Website referrals:** When a visitor arrives at the website by clicking on a link to the site that is on another site (as opposed to a search engine), this is called a site referral or link referral (See Figure 10.8). Some platforms report web domain referrals as well as page referrals; there may be a reason for this involving revenue allocation (when e-commerce is present), and it may also tie into attribution tracking that Google Analytics has become quite adept at providing over the past five years or so. Adobe Analytics (but not Google Analytics) provides the "original referring domain" reporting for attribution tracking. When a visitor returns to the website over several sessions but doesn't arrive from the same source, the analytics platform records all the sourced from which the visitor arrived (via cookie tracking). When the visitor makes a purchase (or conversion), it can be compared based on the attribution model of the last source or the very first source, in any case, the web analytics platform records the source of a visit.

Other referral sources:

- Direct traffic: This type of traffic comes from people (visitors) who have already been to the website before or who know the name of the business/URL and simply type it into their browser address bar.
- Paid search traffic: When an advertiser runs paid search ads (i.e., using Google AdWords), they can set up their advertising along with the landing page. The URLs must be tagged properly with campaign parameters so that web analytics systems can tell the difference between an organic search referral and a paid one.
- Other types of campaign traffic: Can include email campaigns (which also need to be tagged so that the analytics platform can tell what kind of traffic it is – where it originates) as the email client does not usually supply that data to the web analytics platform.
- Social media: Twitter, Facebook, LinkedIn et al. send traffic to websites, but the web analytics might not always be able to tell much more than the channel. Unfortunately, most social media sources of traffic to websites are walled gardens – they supply few details to the analytics platform of the actions that led to the visit. Google Analytics has a data hub that some social media channels participate in allowing for more details of the visitor referral (for example, a visit from Google Blogger provides the exact blog post the visit came from). Meetup.com (a data hub partner) provides the specific meetup group that resulted in a visit, but a session originating from Facebook, Twitter, or LinkedIn does not have that level of data. The sharing of user identity information is a subject in and of itself, not covered in-depth in this book. However, it is evident that social media users want to feel confident that they can use these sites/apps without having their privacy violated. Channels such as Twitter and Facebook limit how much they share of this content.

There are other sources of traffic including mobile visits; most web traffic comes from mobile devices, and since 2015, Google evaluates websites as mobile friendly or not. Web analytics treats mobile sessions as a separate set of reports that doesn't get bundled in with the sources we discussed so far in this section.

Additional Web Analytics Platform Features

Report Visualizations and Dashboards

The commonly used metrics produced by web/data analytics platform are intermediate metrics; to turn the standardized outputs into actionable KPIs, they almost always are customized or transformed. Regardless of the platform, web data is usually displayed in a few standard formats. Metrics have line items that give context and definition to the data along with graphic elements (bar graphs, pie charts, and trends are the most common visual elements). The information imparted is almost identical and has been moving towards having a more standard functionality as an analyst dashboard of sorts that is configurable and extensible (dashboards can be created on the fly, customized, and shared with coworkers with little effort).

Rollups

Web analytics platforms can roll up multiple websites monitored to one comprehensive view, especially useful for large organizations that have many sites tracked by web analytics in separate profiles that also want to compare the performance of each next to one another using the rollup property, in this case (see Figure 10.9).

Report Filtering

The text within analytics reports can be filtered by characters, regular expressions, or Boolean equations to find pages that have the exact or similar patterns. However, filtering can be applied at the profile level in Google Analytics.[11] Filtering is done to include or exclude certain data; typically, this is done to exclude traffic coming from the same domain as the website that is being monitored via web analytics or to exclude referrer spam that has become much more common in analytics reports of late.[12] However, one capability that is lacking from all web analytics platforms is filtering at the content level of a page/website, although this precisely what web search engines provide.

Standard Reporting

There are standard reports that are very similar across platforms – we will not go over them here as there are several books and online videos/tutorials on them. There are differences between Adobe Analytics and Google Analytics regarding the details of setup and details of how the reports are displayed, but at a basic user level they are identical. However, as installations become more customized and higher-end (more

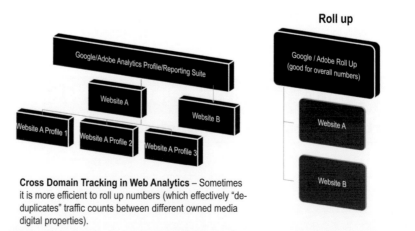

Cross Domain Tracking in Web Analytics – Sometimes it is more efficient to roll up numbers (which effectively "de-duplicates" traffic counts between different owned media digital properties).

Figure 10.9 Cross-Domain Tracking in Web Analytics
Source: Marshall Sponder

expensive and complicated), there may be workflow, feature, and pricing differences (along with financing and license usage rights) that give one platform an advantage over the other.

Real-Time Data

Almost all web analytics platforms provide real-time readouts of traffic with little or no latency. However, standard and custom reports should be assembled from raw data sent over to the analytics server. Thus, it is reasonable to expect some delay of anywhere from a few hours to a day for standard reports. In most cases, it does not matter if the data is real time or not, as organizations rarely act quickly to make changes on their websites. In some cases, having real-time data makes a meaningful difference and is worth having (i.e., a large publisher of *The New York Times* website[13] or a larger retailer like Amazon.com).[14] Analytics platforms that include near- or real-time reporting of web data for organizations are appropriate for those who are willing to pay a significant amount for the real-time data. When an organization has a use case where it needs to make a real time decision based on the data (such as Amazon Web Services) because it helps them save or make more money, then having and acting on real time data is well worth the expense.

"Time Spent" Calculations in Web Analytics

When it comes to calculating how long the visit to a page lasts (called a pageview), when a visit results in a single pageview, it is referred to as a "bounce (bounce rate)". The time spent on a page is not calculated when the visitor does not visit another page. The average time spent is calculated by dividing the total minutes spent on a page from all visits divided by the number of pageviews for that page; the same calculations are done at the site level as well.

Time spent is a metric calculated by comparing the time a visitor spends on a page with the time spent on the next page the user visits during their visit (as shown in Figure 10.10). New features such as new dimensions and reporting are frequently added to Google Analytics 4, and you can keep up-to-date about the changes from the following page (see https://support.google.com/analytics/answer/9164320).

Participation/Contribution/Unique Page Value

Most web analytics platforms assign specific values to pages on the website (for engagement tracking), and when a user lands on that page in their path through the site, the value is added to the counter to calculate how engaged the user is in the website experience (during a visit).

Setting up page scoring (the best name we can come up with for this feature) administrative access to analytics platform is needed.

Designing Dashboards

Reports are created, configured, and annotated so they can be seen in virtually any context that an analyst or stakeholder wants (dashboards are often hard for end users to grapple with unless they are annotated). Every major web analytics platform

How Web Analytics Determines the Time Spent on a Particular Page of a Website

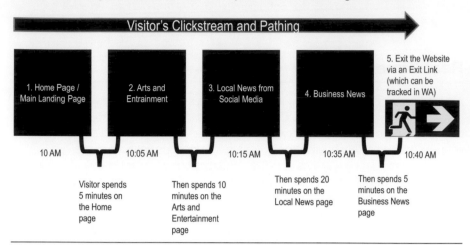

Figure 10.10 Web Analytics Method of Calculating Time Spent on a Page (and of a Visit/Session)

Source: Marshall Sponder inspired by Adobe Education

Participation Grade / Page Scoring Grade

(All web analytics platform have some method of weighting the value of a page towards a particular goal or purpose).

Figure 10.11 Adding Page Scoring to Specific Pages of a Website

Source: Marshall Sponder informed by Adobe Education

has configurable and standard dashboards as well as mobile applications where analytics reports can be viewed. Dashboards are standard fare for web analytics, and they can even be delivered by email and set up to be updated on a regular basis. Certainly, segmentation (custom segments) combined with dashboards makes them more efficient because you can take a magnifying glass and blow up a specific group of visitors (or visits) in the context that a dashboard can highlight (such as geo-location, purchases, etc.). Dashboards can be made up of whatever the analyst or stakeholder wants them to be (see Figure 10.11). If the data is present in the reporting suite or profile (what it is called is depends on the platform), it should be able to be added to a dashboard, especially if there is a defined business need to see the information in a defined context).

Geo-Segmentation

Web analytics platforms can collect as much information about visitors as organizations, and particularly stakeholders' desire. The one segmentation most analytics platforms have *without any customization* is the ability to geo-locate web traffic down to the city level (with additional enablement geo-segmentation can be further refined to focus on lat/long codes, ZIP codes, election districts, neighborhoods, and DMAs, or any custom combination thereof). Geo-segmentation reports can be broken down in several ways, including designated marketing areas (such as greater NYC DMA). Web analytics platforms are flexible in how location is defined, and an analyst (administrator) could even make their own DMA or election district, if desired. Google Analytics allows users to visualize geo-location against almost any metric.

Technologies/Network Segmentation

Another type of segmentation that exists out of the box is the one associated with the service provider that allows visitors to access the Internet. The information from the Internet service provider (ISP) is often taken for granted, but it is much richer as almost any business has its ISP/network address registered in its name. The Technologies/Network Segmentation report, for example, is a standard feature provided by Google Analytics and made available to analytics users. This report provides actual business names of a significant percentage of the website visitors to a website (useful information for generating business leads). Depending on the organization and their goals, knowledge of other businesses visiting the website can provide lead generation information and even drive some degree of content automation.

Campaign Tracking

Campaign tracking is a way to track specific actions that happen on a website with web analytics. Events on websites are assigned by administrators with a campaign code to make it easier to track (usually a link, could be a video or even file download). Campaign tracking requires coordination between stakeholders and administrators. The tracking codes can be set up by the administrator using unique identifiers that are chosen by the marketers, so they are easy to identify within the analytics reports.

Campaign Performance

Like any other URL on a website, a campaign can be examined using the funnel construct (or user flow diagram as shown in Figure 10.7) to see the impact of the campaign (or specific campaign code). Campaign codes with conversion funnels (or user flow diagrams) are a powerful means to track campaign performance. Funnels are useful when there are set ideas of what paths should be traversed by the customer (and in what order) for a campaign to be successful. Funnels work best for organizations with defined business processes and marketing campaigns. Most analytics platforms allow comparisons between two periods of time in most reports they provide: campaign funnels.

Attribution Models

When a visitor comes to a website the first time from a paid search ad and buys something (conversion event), it is evident the attribution is from a paid search campaign (that brought this visitor to the website/landing page).

However, what about when it is not?

What happens when a visitor returns to a site several times (not always by the same channel) before deciding if they engage in a conversion event (buy something, most often) – how do we count it? (See Figure 10.12) Do we give all the credit to the "first touch" attribution (paid search) or "last touch" attribution (say, Facebook)? How organizations decide to count success is more a marketing, and perhaps even a political decision, but it has profound implications in an omnichannel world where the customer journey often is not linear as illustrated in Figure 10.13.

In Figure 10.13, paid search generated a different weighting depending on the last touch (default), first touch, or linear (each channel in the conversion process is assigned equal weight).

There are several types of attribution beyond the first touch, as shown in Figure 10.13, such as last touch attribution, linear, time decay, position-based, and custom attribution that can be set up using web analytics. Rather than discuss each type of attribution in detail, readers who want to know more about multichannel attribution (Figure 10.15) should read a post by Google Analytics Evangelist Avinash Kaushik at his blog, *Occam's Razor*, titled "Multi-Channel Attribution Modeling: The Good, Bad, and Ugly Models".

Which metrics are agreed upon and put in place has profound implications for how organizations function; the subject could be a book in and of itself. Metrics simplify complex situations (for example, see Figure 10.14) but often come with a cost, losing sight of the real end goals.[15]

Tracking Mobile Traffic

Mobile Web traffic is vital. Mobile traffic makes up most web activity that websites receive and is now a Google Search Ranking Factor as of April 21, 2015. The whole

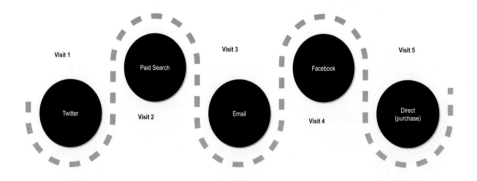

ATTRIBUTION METHODS: DEPENDING ON THE MODEL USED, DIFFERENT PARTS OF A VISITOR'S CLICKSTREAM BECOME MORE OR LESS IMPORTANT FOR DETERMING MARKETING ROI

Figure 10.12 Marketing Attribution
Source: Marshall Sponder

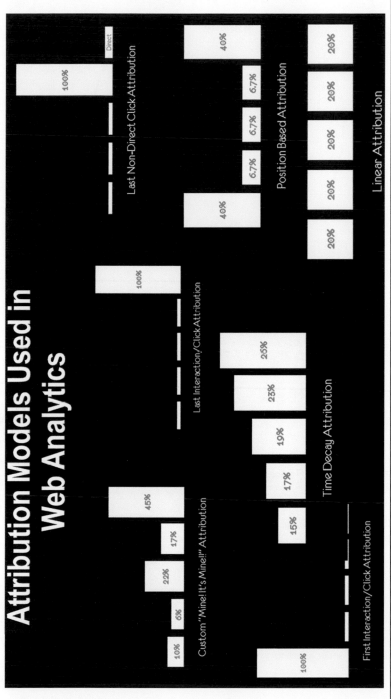

Figure 10.13 Various Attribution Models Commonly Used in Web Analytics Reporting

Source: Marshall Sponder

Calculating the value of social media interactions is possible using platforms such as Google Analytics

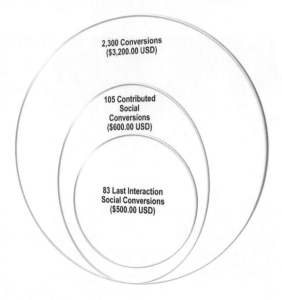

Figure 10.14   Google Analytics – Social Value Report
Source: Marshall Sponder

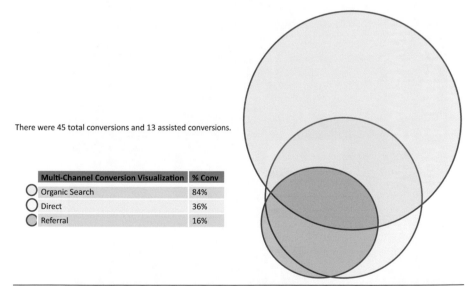

Figure 10.15   Google Analytics – Multichannel Conversion Visualization
Source: Marshall Sponder referencing Google Analytics

idea of what a website is has changed mirroring the development of Web 1.0, 2.0, 3.0 and 4.0 that we studied earlier. How can we ever be sure that web analytics platforms ever track all that activity? We cannot.

There have been several improvements to mobile device tracking in the web analytics platforms since smartphones became so dominant as communications and web browsing medium, including improved visitor identification, better mobile device-specific data collection, and reporting (see Table 10.8).

Table 10.8 shows the variety of reporting on a mobile device that is available in Adobe Analytics, and much the same functionality exists in Google Analytics, although the specific reports might have different names. The key lies in mapping business.

needs with reporting capabilities (and then reporting it back to stakeholders in a language they understand).

Visitor Retention

Determining the activity of loyal customers (those who have made a purchase or registered on the website) in web analytics is commonly defined by the frequency with which a customer returns to the site, how long they spend during their visit, and how many pages they view. The number of products or services purchased on a recurring basis is examined in customer loyalty reports as well.

Return/Frequency

Adobe and Google Analytics provide similar readouts and segments showing the days between the last visit/session where the user took a specific action; in Google Analytics, this report is generated by running the "days since last session" report.

Visit Number Reports

Visit numbers, when combined with additional conversion metrics, can be very useful readouts. By combining visit numbers with other custom metrics, such as registrations, stakeholders can find the moment of maximum profitability for a marketing activity.

Table 10.8 Similarities and Differences between the Mobile Web vs. Mobile Apps

	Mobile Web	Mobile Apps
DIFFERENT	• Unique mobile reports/ dimensions • GPS locations (HTML5) • Smaller and more diverse form factors • Touch and Gesture Interactions	• Cohort analysis • SDKs for tracking code • Version fragmentation • Screen views and similar metrics • Offline usage • Shorter session timeout
SIMILAR	• JavaScript tagging • Conversion, traffic, and engagement KPIs	• Campaign tracking • Event tracking • Engagement and conversion metrics

Source: Authors

Table 10.9 Mobile Device Reports That Web Analytics Platforms Typically Provide

Report Type	Device Data That Is Reported on in Web Analytics
Mobile Devices	By vendor, by device model
Device Type	Is the device a phone, tablet, gaming console or e-reader, etc.?
Device Manufacturer	The vendor that manufactured the device such as Samsung, Apple, etc.
Screen Size	Display width x display height for all the devices detected by the web analytics platform
Screen Height	Height of the mobile device display
Screen Width	Width of the mobile device display
Cookie Support	Display the cookies that are/aren't supported by the device model/operating system of the device
Image Support	Various types of image display times such as GIF, PNG, JPG, etc.
Audio Format	Various types of audio files that the mobile device accessing the website is able store such as MP3, etc.
Screen Color Depth	The number of colors a device can display
Video Format	Various video file formats that are able to be stored and played by the mobile device

Source: Authors, from Adobe Education

Sales Cycle Report (Adobe)

This report is unique to Adobe Analytics (platforms often have unique features and reports) but can be replicated in most other web analytics platforms. In this report, the variable "**s. Purchase**" needs to be set up to track consumer purchases by the administrator of the system and is best suited for retail sites. There are a couple of variations of the report, one for new, repeat, and loyal customers, and others that relate to the days before and after the first or last purchase.

Customer loyalty reports (see Figure 10.16) provides site owners with a good idea of how much of the revenue collected on the website is happening on the first visit versus subsequent visits. However, the real question is how a loyal customer is defined.

- New customers = first purchase on the website
- Return customers = second purchase on the site
- Loyal customers = third purchase and more on the site

Metrics definition could be tweaked to say that loyal customers are only those who buy more than four or five times, but that is a marketing decision, not an analytics decision.

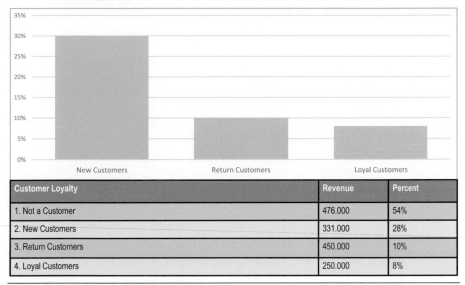

Customer Loyalty Report

Customer Loyalty	Revenue	Percent
1. Not a Customer	476.000	54%
2. New Customers	331.000	28%
3. Return Customers	450.000	10%
4. Loyal Customers	250.000	8%

Figure 10.16 Customer Loyalty Report
Source: Marshall Sponder, deriving information from Adobe Education

Setting Targets

Adobe Analytics can report how website performance measures stated goals. Targets enable stakeholders to track the progress of each site goal they create, and targets can be added to any dashboard. Adobe Analytics allows additional flexibility in how targets are set up. The analyst or stakeholder set up the targets, so any value over zero would have been above the target. Google Analytics does not have targets (at least, not in this sense) but there are other third-party integrations such as Klipfolio that provide report targets appropriate for dashboard reports.

Points to Remember Before We Dive Into Using Google Analytics 4 for Insights Work

- The data you get out of GA4 will never be 100% accurate when compared to your back-end accounting and database system(s), in that case, for financials, defer to your back-end billing or database systems over the GA4 data.
- GA4 provides partial data that we can perform analysis on for patterns and trends of user's behavior on a monitored website or app.
- Don't rush to immediately analyze your data after just implementing GA4 because for proper analysis you would need at least a month or more of data. One week would not be enough time for a variety of reasons (outliers, holidays, etc.) – good analytics requires a certain amount of time and patience. A month of data gives analysts and stakeholders a more complete picture of what is going on in the website or app.
- For analyzing attribution modeling, wait at least two months.

Points to Remember About the Questions You Ask When Working With Analytics Stakeholders and Clients

1. **Specific questions are better than general questions:**

   - Specific questions that can be related to specific reporting in Google Analytics 4 (and beyond it) are a good way to start. Now that we are familiar with the kind of reporting we see in web analytics, we can also the kind of questions that lead to answers we can provide (hopefully) using specific reports and dimensions with Google Analytics 4 or Adobe Analytics.
   - Now that we understand web analytics reporting, we can start asking questions that relate to the kind of information almost any web analytics platform can provide.

     - *I know this sounds contra-intuitive,* but unless you know what data is in the analytics reporting, what kind of information you can capture and produce, how can we possibly answer any questions with these platforms?
     - ***It's almost as if you could go through each feature of a web analytics and suggest the questions this report could answer.***

2. **Prepare an action plan about what you're going to do next when working with a client. Ensure that the answers you provide lead to solutions you can suggest or put into place for the client based on a series of reports the analyst will run with their analytics platform.**

   - Before asking your questions have an idea of what you are going to do with the information once you get the answers.
   - Generally speaking, if you can answer a stakeholder's question(s) with a simple vanity metric out from GA4 or Adobe Analytics, you have added no value or insights.

     - Analytics platforms provide plenty of vanity metrics, but these alone provide no insight or action plan, and we don't even know if the metric results are good or bad.
     - Once you can figure out what may account for the success of a product, you can try to replicate it with a different product. Then, wait a few weeks and check GA4 and see if the product we tested our hypothesis on sold better than before.

   - Ask questions that reveal vulnerabilities in a business's income/conversion.

     - For example, if a business's top source (~90%?) of traffic conversions is Google Organic search and something happens with the algorithm in the future, that business's income is jeopardized.
     - You can suggest a campaign budget that can help remedy the vulnerability.
     - Try to identify sources of traffic that don't necessarily convert immediately but get more people in the top of the funnel for the buying cycle of the client's website, such as Facebook ads.

3. **When asking your analytics-based questions, stay focused on the clients or businesses' initial business marketing targets.**

   - Look at the previous quarter and see if the client's targets were met, and if not, dig deeper to find out why.

4. **When clients ask for specific numbers about performance, before answering their questions ask them how they plan to use the information.**

   - The client/stakeholder's answers can provide the analyst with additional context, and the context is the key to answering their questions with information that is actionable.

5. **Start the analysis with what is already working on a client's website and figure out why and how it is working – look for patterns that highlight the Pareto principal or the 80/20 rule.**

   - The Pareto principal as applied win web analytics predicts that 80% of the revenue comes from 20% of the products, and that is usually the case for many large e-commerce websites.

6. **Next, once you have gotten done figuring out what is working, go after technical issues on the website or app and try to figure out if those factors are impacting the conversion rates of the products, and if so, get them fixed.**

   - One way to do this is to use funnel reports with different products and use device category as a dimension in your analysis to identify the drop-offs.

7. **Finally, focus on what is working worse, which is harder than improving what is already working well.**

Producing an Initial Analytics Audit to See What is Working as the Basis to Ask More Questions to Client/Stakeholders

Start your initial analysis by looking for patterns in the web analytics platform (assuming one is already set up and in place) and record them in a simple Excel table or Google Sheet.

- **Identify the performing products and services using the clients' web analytics** (if no web analytics is set up, then you must set up a basic implementation of web analytics on a chosen platform and wait a few weeks for enough data to be collected to do an analysis).

  - Analyze top traffic sources first and find the top 5 or 10 performers with at least a 90-day period.
  - Look for the countries and regions that deliver the most traffic and revenue.
  - Look for the top landing pages of the website.
  - Look for the top keywords (organic and Paid keywords).
  - Look for the top traffic sources, ad campaigns.

- **Now look at the various standard reports in the web analytics platform to** see where there are gaps between the products that are most popular by views vs, those that sell the best (when this is an e-commerce website).
- **Look at the various product performance reports in the web analytics platform** and see if there are technical issues or gaps in the reporting.
- **Look at the site search reports when present to see what products or services that** searchers are looking for on the website or app and identify gaps where what searchers are looking for is not present or not shown in the top of the search results.

This initial audit will give the analyst the specific questions they need to begin the analytics engagement and to improve the business results of the website or app.

Additional Analytics Resource for Google Analytics 4: GA4 EXPLORER PLAYBOOK

See – https://support.google.com/analytics/answer/12664847#zippy=%2Cin-this-article EXPLORER PLAYBOOK – build this into your course for assignments and extra credits.

Academic Research Synopsis: "Journalism is Twerking? How Web Analytics is Changing the Process of Gatekeeping"[16]

Most online publishers also use web analytics to monitor the performance of their website/publishing portal, they can also use the data to evaluate the performance of specific news stories and articles along with the specific journalists who create the information is available as first-party data to the publisher. As news and magazine publishers have seen vast changes in their industries due to the Internet and social media, there have been many attempts to reward journalists for creating content that draws many page views and visits. Advertising can be displayed, and the publisher makes revenue based on the advertising and subscriptions.

Twerking, as mentioned in the title of the paper refers to an incident in 2013 when Miley Cyrus shocked people with her performance at the *MTV Video Music Awards*. MTV uploaded a story about the stunt, and CNN used the article as a story on their homepage. It was an attempt to drive up their web traffic, which in turn would allow CNN to increase their advertising revenue.

Measuring web traffic via web analytics is now common, and in newsrooms traffic generation has become a requirement of the job – if the journalist does not generate enough relevant traffic because of their articles, they may lose their job. Publishers are using web analytics (along with search engine optimization) to choose the subjects, phrases, and keywords that the journalist is asked to write. The following is a summary of a research paper on the way newsroom publishers use web analytics to decide what to publish (and what not to publish).

Questions/Hypothesis

- How do journalists use web analytics in their news work? (Restated – there are several use cases where web analytics is used for news work, and it has influenced journalism.)
- What factors influence journalists to use web analytics in their news work?

Gatekeeping: Content Curation

This paper uses the term "gatekeeping" rather than another that we prefer called "content curation". Gatekeeping is "the process of selecting, writing, editing, positioning, scheduling, repeating, and otherwise, messaging information to become news", both terms are synonymous for this peer-research review.

Caveat, as more news aggregators/publishers use clickbait titles, it could be difficult to determine if the audience enjoyed the content. In such instances, other metrics such as session duration and time spent on page (collected by web analytics) can be deployed to get a better understanding of content effectiveness.

Using Web Analytics in Newsrooms

Publishers and newsrooms use web analytics to understand how their published content is being received by their online audience. The intermediate metrics produced by web analytics are used to determine, in many cases, how compelling a news story is. Not all writers or editors write for audience impact, but increasingly (to the researcher's alarm) more are doing so.

Ethnographic Research Methodology

The researcher conducted 30 interviews with three news publishers in Singapore. The observations from the interviews were coded into a text analytics platform called Nvivo. The paper cites a case where the editor of one of the three newsrooms chose a story about the Pope to run over the weekend. Their story was published because web analytics reports indicated it was receiving more traffic.

> "There's much interest over the weekend about the Pope being a 'regular' guy", the editor said, adding that stories on the new Pope did well on Chartbeat. "It was resonating over the weekend."[17]

Web Analytics Platforms Referred to in the Study

- **Adobe analytics:** Omniture – essentially web analytics. Adobe Analytics provides basic web statistics and clickstream data on articles, column pages, and the overall online publication – it may also provide advertising and revenue reports.
- **Chartbeat:** Web analytics with real-time visual diagrams – closer to heat maps with analytics data superimposed.

Example:

> A Web editor at the other newsroom took out a business story from the homepage to make space for a new sports story he was sure would get much more traffic. However, when he checked Chartbeat again, the business story he had taken out was the eighth most viewed story so far. He decided to put it back. Instead, he took out a story on a girl who was shot dead, saying, "If it does not get any traction in 20–30 minutes, we usually pull it out".[17] Note that online news publishers make money on stories that have an extremely short shelf life; decisions on where to place the story need to be done very quickly to maximize the value of the story.

- **Visual Revenue** (news story placement and advertising analytics): VR determines how interested online audience is in a story that is currently on the news site. It considers when the story has been online too long, not long enough, or whether it was properly placed, and calculates the revenue impact of those decisions around where to place the story and how to preview/change the title of the story, so it gets more audience attention – one of the co-authors knows with the founder of this platform. In 2014 Visual Revenue was acquired by OutBrain, another advertising platform.

Example:

A web editor talked about a story that quoted a football player saying "bad barbecue makes me want to fight". The article was a blog post buried in the sports page and had gone unnoticed by the homepage editors. However, then, out of the blue, Visual Revenue recommended putting it on the homepage. The web editor followed the recommendation, took an underperforming story out and replaced it with the "bad barbecue" story which ended up being the day's most viewed story.[17]

Findings

Question 1: How Do Journalists Use Web Analytics in Their News Work?

While journalists are not known to be early adopters of technology, as they adopt new technologies, they fit them to into their existing norms and routines.

- **Newsroom editors discussed what topics were popular on social media at the current moment with the social media manager or assistant managing editor**. Stories that had generated good traffic, based on web analytics reporting, get more frequent updates and follow-ups from editors. Topics that have done well in the past also tend to be assigned to reporters, again and again.
- **Selection and de-selection of news stories on the home page was impacted by web analytics metrics and algorithms (via Visual Revenue)**. Visual Revenue, using its own built-in web analytics, allows editors to determine which stories to run based their profitability for the publisher.
- **Algorithms are being used to suggest the best titles of a story and its framing**. The researcher observed a web editor in the act of choosing two possible headlines for the same thing. Visual Revenue randomly exposed readers to one of the two headlines. The first version got a 9% rating while the other version got 42%. The editor decided to go with the second headline based on Visual Revenue's recommendation.
- **While social media can be used to improve stories already online, the observed publications treated it as another traffic delivery mechanism**. The stories promoted the most were those shared on social media as clickbait.
- **What the audience wants is now understood through which stories generate traffic**. Generating significant web traffic was equated to a job well done by the article's author.

Question 2: In What Other Ways Does Web Analytics Affect Newsrooms?

- Editors no longer ignore audiences, although they appeared to be more interested in what the audience clicked on than what they thought about the stories.
- Newspapers have become online publishers, with the belief that the revenues they generate will be enough for them to stay in business.
- The editors observed for this study professed that they cared more about good journalism than web traffic. However, their behavior told a different story. Editors looked at their web traffic dashboards most of the day, and they were deciding the stories to publish based their traffic potential.

Limitations of This Research Study

- Ethnographic observations made by one researcher on three newsrooms in Singapore.

Review Questions

1. What is segmentation and define the steps to go into creating a custom segment in web analytics?
2. Do web analytics platforms already have some predefined segments out of the box, or does the user should define all the segments they use?
3. Name the two types of reports in web analytics.

Chapter 10 Citations

1. Fattah, A. "IBM big data & analytics hub." www.ibmbigdatahub.com/blog/author/ahmed-fattah. Accessed May 30, 2023.

2. Kaushik, A. "Digital marketing and measurement model: Web Analytics." www.kaushik.net/avinash/digital-marketing-and-measurement-model. Accessed May 30, 2023.

3. Angel, G. (2016) *Measuring the Digital World: Using Digital Analytics to Drive Better Digital Experiences*. Upper Saddle River, NJ: Pearson Education, Inc.

4. https://support.google.com/analytics/answer/10597962#zippy=%2Cin-this-article. Accessed June 2, 2023.

5. See https://cunderwood.dev/2022/01/16/is-google-analytics-illegal/ and See https://www.wired.com/story/google-analytics-europe-austria-privacy-shield/. Accessed June 2, 2023.

6. https://www.analyticsmania.com/. Accessed June 2, 2023.

7. https://digiday.com/media-buying/as-gdpr-turns-5-years-old-the-u-s-ad-industry-seeks-to-peddle-influence/. Accessed June 2, 2023.

8. http//digiday.com/media/digiday-research-deep-dive-publishers-large-and-small-put-their-resources-into-first-party-data/. Accessed June 2, 2023.

9. https://digiday.com/marketing/inside-nhls-content-strategy-ahead-of-the-stanley-cup-finals/. Accessed June 2, 2023.

10. "Create a filter in Google Analytics." *Wikihow*. January 18, 2017. www.wikihow.com/Create-a-Filter-in-Google-Analytics. Accessed April 15, 2016.

11. Escalera, C. "Stop ghost spam in Google Analytics with one filter." August 3, 2015. https://moz.com/blog/stop-ghost-spam-in-google-analytics-with-one-filter. Accessed April 15, 2017.

12. Hunter, L. "New York Times chief data scientist Chris Wiggins on the way we create and consume content now." July 24, 2014. www.fastcompany.com/3033254/most-creative-people/new-york-times-chief-data-scientist-chris-wiggins-on-the-way-we-create-. Accessed April 15, 2017.

13. Gothwa, A. "All you wanted to know about analytics in e-commerce." February 7, 2015. www.slideshare.net/anjugothwal/all-you-wanted-to-know-about-analytics-in-e-commerce-amazon-ebay-flipkart-44396611. Accessed April 15, 2017.

14. Kaushik, A. "Multi-channel attribution modeling: The good, bad, and ugly models." November 8, 2013. www.kaushik.net/avinash/multi-channel-attributionmodeling-good-bad-ugly-models. Accessed April 15, 2017.

15. Fowler, M. "An appropriate use of metrics." February 19, 2013. http://martinfowler.com/articles/useOfMetrics.html. Accessed April 15, 2017.

16. "Journalism is twerking? How Web Analytics is changing the process of gatekeeping." April 11, 2014. http://nms.sagepub.com/content/16/4/559.abstract. Accessed April 15, 2017.

17. "Journalism is twerking?", p. 568.

Aligning Digital Marketing With Business Strategy

CHAPTER OBJECTIVES

After reading this chapter, readers should understand the following:

- The need to align digital marketing and with business goals
- How to perform a social media audit from several perspectives
- Steps that can be taken to minimalize the business risk arising from the deployment and use of social media

---

Today's digital landscapes are evolving constantly. We saw the emerging number of tools and new digital technologies that are available these days for organizations for employ in digital marketing activities. However, these tools and technologies alone are not sufficient for effectively achieving marketing goals. Hence, it is highly imperative that organizations align their digital marketing goals and tactics and with the overall business strategy. This way organizations can focus on activities that drive value and efficiently allocate resources. The alignment of the two enables organizations to target their audience more effectively by ensuring that marketing campaigns carry the same message (value) that the organization strives to through its vision. It also facilitates optimal resource allocation, ensuring that budgets and staffing are directed towards initiatives that align with strategic goals.

In this chapter we give specific examples from social media (a component of digital marketing) and its alignment with the business strategy of an organization.

Reasons for Aligning Social Media With Business Goals and Use Cases

- Improve search engine rankings of a business's website
- Listen to and communicate with customers (increase customer satisfaction)
- Gain audience insights and provide market research (social media analytics)
- Drive influencer marketing and communicate with influential individuals
- Provide customer support and advocacy services

DOI: 10.4324/9781003025351-11

Figure 11.1 Aligning Social Media Analytics with Business Goals (Yin and Yang Philosophy)
Source: Gohar F. Khan

Aligning social media objectives and goals with the organization's objectives should be the starting point of any social media analytics initiative. In fact, the marketing strategy may fail without that alignment. Aligning social media analytics with business objectives is analogous to the well-known Chinese yin and yang philosophy, where two seemingly opposing forces (in this case, social media and business) complement each other, as shown in Figure 11.1.

Table 11.1 provides example scenarios for aligning social media with business objectives. If the business goal is to understand customer sentiments expressed over social media, the social media analytics should be designed to facilitate this aim. It may require, for instance, tools and skills for extracting and analyzing tweets or comments posted on a Facebook fan page. Alternatively, when the objective is to identify important social media customers and their position in the network, the focus should be on social media networks.

Social Media Analytics Alignment Matrix

Several factors determine the alignment of social media analytics with business goals. The factors impacting the alignment include the availability of technical, financial, and administrative resources appropriate to achieve the business goals. Aligning information technologies with business objectives has been a widely studied field. However, aligning social media analytics with business objectives may require a comprehensive approach to the strategic alignment model suggested by Henderson and Venkatraman.[1]

In this book, we used a simplified social media analytics alignment matrix, as provided in Figure 11.2. On the Y axis of the matrix is "resource availability", which refers to the availability of financial, technical, administrative, and leadership resources for social media analytics. On the X axis of the matrix is the impact of social media analytics alignment regarding its potential to achieve business goals

Table 11.1 Aligning Analytics With Business Objectives

Example Business Question	Layer of Interest	Data Source	Tool Example
Is the social media conversation about our company or service positive, negative or neutral?	Text Analytics	Tweets, Comments, Retweets, Reviews	Discovertext, Lexalytics, Semantria, Brandwatch
Which content posted over social media is resonating with my customers?	Actions Analytics	Likes, Shares, Mentions, etc.	Google Analytics, Hootsuite
Who are the most influential network nodes and what is their position in the network?	Network Analytics	Fans, Followers, Network, etc.	NodeXL, Netlytic, Mentionmapp, etc.
How is our mobile app performing?	Mobile Analytics	Total Sessions, New Users, Time Spent, etc.	Count.ly, Mixpanel, Google Mobile Analytics
Where are our customers on social media located?	Location Analytics	Geo-Map, IP Address, GPS, etc.	Google Fusion Tables, Followerwonk, Tweepsmap, Picodash, etc.
What social media platforms are driving the most traffic to our corporate website?	Hyperlink Analytics	Hyperlinks, In-Links, Co-Links, etc.	VOSON, Webometrics Analyst, etc.
Which keywords or terms are trending?	Search Engine Analytics	Trending Topics	Google Trends, etc.

Source: Gohar F. Khan

(or its potential to generate economic value and return on investment). Depending on the two variables (i.e., resources availability and its potential), an organization's social media analytics alignment with business goals can fall into four possible quadrants.

When the alignment resides in the "highly aligned" quadrant of Figure 11.2, leadership, financial, administrative, and technical resources are available within the organization to leverage and (sustain) social media analytics. Also, the potential is high in regard to achieving business goals. For instance, mining the layers of social media data is technically and financially demanding, but rewarding to the organization. Moreover, the social media analytics alignment efforts reside in the "not aligned" quadrant when its potential to achieve business goals and the organization's resource availability is low.

Overall, an organization's analytics efforts ought to focus on highly aligned and high-impact alternatives. Nevertheless, the business goals and availability of resources will play a major role in determining the depth of the analytical efforts and resulting quadrant in the matrix. For instance, using Facebook's built-in analytical tools is financially and technically less challenging than using a sophisticated Facebook analytics tool, such as SocialBakers, Quintly, and Razorsocial,[2] which may require technical and financial resources, but are more helpful to achieve the stated business goals.

The alignment matrix visualized in Figure 11.2 is very flexible. We can replace the variables at both the axes with any other variables of interest. For example, by placing the criticality of social media analytics (the extent to which the analytics is critical to the business) on the Y axis and sensitivity of the analytics (e.g., regarding security, privacy, or ethics) on the X axis and determine the extent of your alignment. The social media analytics alignment matrix will assist in the formulation of the business strategies needed to achieve the business goals, as illustrated in Figure 11.3.

Senior IT executives, particularly the CIO, play a major role in envisioning and creating aligned social media analytics strategy. The CIO is the person in charge of managing and aligning information communications technologies (ICTs) to achieve business-wide goals. The role of CIO has evolved from a technical guru to an informed leader, communicator, and strategic thinker. For a sustained strategic IT-business goals alignment, a CIO should possess the following skills and competencies:[3]

Figure 11.2 Social Media Alignment Matrix
Source: Gohar F. Khan

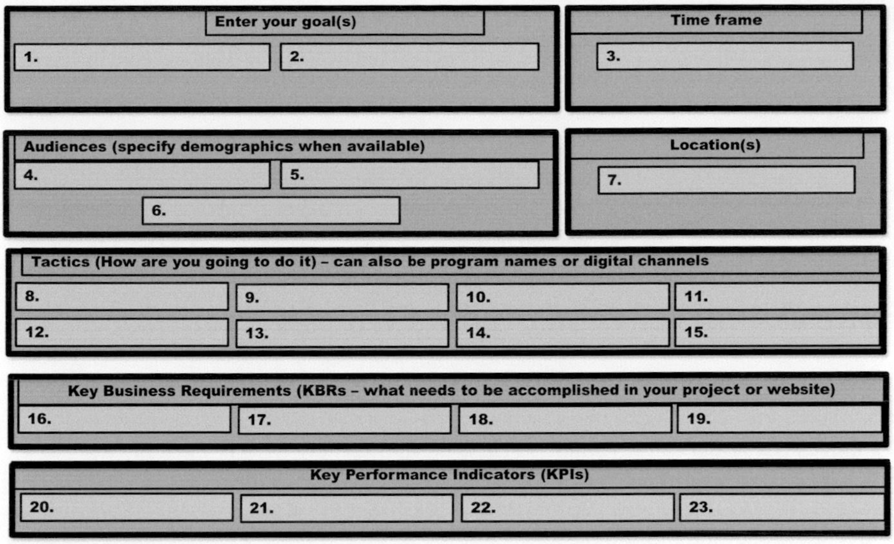

Enter your goal(s)		Time frame
1.	2.	3.

Audiences (specify demographics when available)		Location(s)
4.	5.	7.
	6.	

Tactics (How are you going to do it) – can also be program names or digital channels

8.	9.	10.	11.
12.	13.	14.	15.

Key Business Requirements (KBRs – what needs to be accomplished in your project or website)

16.	17.	18.	19.

Key Performance Indicators (KPIs)

20.	21.	22.	23.

Figure 11.3 Social Media Analytics Strategy Alignment Process
Source: Authors

Strategic Thinking and Evaluation

- Business and policy reasoning
- IT investment for value creation
- Performance assessment
- Evaluation and adjustment

Systems Orientation

- Environmental awareness
- System and social dynamics
- Stakeholders and users
- Business processes
- Information flow and workflow

Appreciation for Complexity

- Communication
- Negotiation
- Cross-boundary relationships
- Risk assessment and management
- Problem-solving

Information Stewardship

- Information policies
- Data management
- Data quality
- Information sharing and integration
- Records management
- Information preservation

Technical Leadership

- Communication and education
- Architecture
- Infrastructure
- Information and systems security
- Support and services
- IT workforce investments

Formulating a Social Media Strategy

The purpose of formulating a social media strategy is to create business rules and procedures that align social media with stated business goals (such as reaching out to a target market to increase the business's awareness and popularity with that audience). Planning an aligned social media strategy should follow a strategy formulation process like that used by IT management, as suggested by Luftman et al.,[4] although some additional steps are needed to account for the unique nature of social media technologies.

Steps in Formulating a Social Media Strategy

The following steps will lead to the formulation of a sound social media strategy.

- **Get hold of an executive champion:** For any organizational strategy development and implementation, the sponsorship of a senior-level executive is crucial. The most important factor for success in social media analytics is not technology, but leadership and top management commitment. Success is possible only when the transformation is steered through strong leadership, setting in the right direction, building momentum, and ensuring the disciplined execution of an inspiring vision and ambitious plans (i.e., Steve Jobs comes to mind with the way he promoted Apple products in his product launch videos). A social media executive champion will be someone with charisma and the power to enforce social media strategy in the organization. It usually is the head of the department or the government chief information officer (GCIO). Enlisting the support of a champion is crucial for social media efforts to be fruitful.
- **Build a cross-functional team:** The first step in formulating a social media strategy is to create a cross-functional team Wi-Fi senior management members from all the departments, including the IT department; Ideally, this team should be led by a CIO. Having a cross-functional team will make sure that all the stakeholders have their say and have ownership of the social media analytics initiative.
- **Assessing organizational culture:** Is the organization ready to embrace social media analytics? What are the organization's assumptions and beliefs about social media analytics? Embracing social media in all aspects of the business requires organizational cultural transformation at all levels. Corporate culture refers to the shared values, attitudes, standards, and beliefs of the members of an organization. By first seeking to understand the current state of the corporate culture, it becomes much easier to determine how to improve it. Understanding a corporate culture and transforming it is a very complex task and is beyond the

scope of this book. A roundtable with the team members may provide some clues on the organization's social media readiness. Perhaps the age of members is a factor; note that organizations with younger management tend to use social media more effectively, and are thus more, open to using it than senior execs. Also, a variety of organizational culture assessment and change tools are available on the market that can be used to access and highlight the need for a cultural shift. For example, the Organizational Culture Assessment Instrument (OCAI) is a free tool for diagnosing organizational culture (developed by Professors Robert Quinn and Kim Cameron) and Culture Builder Toolkit prepared by Corporate Culture Pros.[5] The bottom line is that with the cultural assessment, business users and stakeholders may want to ensure that their organization is ready to embrace social media and that it has the necessary vision and will to leverage it (i.e., by targeting specific users' attention and building a following via social media).

- **Review the current social media presence:** Before formulating a social media strategy, stakeholders need to document their current social media use and presence (i.e., by using some of the platforms in previous chapters of this book). Start by asking team members about their current social media status and by conducting, a search for social media pages representing their organization. The best way to do it would be to arrange small, interactive seminars. The objective is to find out all the officially sanctioned and unauthorized social media outlets, including blogs, wikis, fan pages, and Twitter pages that use the organization's name. For example, they may use topsy.com to search for social media profiles representing the organization. They can also employ a SWOT (strength, weakness, opportunities, and threats) analysis to determine their current social media landscape. Documenting the status will determine a baseline and help stakeholders streamline their organization's' social media presence.

- **Determining business objectives:** Once we measure and understand the baseline social media presence, the next step is to create a list of the targets and goals to achieve through that social media presence. With a clear idea of what stakeholders want to accomplish with social media, they are likely to put together a sound social media strategy. Clearly defining business goals and objectives is important, as different social media goals require different sets of actions and tools. In a worst-case scenario, having teams with divergent views and goals in mind will make it next to impossible to get anything done. Making sure everyone is on the same page is one of the keys to successful business enterprise.

Some Possible Social Media Business Tactics

- Attract customers by driving traffic with high-quality content on social media platforms, such as LinkedIn that links back to corporate websites.
- Share news, alerts, and updates through social media platforms, including Twitter, Facebook, and YouTube (i.e., statistics show millennials are more likely to check social media platforms for the news rather than mainstream media news sites).
- Implement a participatory platform (e.g., blog) where customers can submit ideas and suggestions, providing them with the opportunity to participate in business strategy-making.
- Increase awareness about products/services by disseminating information on social media platforms.
- Provide customer service and resolve issues.

Each department may have different goals and objectives to be achieved through social media platforms, so creating a broader social media policy will make sure each department has its say. The social media engagement matrix introduced earlier can be used here to determine the ease of achieving an objective against its impact.

Aligning Social Media Goals With Business Goals

As mentioned earlier, aligning social media goals with business goals is vital. First, each goal must be specific, realistic, and measurable. Next, each goal should be brought into line with the existing business goals and strategy. If the organizational goal is to network with customers via social media platforms, the social media strategy should be aligned with this objective.

Developing a Content Strategy

Establishing a social media presence is the easy part; sustaining it is the real challenge (i.e., the problem of getting new followers as well as keeping them). Developing a sound content strategy will make sure stakeholders know what to post and when to post, and how to post the right content. Content strategy is tied to the business goals, and only the content that supports the goals should be developed and posted. Organizations should know how to target a specific audience by using the correct form of social media and tweak their content to fit the demographics and psychographics of the target audience.

A sound content strategy should at the minimum answer the following questions:

- What type of content should we post to social media; for example, news, updates, alerts?
- How often should we post the content? Daily or weekly?
- Who will create the content?
- Does the organization approve the content?
- Who will respond to follow-up suggestions and comments?
- How will the feedback be handled?

Platform Strategy

A successful platform strategy should detail the type of social media platforms that are being utilized to achieve business objectives. The platforms being used should be matched to the business goals and objectives. For example, if the aim is to share news, alerts, and updates, choose existing mainstream social media platforms, such as Twitter, Facebook, and YouTube. However, if the goal is to crowdsource ideas, a custom-built Web 2.0 or Web 3.0 platform may be needed; the strategy goals and objectives will determine what type of resources are required.

Resource Considerations

Social media is the place for organizations to interact with their consumers. It increases the touchpoints throughout the customer journey. It is crucial to understand the desired level of social media engagement, as it will determine the kind of resources (technical, human, and financial) that are required. For example, if the goal is to establish an idea generation platform to solicit creative ideas in-house, the purpose-built platform may be necessary. Bear in mind that creating and sustaining a Facebook fan page requires planning, along with human, financial, and technical resources. Facebook pages should contain posts, updates, and answers to customer complaints. Extraction and analysis of data (tweets or comments) should be used for better decision-making. Facebook business pages will also display how quickly they typically respond to customer's messages. However, Hootsuite and Buffer are among the platforms that can help business users create and distribute their content. Both platforms can send out tweets at certain, preconfigured times. While it may sound easy to create an engaging social media presence, in practice it is time-consuming and repetitive. That is why organizations form dedicated teams to tackle all the work associated with maintaining a successful social media presence.

Establish a Social Media Security Policy

A social media ownership plan and policy should outline the rights and responsibilities of employers and employees. Security plans cover social media ownership regarding both accounts and activities such as accounts themselves, individual and pages profiles, platform content, and posting activity. Policies related to social media clarify issues related to personal and professional use, trade secrets, intellectual property, confidentiality, etc. Courtney Hunt[6] has done an excellent job of providing social media ownership guidelines. The guidelines touch on the following areas related to social media ownership.

- **Organizations accounts and profiles:** This part of the ownership plan deals with all the social media accounts and activities, such as accounts themselves, individual and page profiles, platform content, and posting activity. Ideally, all the organization's social media profiles should be owned by the organization.
- **Individual profiles:** The individuals' personal social media profiles; businesses should provide employees with comprehensive social media guidelines for how they are permitted to use social media while working for the company. Employees should consider setting their social media profiles to be private to protect their image/reputation (especially in the age we live in, where privacy barely exists). Employees are representations, of the company and what they do outside of work, although personal, can be a direct influence on the company's image. One can never be too careful about content posted on social media.
- **Contact information:** Social media allows people to have multiple contact addresses (e.g., email), and this policy should specify which communication medium the employee should display on their personal profile. A good practice is that employees include both a personal and a professional address.
- **Contacts:** This policy should specify the rules for social media contacts made during the employment period (e.g., through LinkedIn). For example, business owners might specify that the contacts made are joint property, but that employees can keep their contacts after leaving the organization. However, organizations should have a contact management system to capture the valuable contacts or leads, such as Salesforce.
- **Comments:** Ownership strategy should also provide policies and guidelines on whether and how employees can comment on a variety of social media platforms.

For example, when commenting, employees should make it clear whether they are commenting on behalf of the organization or expressing their personal thoughts.

- **Posting:** What should and should not be posted to the social media platform is covered here. Clearly defining posting rules can help avoid issues with trade secrets, intellectual property, confidentiality defamation, etc.
- **Groups:** Organizations may establish policies and guidelines about the kind of groups employees can join or be members of. Allowing employees to join groups that promote business goals is encouraged.
- **Privacy settings:** By setting guidelines for social media privacy settings, agencies may encourage employees to set their social media privacy settings in the best interest of the both individuals and the organization.

A paper published by Socialfish.org on the risks connected with social media provides further useful guidelines on the structure and characteristics of a sound social media policy.[7]

Select Success Metrics

Success metrics such as likes, shares, tweets, retweets, followers, and following will help stakeholders evaluate their social media strategy's effectiveness. Defined metrics should be put in place to measure the success of social media in the organization. Metrics will help determine whether social media is making a difference in the business. Depending on the type of social media engagement, success metrics may vary. For example, if the prime objective of the social media use is to engage customers in dialogue, the number of comments may be utilized as a metric. Alternatively, if it is to promote awareness, then the number of likes, shares, and pageviews may provide some indication.

Use Analytics to Track Progress

Social media analytics should be used to evaluate social media presence and determine how the organization is performing. For example, Google Analytics can provide useful web metrics, such as visits and conversions, Hootsuite Pro also offers advanced analytics and reporting for social media measurement needs. The important thing to note is that the analytical tools should be properly configured to match the organization's success metrics and business goals. Organizations almost always have a vast amount of internal and external data at their disposal, but it is not always captured in a usable form. For instance, customer call center complaints from the Macys.com retail site that are initiated by customers, but not cross-referenced to their website visits where their issues-first occurred. It is probably best to perform an audit to understand better what data exists in the organization, where it is located, who owns the data, and how to access it.

Social Media Strategy Implementation Plan

A strategy implementation plan is an essential part of the social media strategy formulation process. This plan lays out strategies and tactics to put the strategic plans into action. The strategy implementation process can vary from organization to organization and depends on a variety of factors, including support from senior executives and involvement of members from key departments. Four major barriers to strategic implementation are:[8]

- 85% of executive teams spend less than one hour per month discussing strategy
- 60% of strategic plans are not linked to budgets
- 25% of managers have incentives linked to strategy
- 5% of the workforce understands the strategy

The best way to go is to select team members from key departments who understand the purpose of the plan and the steps involved in implementing it. Establish a mechanism to discuss progress reports and let team members know what has been accomplished. Communicate the plan throughout the organization and clearly specify ownerships, deadlines, and accountabilities.

Periodic Review

In the face of rapid technological, business, and social changes, the social media strategy should be periodically reviewed. The review will make sure that the initial assumption made about the external and internal factors (e.g., technology, vision, budgets) are still relevant.

Protecting Business and Data Security

The rise of social media and its pervasive use introduces new challenges for marketers. Persistent challenges to privacy, security, data management, accessibility, social inclusion, governance, information security, cyber-warfare, and fake news sites have arisen. It has become important to protect online assets in much the same way that offline, brick-and-mortar operations have traditionally been guarded. For example, damage caused by the Sony Pictures hack in late 2014, allegedly perpetrated by North Korea, ran into several million dollars for the movie studio.[9]

The risk is defined as the possibility of losing something of value, such as intellectual or physical capital. A comprehensive definition of risk is provided by National Institute of Standards and Technology (NIST), which states that "risk is a function of the likelihood of a given threat sources exercising a particular potential vulnerability, and the resulting impact of that adverse event on the organization". (For more information please see: http://nvlpubs.nist.gov/nistpubs/Legacy/SP/nistspecialpublication800-30r1.pdf.)

Here we will focus on the risks associated with social media usage and define it as the potential of losing something of value (such as intellectual property, information, reputation, or goodwill).

Social media-related risks need to be managed properly, both from the strategic and technological point of view. Organizations need a set of proactive social media risk management strategies.

A simple but effective way to proactively manage social media risks is through the social media crisis management loop (Figure 11.4), which includes four iterative steps:

1. **Identify:** Potential risks are identified.
2. **Assess:** Risks are assessed and prioritized regarding the probability of occurrence and impact on the organization.

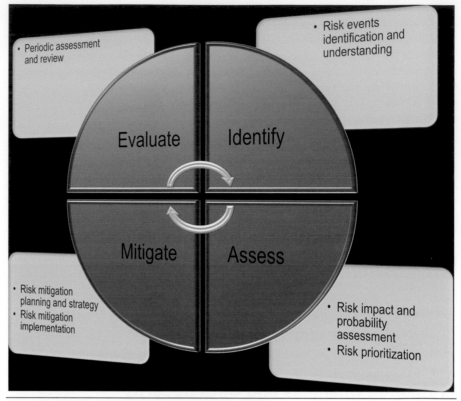

Figure 11.4 Social Media Risk Management Framework
Source: Gohar F. Khan

3. **Mitigate:** Risk reduction strategies are formulated and implemented.
4. **Evaluate:** Periodic assessment and reviews are carried out.

Below, we discuss each step.

Risk Identification

- Risk identification is the process of identifying social media threats (such as friending fake social media accounts, fake news, and malware) regarding vulnerabilities and exploits that could potentially inhibit the organization from achieving its objectives. At this stage, the goal is to determine potential accidental or malicious risks that can come from within or outside the company. Examples of common (but not necessarily malicious) social media-related security breaches are hacking, information leaks, phishing (defrauding an online account holder of financial information by posing as a legitimate company), and impersonation. Phishing and hacking are examples of malicious outsider attacks.

Two examples of malicious security breaches:

- A Snapchat employee in the payroll department fell for a phishing attack and ended up exposing information on several current and former employees.[10] In response, Snapchat contacted affected employees and offered two years of identity theft monitoring and insurance. Additionally, Snapchat improved its security education efforts for employees.

- A growing number of incidents at hospitals across the country have revealed PHI, PII, and other sensitive information. Three incidents were caused by a phishing attack, unauthorized access to a database, and an improper mailing, revealing the cost of human error in breaches.[11]

Well-known social media platforms (such as Facebook, Twitter, and YouTube) are at high risk for security breaches. According to a study based on surveys and interviews with 99 professionals and 36 companies,[12] the main social media risks identified are the following:

- Damage to reputation and trust
- The release of confidential information
- Legal, regulatory, and compliance violations
- Identity theft and hijacking
- Loss of intellectual property
- Loss of privacy
- Social engineering attacks

While not exactly a social media platform, 500 million Yahoo! accounts were breached in 2014, but the public did not find out about it until the news was announced in February 2016.[13] The theft included names, email addresses, telephone numbers, dates of birth, and in some cases, encrypted or unencrypted security questions and answers. Yahoo believed the theft (the largest security breach ever to have taken place in the history of the United States) was state-sponsored (i.e., by Russia, China, Iran, etc.). Let's not forget to briefly mention the political upheaval, security hacks, and fake news (spread via social and mainstream media) that dominated the 2016 US presidential election occurred at an extremely high visibility level that had never been seen before.[14] The implications are that no computer system is fully immune from being hacked, and soon we are likely to see even more privacy violations at every level, similar to what occurred in 2015 and 2016, leading up to and during the election.[15]

Risk Assessment

Risk assessment is "the process of assessing the probabilities and consequences of risk events if they are realized".[16] The risk evaluation process determines the likelihood of a social media risk event that could impact the organization economically and socially. The potential risks identified in the earlier step are priorities and ranked based on the probability of occurrence and impact on an organization.

Probability (P) is the likelihood of occurrence of a risk event and can take a value from 0 to 1. Probability can, for example, be assigned to risks events as follows:

- **Certain to occur (P=1):** The risks with a P value equal to 1 are the risks that will certainly happen. In other words, they have a 100% chance of occurring.
- **Extremely sure to occur (P=> 95 <1):** The risks, for example, with a probability value greater than 0.95 and less than 1.0 can be considered as "extremely sure to happen" risks. In other words, they have a 95–100% chance of occurring.
- **Almost sure to occur (P= > 0.85 <= 0.95):** The risks with a probability value greater than 0.85 and less than or equal to 0.95 can be considered as "very likely to occur" risks. They can be said to have an 85–95% chance of occurring.
- **Very likely to occur (P=> 0.75 <=0.85):** These are the risks with a 75–85% chance of occurring.

- **Likely to occur (P=> 0.65 <=0.75):** These are the risks with a 65–75% chance of occurring.
- **Slightly likely to occur (P=> 0.55 <=0.65):** These are the risks with a 55–65% chance of occurring.
- **Evenly likely to occur (P=> 0.45 <=0.55):** These are the risks with a 45–55% chance of occurring.

As shown in Table 11.2, stakeholders can assign other probabilities similarly.

The impact of a risk event can be characterized as

1. Severe
2. Significant
3. Moderate
4. Minor
5. Minimal

A risk event is considered severe if it has devastating economic, technological, political, or social impact on the organization. Moreover, a risk is deemed minimal if its impact is minimal or negligible.

Based on the incidence and probability, social media risks can be prioritized as

1. High
2. Medium
3. Low

- **High-priority hazards:** Risks that will have a severe impact on the organization. These are risks that need immediate attention and should be managed carefully.

Table 11.2 Risk Probability and Prioritization Assessment

Probability (P)		Chance of Occurrence		Priority
P = 1		Certain to occur		High-Priority Risks
P = 0.95 1		Extremely sure to occur		High-Priority Risks
P = 0.85 = 0.95		Almost sure to occur		High-Priority Risks
P = 0.75 =0.85		Very likely to occur		High-Priority Risks
P = 0.65 =0.75		Likely to occur		High-Priority Risks
P = 0.55 =0.65		Slightly likely to occur		Medium-Priority Risks
P = 0.45 =0.55		Evenly likely to occur		Medium-Priority Risks
P = 0.35 =0.45		Less than an even chance		Medium-Priority Risks
P = 0.25 =0.35		Less likely to occur		Low-Priority Risks
P = 0.15 =0.25		Not likely to occur		Low-Priority Risks
P = 0.00 =0.15		Certainly sure not to occur		Low-Priority Risks

Source: Gohar F. Khan, based on Mitre methodology

- **Medium priority risks:** Medium-probability risks that have a considerable impact on the organization.
- **Low priority risks:** Low probability risks that have a low impact on the organization.

Risk Mitigation

The risks prioritized and ranked in the earlier stage should be physical, technically, and procedurally managed, eliminated, or reduced to an acceptable level. Depending on the nature of the risks, different strategies should be used. The accidental risks posed by employees (e.g., posting copyrighted material online or tweeting confidential information) can be eliminated by a training and awareness program. It also helps to have a sound social media policy in place to minimize risks. Hacking attacks are another type of security risk that is mitigated using updated antivirus systems and by creating an extra layer of security. In fact, that is why so many jobs have a firewall of what sites can be accessed at work – several ban all social media sites.

Measures to Decrease Risk

- **Risks management governance:** New governance structures, roles, and policies are created within the business for properly managing social media risks. These activities may involve identifying and empowering a social media risk management manager, developing a business-wide risk management strategy, the identification of actions and steps needed to implement the strategy, and determining the resources required to mitigate the risks.[17] This risk assessment should include IT, finance, public relations, human resources, legal, and communications. These components play a major role in identifying and mitigating social media risks.
- **Training and awareness:** Provide education and spread awareness on legal issues such as copyright, intellectual property, defamation, slander, and antitrust issues.
- **Social media policy:** Create a sound and easily accessible social media policy that outlines the related rights and responsibilities of employers and employees. As of 2013, 72% of US companies did not have a social media security policy for employees.[18]
- **Secure social media platforms:** Secure social media platforms to minimize the impact or likelihood of the security risk from occurring.

Security measures are set up at the platform level (i.e., Facebook sets up its security protocols), but some programs can scan social media accounts, such as Facebook pages, see malicious words in visitor posts. When malicious words are detected, the posts are automatically flagged and hidden from view until the page owner examines them.

Creating Strong Passwords

The following techniques will help secure various social media platforms:

- Password should be at least ten characters long.
- Password should contain a combination of uppercase and lowercase letters, numbers, and symbols.
- Password should not include personal information such as phone numbers, birthdays, name, etc.
- Password should not contain common words (such as "and", "or", "but", "the", etc.).

- Password should not use alphabetical sequences (such as "abcd1234") or keyboard sequences (such as "qwerty").
- Password should not be reused across websites; for example, the Twitter account password should be unique to Twitter.
- Password should be memorized and kept in a safe place if written down.

Risk Evaluation

Social media risk management is a rigorous process that requires professional stakeholders who are kept informed. In the face of rapid technological, political, and social change, social media risks should be periodically reviewed. The continuous evaluation and monitoring efforts will make sure that the initial assumption made about the external and internal risks are still relevant.

Summary

This chapter covered the some of the essential elements of aligning business goals with social media and introduced the social media alignment matrix. Also, we discussed a way to evaluate the risks involved that are connected with social media analytics using the Mitre framework. To reduce risk, organizations should take stringent steps to protect passwords, personal and business accounts, and infrastructure from various security threats, including network and computer hacking.

Review Questions

1. What are some common social media risks?
2. Explain the four steps in social media risk management.
3. Explain common social media risk mitigation strategies.
4. Explain different techniques to secure social media accounts.
5. What is the goal of aligning social media analytics with business objectives?
6. Explain the social media alignment matrix.
7. Briefly explain the role of CIO in aligning analytics with business objectives.
8. What is the purpose of a social media strategy?
9. Explain the steps needed to formulate a social media strategy.

Chapter 11 Citations

1. Henderson, J.C. and N. Venkatraman. "Strategic alignment: Leveraging information technology for transforming organizations." https://ieeexplore.ieee.org/document/5387398. Accessed May 30, 2023.
2. Cleary, I. "Facebook analytics tools: 7 alternatives to Facebook Insights." August 19, 2016. www.razorsocial.com/facebook-analytics-tools. Accessed May 30, 2023.
3. Dawes, S.S. (2008). "What makes a successful CIO?" *Intergovernmental Solutions Newsletter*, GSA Office of Citizen Services and Communications. *21*.

4. Luftman, J.N., C.V. Bullen, et al. (2004). *Managing the Information Technology Resource: Leadership in the Information Age*. New York: Prentice Hall.

5. "OCAI online." www.ocai-online.com. Accessed May 30, 2023.

6. Hunt, C. "Social media ownership: Recommendations for employers." http://denovati.com/2014/02/social-media-ownership. Accessed May 30, 2023.

7. Dreyer, L., M. Grant, and L.T. White. "Social media, risk, and policies for associations." *SocialFish*. www.socialfish.org/wp-content/downloads/socialfishpolicies-whitepaper.pdf. Accessed May 30, 2023.

8. Kaplan, R.S. and D.P. Norton. "The strategy-focused organization." http://iveybusinessjournal.com/publication/building-a-strategy-focused-organization. Accessed May 30, 2023.

9. Musil, S. "Sony Pictures hack has cost the company only $15 million so far." *CNET*. February 4, 2015. www.cnet.com/news/sony-pictures-hack-to-cost-the-company-only-15-million. Accessed May 30, 2023.

10. King, H. "Snapchat employee fell for a phishing scam." *CNN*. February 29, 2016. http://money.cnn.com/2016/02/29/technology/snapchat-phishing-scam. Accessed April 15, 2017.

11. Bailey, M. "The latest in phishing: March 2016." *Wombat Security*. March 16, 2016. https://info.wombatsecurity.com/blog/the-latest-in-phishing-march-2016. Accessed April 15, 2017.

12. Webber, A. "Guarding the social gates: The imperative for social media risk management." www.slideshare.net/Altimeter/guarding-the-social-gates-the-imperative-for-social-media-risk-management. Accessed April 15, 2017.

13. Snider, M. and E. Weise. "500 million Yahoo accounts breached." *USA Today*. September 22, 2016. www.usatoday.com/story/tech/2016/09/22/report-yahoo-may-confirm-massive-data-breach/90824934. Accessed April 15, 2017.

14. Gallagher, S. "Did the Russians 'hack' the election? A look at the established facts." *Ars Technica*. December 12, 2016. http://arstechnica.com/security/2016/12/the-public-evidence-behind-claims-russia-hacked-for-trump. Accessed April 15, 2017.

15. "2015–2016 US politics hacking." www.thompsontimeline.com/tag/2015-2016-us-politics-hacking. Accessed April 15, 2017.

16. "Risk impact assessment and prioritization." www.mitre.org/publications/systems-engineering-guide/acquisition-systems-engineering/risk-management/risk-impact-assessment-and-prioritization. Accessed April 15, 2017.

17. Garvey, P.R. (2008). *Analytical Methods for Risk Management: A Systems Engineering Perspective*. New York: Taylor & Francis Group.

18. "73% of companies do not have employee social media policies." April 9, 2013. http://leaderswest.com/2013/04/09/study-68-of-companies-dont-share-the-purpose-of-social-media-with-employees. Accessed April 15, 2017.

12

Deriving Strategic Insights and "Digital Value" From Digital Marketing Analytics

---

CHAPTER OBJECTIVES

After reading this chapter, readers should understand the following:

- Data-driven marketing
- Insights transformation cycle
- Forms of "digital value"
- Improvement of overall strategy

Data-Driven Marketing

Data is gold for digital marketing. Data-driven marketing is highly warranted by businesses as it is a way to improve customer engagement and loyalty, enhance brand awareness, and increase revenue and market share. Unlike traditional marketing, data-driven marketing seeks to gain a deep understanding of the target audience and the market first, identify and anticipate customer needs, and then orchestrate marketing strategies.[1, 2] Data-driven marketing enables organizations to highly personalize the customer journey, measure the impact of their marketing campaigns, and improve their strategy in real time.[3, 4] However, it requires careful analysis and interpretation of data, as well as strong data governance practices to ensure the data being used is accurate and relevant. Hence, organizational capabilities and resources are important.[5, 6]

Robust data and analytical capabilities help organizations to have a competitive edge with better insights into the market and the customers. It is imperative to understand that collecting and analyzing the right data matters. There are numerous sources for data collection that can prove valuable for organizations such as customer interactions, market trends, and social media activity. Given the complexity of today's markets and industries and consumer trends, organizations will have to take various dimensions into account, such as behavioral aspects, location-based analytics, competitors' position, and business environment, etc. AI-based predictive analytics models can help organizations to streamline data analysis processes and guide

DOI: 10.4324/9781003025351-12

marketing decisions. We touched on AI-based marketing in Chapter 1 and later in Chapter 8. We dive into how the process of deriving insights from analytics works and how organizations can use those insights for creating value for customers.

Deriving Insights From Digital Marketing Analytics

In the previous chapters, we mainly focused on the tools and analytics techniques for digital marketing. Those tools and techniques alone bring no value for organizations. Hence, deriving insights from digital marketing analytics is paramount for culmination of maximum return value to the organizations. Analyzing and interpreting the data collected from various digital marketing channels to gain valuable insights can result in the successful implementation of the overall marketing and business strategies. This whole process, we call it the "Insights Transformation (IT)", occurs in six steps are shown in Figure 12.1;

Insight Transformation Cycle

As a process of turning data into insights and action, the insight transformation cycle, involves the collection and analysis of data, identification of insights, reporting the findings and the implementation of digital marketing strategies based on those insights. As we saw in the earlier chapters, a plethora of tools and technologies are available for digital marketing analytics. However, those tools are not valuable

Figure 12.1 Insight Transformation Cycle
Source: Authors

if not utilized properly. Collecting and analyzing the right data the right way from these sources can provide organization with insights into customer behavior and preferences that can result in improving the marketing performance.

Note: The insight transformation cycle discussed here may vary across different organizations. The steps involved could also differ in scale or order. We put together this cycle based on our research and experiences.

Data Collection and Analysis

Data collection is the first step to understand your customers. It involves gathering information and relevant data from various sources. Collecting the data related to customers, target markets, consumer behavior, and other relevant factors is important as it will give you a holistic view. The data collected can include structured data (e.g., sales figures, customer feedback) and unstructured data (e.g., social media mentions, customer reviews). We discussed working with third party and unstructured data in Chapter 5. The analytics tools discussed in Chapters 4, 9, and 10 can help with gathering customer data from external sources. Some examples of external sources that we discussed in this book include webs analytics and social media analytics. They also include, email marketing campaigns, competitor analysis, and online reviews and ratings.

In addition, data from internal sources should also be considered for analysis. Internal data is usually very structured and accurate in nature as compared to unstructured external data. Hence, internal data can be highly reliable in terms of deriving insights specific to the core business/operations of the organization. Internal data can offer contextual understanding and can be benchmarked for evaluating the performance of digital marketing campaign. It can also help organization to identify any weakness and opportunities for improvements. Integrating internal data with digital marketing analytics maximizes the effectiveness and impact of marketing efforts. The internal data sources include, financial statement, sales and revenue reports, customer support tickets and interactions, employee surveys, performance metrics, inventory and supply chain data, etc. Once all the data is collected, it should be prepared for analysis (Table 12.1).

Findings and Reporting

Good on-time reporting, communicating, and presenting the findings is crucial for decision-making. Effective communication and presentation ensure that the key stakeholders, leadership, and middle management clearly see the effectiveness of digital marketing campaigns. Easy presentation and visual reporting are also essential to ensure that the insights and conclusions derived from data analysis are clearly understood and actionable. Presenting findings to the upper leadership can be tricky especially when important decision-making rest on the data being presented. Hence, it is highly advisable to structure the communication around a narrative that tells a compelling story with a clear beginning, middle, and end. This helps engage the audience and makes the findings more relatable and memorable. The upper management has to buy your story in order for them to act based on your data.

Table 12.1 Steps in Data Cleaning and Analysis for Digital Marketing

No.	Steps	Description	Tools
1.	Data Cleaning and Preparation	This step involves the inspection, cleaning, and transformation of the collected data. Clean, complete and accurate data is important for reliable analysis. This process ensures that the data is well organized and any duplicate entries have been removed.	Excel, OpenRefine, Python
2.	Data Exploration and Visualization	In this step, a preliminary understanding of data characteristics is gained and some patterns and trends are identified. For example, creating visualizations of website traffic over time can provide a visual picture of the data.	Google Analytics 4, Tableau, Power BI,
3.	Statistical Analysis and Modeling	In this step, statistical techniques and tools are employed to explore relationships. In digital marketing, this step can be helpful in comparing two different marketing techniques and judging their effectiveness.	AI-driven tools, R, SPSS
4.	Findings and reporting	Finally, the data is interpreted, and the findings are ready to be reported. Communicating the results in an effective manner is important.	Data visualization tools, Microsoft PowerPoint, Google Slides,

In Chapters 6 and 7, we saw different analytics tools that can be used to identify patterns, trends, and insights from the collected data from various sources. Tools such as Google Analytics 4 and Excel to visualize the data makes it easier to understand enabling data-driven decision-making for future digital marketing efforts. Emphasizing the significance of communication cannot be overstated. Effective communication and reporting of the results can expedite the process of identifying what is working well and what needs improvement in terms of digital marketing campaigns. On-time and clear communication of resulting from analytics promotes organization-wide collaboration, facilitates coordination, and encourages a unified approach towards achieving digital marketing objectives. It also fosters a shared understanding within the organization, ensuring that all relevant teams and departments are aligned and on the same page regarding digital marketing performance and goals.

Communicating the results of the digital marketing analytics to key stakeholders, including the marketing team, management, and other teams, ensures that everyone is informed and aware of the impact of the campaigns. Additionally, communicating findings helps build trust and credibility by providing evidence-based insights. When communicating the results to the upper management, it is advised to use real-world examples and case studies to demonstrate how the findings can be applied to solve business challenges or improve decision-making. It illustrates the practical value of the insights and allows stakeholders to see the value of digital marketing analytics and understand the impact on business outcomes, leading to increased confidence in digital marketing strategies and investments in digital analytics tools. Ultimately, effective communication of digital marketing analytics findings empowers organizations to make informed decisions, optimize marketing efforts, and drive business growth in an increasingly data-driven digital landscape.

Application and Optimization

Once the results are reported and communicated to key stakeholders, now it's time to apply the insights to optimize digital marketing campaigns. In an organizational setting, multiple departments will have to work together to translate insights into actual actions. This may involve adjusting the targeting, messaging, or channels used, to improve the performance and achieve the business objectives. The whole process should start with identifying specific areas within digital marketing campaigns that can be optimized based on the insights gained. This could involve refining audience targeting, adjusting ad creatives, modifying landing pages, optimizing bidding strategies, or reallocating budget towards top-performing channels or segments. Continuously monitor and track the performance of the digital marketing campaigns using the KPIs defined in Chapter 2.

Improvements and Feedback

Once new insights are applied and areas for optimization are identified, more ideas can be generated from the tools previously discussed to make ongoing improvements and optimize the campaigns for better results. Internally, the feedback from various departments and stakeholders directly or indirectly involved in digital marketing initiatives is important for bringing improvements in the marketing campaigns. Internal feedback provides an internal perspective that can help the marketing team to align strategies with organizational goals more efficiently.[7, 8] External feedback is also crucial. It helps businesses understand customer preferences, needs, and satisfaction levels. External feedback provides valuable perspectives from the outside and can highlight opportunities for improvement. In the previous chapters, we discussed tools that can help in this regard. For example, in Chapter 9 and 10, we saw how web analytics can to estimate how the traffic goes at different times of the day, by tracking information about the number of visitors of the app and the number of page views. The main purpose of web analytics is to report and optimize web usage by measuring web traffic. It can also be used it as a tool for business and market research in order to improve the effectiveness digital marketing techniques. Another example is that of geo-analytics. Marketing and data-driven location analytics, deals with mapping, visualizing, and mining of location data to reveal patterns, trends, and relationships hidden in tabular business data. The applications of location data vary by country.

Capitalizing on the data stored in a company database, location analytics can map and capture vast amounts of geo-specific data. The geo-data provides information, products, and services that are based on where the customers.

Adjustments and Repositioning

The next step involves using internal and external feedback to make data-driven adjustments to digital marketing campaigns. This could involve refining online targeting parameters, modifying digital content, optimizing web analytics techniques, or adjusting social media strategies based on performance trends.

The adjustments and repositioning of digital marketing analytics based on internal and external feedback empower organizations to make data-driven decisions and adapt their strategies to meet the evolving needs of their customers. It allows for continuous improvement, optimization, and innovation in digital marketing initiatives. By leveraging both internal and external feedback, organizations can ensure that their digital marketing analytics efforts are effective, relevant, and impactful, resulting in improved marketing performance, enhanced customer experiences, and sustained business growth.

Creating and Capturing Digital Value

Leveraging digital technologies, digital marketing analytics, assets, and strategies to generate and extract value for businesses and customers is what we refer to as "digital value".[9, 10] This is the final step in our insight transformation cycle. The digital analytics tools for marketing discussed in the previous chapters coupled with other digital technologies can create value for organizations in different forms (Figure 12.2).

In the previous chapters, we saw how various digital marketing analytics tools can be used to measure performance, identify techniques for targeting the right audience, optimize marketing channels, and analyze attribution and ROI. All this coupled with the ability to measure real-time trends, make data-driven decisions, and allocate resources more efficiently can lead to the overall effectiveness digital marketing techniques.[1, 11] All these constitute digital value derived from digital marketing analytics (Table 12.2).

Improving Overall Strategy

The utilization of digital marketing analytics tools and techniques discussed in the previous chapter in an effective manner can significantly improve the overall marketing strategy. Leveraging data-driven insights generated from analytics can enable organizations to make informed decisions, enhance the quality of digital marketing campaigns, and obtain better performance and results. Organization should wisely use the insights gained from the digital marketing analytics to improve the overall marketing strategy and make continuous improvements in digital marketing campaigns.

Figure 12.2 Forms of "Digital Value" From Digital Marketing Analytics
Source: Authors

Table 12.2 Forms of Digital Value From Digital Marketing Analytics for Organizations

No.	Forms of Digital Value	Expiations and Examples
1.	Informed Marketing Decisions	Informed decision-making is key to the success of digital marketing. Digital marketing analytics enable marketers to act upon the insights gained from data to make informed and improved decisions. When marketers have gained the insights, they can be used to target the right audience, measure campaign performance, allocate resources effectively, and continually optimize marketing efforts. For example, marketers can use predictive analytics to forecast demand and adjust pricing strategies accordingly.
2.	Streamlined Marketing Operations	Digital marketing analytics empowers organizations to make data-driven decisions, optimize marketing strategies, and improve the efficiency of their marketing activities. For example, using advanced AI-driven chatbots to offer 24/7 customer support and quick responses to queries can enhance customer experiences and reduce costs for organizations.

(Continued)

Table 12.2 *(Continued)*

No.	Forms of Digital Value	Expiations and Examples
3.	Innovation and Differentiations	Acting upon the insights gained from analytics, marketers can generate ideas for new products, services, business models and value creating processes can set the organization apart from its competitors and drive innovation.
4.	Efficiency and Productivity	Digital marketing analytics enable organizations to automate marketing tasks, enhance the quality of digital content, and optimize marketing operations. This can result in improved efficiency and productivity of marketing campaigns. For example, utilizing machine learning algorithms to automate data analysis and generate insights faster is one way to bring efficiency in marketing efforts.
5.	Agility and Adaptability	Organizations should embrace digital marketing technologies and develop capabilities to quickly adapt and respond to changes in the market, customer needs, and competitive landscape. This digital value comes from digital marketing analytics in the form of how organization able to use the gained strategic insights and identify emerging trends and modify marketing strategies accordingly.

In Chapter 2, we talked about establishing the key performance indicators (KPIs) that align with the organizational goals. We talked about various metrics such as website traffic and conversion rates, etc. It crucial to elect the KPIs that are most relevant to the objectives of the organization. KPIs provide meaningful insights into marketing performance and can help in aligning the overall marketing strategy with digital marketing analytics efforts. Speaking from a marketing perspective, the success of organization is tied with the satisfaction of consumers. Digital marketing technologies can enhance that. For example, in terms of remote accessibility, organizations can utilize digital technologies to create tools to manage vendor relationships and build strong bonds with the consumers. Similarly, in the previous chapters, we saw how implementing tools like Google Analytics, social media analytics platforms, or marketing automation systems can help in making the right marketing decisions by enabling organizations to track and capture data accurately. Utilizing digital marketing analytics effectively and efficiently is key to the success of all the marketing efforts in an organization!

Review Questions

1. What is insights transformation cycle?
2. What is digital value that comes from digital marketing analytics?

3. Explain the steps in cleaning and preparing data for analysis
4. How can digital marketing analytics help in improving the overall marketing strategy of an organization?

Chapter 12 Citations

1. D. Shah and B. P. S. Murthi, "Marketing in a data-driven digital world: Implications for the role and scope of marketing," *J. Bus. Res.*, vol. 125, no. June 2020, pp. 772–779, 2021, doi: 10.1016/j.jbusres.2020.06.062.

2. S. Sleep, P. Gala, and D. E. Harrison, "Removing silos to enable data-driven decisions: The importance of marketing and IT knowledge, cooperation, and information quality," *J. Bus. Res.*, vol. 156, no. November 2022, p. 113471, 2023, doi: 10.1016/j.jbusres.2022.113471.

3. C. Yu, Z. Zhang, C. Lin, and Y. J. Wu, "Can data-driven precision marketing promote user ad clicks? Evidence from advertising in WeChat moments," *Ind. Mark. Manag.*, vol. 90, no. May 2019, pp. 481–492, 2019, doi: 10.1016/j.indmarman.2019.05.001.

4. A. Jabbar, P. Akhtar, and S. Dani, "Real-time big data processing for instantaneous marketing decisions: A problematization approach," *Ind. Mark. Manag.*, vol. 90, no. September 2019, pp. 558–569, 2020, doi: 10.1016/j.indmarman.2019.09.001.

5. C. Brewis, S. Dibb, and M. Meadows, "Technological Forecasting & Social Change Leveraging big data for strategic marketing: A dynamic capabilities model for incumbent firms," *Technol. Forecast. Soc. Chang.*, vol. 190, no. December 2022, p. 122402, 2023, doi: 10.1016/j.techfore.2023.122402.

6. T. (Ya) Tang, S. (Katee) Zhang, and J. Peng, "The value of marketing innovation: Market-driven versus market-driving," *J. Bus. Res.*, vol. 126, no. October 2019, pp. 88–98, 2021, doi: 10.1016/j.jbusres.2020.12.067.

7. X. Wang and T. Lou, "The effect of performance feedback on firms' unplanned marketing investments," *J. Bus. Res.*, vol. 118, no. August 2019, pp. 441–451, 2020, doi: 10.1016/j.jbusres.2020.07.015.

8. G. Agag *et al.*, "Understanding the link between customer feedback metrics and firm performance," *J. Retail. Consum. Serv.*, vol. 73, no. December 2022, p. 103301, 2023, doi: 10.1016/j.jretconser.2023.103301.

9. D. Chaffey and M. Patron, "From web analytics to digital marketing optimization: Increasing the commercial value of digital analytics," *J. Direct, Data Digit. Mark. Pract.*, vol. 14, no. 1, pp. 30–45, 2012, doi: 10.1057/dddmp.2012.20.

10. M. Alwan and M. Alshurideh, "The effect of digital marketing on value creation and customer satisfaction," *Int. J. Data Netw. Sci.*, vol. 6, no. 4, pp. 1557–1566, 2022, doi: 10.5267/j.ijdns.2022.4.021.

11. M. Lytras, A. Visvizi, X. Zhang, and N. R. Aljohani, "Cognitive computing, Big Data Analytics and data driven industrial marketing," *Ind. Mark. Manag.*, vol. 90, no. April, pp. 663–666, 2020, doi: 10.1016/j.indmarman.2020.03.024.

Index